Studien zur Mustererkennung

Band 50

Studien zur Mustererkennung

Band 50

Herausgegeben von

Prof. Dr.-Ing. Heinrich Niemann
Prof. Dr.-Ing. Elmar Nöth

Tomás Arias-Vergara

Analysis of Pathological Speech Signals

Logos Verlag Berlin

λογος

Bibliografische Information der Deutschen Nationalbibliothek

Die Deutsche Nationalbibliothek verzeichnet diese Publikation in der
Deutschen Nationalbibliografie; detaillierte bibliografische Daten sind
im Internet über http://dnb.d-nb.de abrufbar.

978-3-8325-5561-0
ISSN 1617-0695

Logos Verlag Berlin GmbH
Georg-Knorr-Str. 4, Geb. 10, 12681 Berlin

Tel.:   +49 (0)30 / 42 85 10 90
Fax: +49 (0)30 / 42 85 10 92

https://www.logos-verlag.de

Acknowledgments

The development of this thesis wouldn't be possible without the help and support of many people. I'm very thankful to my family for their support during all my academic life. Especially to my mom for her wisdom and guidance. She has always given me reasons to keep going, go beyond my limits, and dream for the best. Thanks to my brothers, Matias and Simon, for their invaluable support in many difficult situations that I could have never faced alone.

I'm very grateful to my supervisor Prof. Dr.-Ing. Juan Rafael Orozco-Arroyave, Prof. Dr.-Ing. Elmar Nöth, and Prof. Dr. med. Maria Schuster. I can only offer my sincere appreciation for all of their advice, encouragement, and learning opportunities to them. Rafa has been my supervisor since I was an undergraduate student. He allowed me to explore the world of academic research. His guidance helped me accomplish several of my career goals and influenced many of my life decisions. Elmar opened the doors of the Pattern Recognition Lab and from the very first moment I arrived in Germany, he was very supportive academically and personally. I'm very thankful for all the fruitful discussions we had and his time helping me be a better researcher. I'm thankful to Maria and the trust she put in me to carry on this project. She always encouraged me to get the best out of every task I've performed and offered me the best conditions to accomplish my goals.

I also want to thank my colleagues from the GITA lab, Camilo, Paula, Parra, Patricia, Orlando, Cristian, Daniel, Lucho, Manuel, and Nicanor. In particular, I'm very thankful to Camilo and Paula. Together with Camilo, we developed new ideas, discussed the results of many experiments, and shared many great moments. Although, in the end, we went on different paths, I will always be grateful to him for all of the help. I'm also very thankful to Paula. There were difficult moments towards the end of my Ph.D. where she was my only support and the one that gave me the strength to continue given the circumstances. She became my "partner in crime" and I hope to support her as much as she did to me, now that she started her Ph.D.

I would like to thank my colleagues at the Pattern Recognition Lab, Philipp, Sebastian, Tino, Hendrik, and Dalia. They helped me a lot when I arrived in Germany and always were very kind and friendly. I want to express my deep gratitude to Philipp. He has helped me a lot with different technical and general things during my stay in Germany. I consider him a close friend of mine, and I'm glad for the opportunity to have worked with him at the Pattern Recognition Lab.

And last but not least, I want to thank the patients and volunteers of the Fundalianza Parkinson Colombia, the Clinic of the Ludwig-Maximillians University in Munich, and the people from the Augustinum retirement home. Without their help and willingness to collaborate in this work, none of this could have been possible. Thanks to them for letting me be part of their group.

Abstract

The present thesis addresses the automatic analysis of speech disorders resulting from Parkinson's disease and hearing loss. For Parkinson's disease, the progression of speech symptoms are evaluated considering speech recordings captured in the short-term (4 months) and long-term (5 years). Machine learning methods are used to perform three tasks: (1) automatic classification of patients vs. healthy speakers, (2) regression analysis to predict the dysarthria level and neurological state, and (3) speaker embeddings to analyze the progression of the speech symptoms over time. For hearing loss, automatic acoustic analysis is performed to evaluate whether the duration and onset of deafness (before or after speech acquisition) influences the speech production of cochlear implant users. Additionally, articulation, prosody, and phonemic analyses are performed to show that cochlear implant users present altered speech production even after hearing rehabilitation.

Automatic acoustic analysis is performed considering phonation, articulation, prosody, and phonemic features. Phoneme precision is characterized using the posterior probabilities obtained from recurrent neural networks trained in German and Spanish. The phonemic analysis considers three main dimensions: manner of articulation, place of articulation, and voicing. This thesis also proposes a methodology for automatically detecting voice onset time in voiceless stop consonants.

Furthermore, this thesis studies the acoustic cues that reflect changes in elderly people due to the aging process. Regression analysis is performed to estimate a person's age using the phonation, articulation, prosody, and phonemic features. Additionally, the use of smartphones for health care applications is considered here.

Zusammenfassung

Die vorliegende Dissertation befasst sich mit der automatischen Analyse von Sprachstörungen infolge von Parkinson und Hörverlust. Bei der Parkinson-Krankheit wird der Verlauf der Sprachsymptome anhand von Sprachaufzeichnungen bewertet, die kurzzeitig (4 Monate) und langfristig (5 Jahre) aufgenommen wurden. Methoden des maschinellen Lernens werden verwendet, um drei Aufgaben zu erfüllen: (1) automatische Klassifikation von Patienten vs. gesunde Sprecher, (2) Regressionsanalyse zur Vorhersage des Dysarthrie-Levels und des neurologischen Zustands und (3) Sprechereinbettungen zur Analyse des Verlaufs der Sprachsymptome im Laufe der Zeit. Bei den Patienten mit Hörverlust wird eine automatische akustische Sprachanalyse durchgeführt, um zu beurteilen, ob die Dauer und das Einsetzen der Taubheit (vor oder nach dem Spracherwerb) die Sprachproduktion von Cochlea-Implantat-Trägern beeinflusst. Darüber hinaus werden Artikulations-, Prosodie- und Phonemanalysen durchgeführt, um zu zeigen, dass Träger von Cochlea-Implantaten auch nach einer Hörrehabilitation eine veränderte Sprachproduktion unterschiedlichen Ausmasses aufweisen.

Für automatischen akustischen Analysen werden wird Phonation, Artikulation, Prosodie und phonemischen Merkmalen berücksichtigt. Die Phonempräzision wird durch die Posterior-Wahrscheinlichkeiten charakterisiert, die aus rekurrenten neuronalen Netzen gewonnen werden, die auf Deutsch und Spanisch trainiert wurden. Die phonemische Analyse fokussiert auf drei Hauptdimensionen: Artikulationsart, Artikulationsort und Stimmgebung. Diese Arbeit schlägt auch eine Methodik zur automatischen Erkennung der Stimmeinsatzes nach stimmlosen Stoppkonsonanten vor.

Darüber hinaus untersucht diese Arbeit die akustischen sprachlichen Charakteristika, die Veränderungen bei älteren Menschen aufgrund des Alterungsprozesses widerspiegeln. Eine Regressionsanalyse wird durchgeführt, um das Alter einer Person unter Verwendung der Phonation, Artikulation, Prosodie und phonemischen Merkmale zu schätzen. Darüber hinaus wird hier der Einsatz von Smartphones für Anwendungen im Gesundheitswesen betrachtet.

Resumen

La presente tesis aborda el análisis automático de los trastornos del habla derivados de la enfermedad de Parkinson y la pérdida auditiva. En el caso de la enfermedad de Parkinson, el progreso de los síntomas del habla se evalúa considerando las grabaciones capturadas a corto (4 meses) y largo plazo (5 años). Métodos de aprendizaje automático son utilizados para realizar tres tareas: (1) clasificación automática de pacientes contra a hablantes sanos, (2) análisis de regresión para predecir el nivel de disartria y el estado neurológico, y (3) modelos de hablante para análisis longitudinal del progreso de los desórdenes en la voz. En el caso de la pérdida auditiva, se realiza un análisis acústico automático para evaluar si la duración y el inicio de la sordera (antes o después de la adquisición del habla) influye en la producción del habla de los usuarios de implantes cocleares. Además, se realizan análisis de articulación, prosodia y fonémicos para demostrar que los usuarios de implantes cocleares presentan una producción del habla alterada incluso después de la rehabilitación auditiva.

El análisis acústico automático se realiza considerando fonación, articulación, prosodia y características fonémicas. La precisión de la producción de fonemas se caracteriza mediante el cálculo de las probabilidades obtenidas de redes neuronales recurrentes entrenadas en Alemán y Español. El análisis fonémico considera tres dimensiones principales: forma de articulación, lugar de articulación y sonorización. Esta tesis también propone una metodología para la detección automática del tiempo de inicio de la voz en consonantes oclusivas sordas.

Además, en este trabajo se analiza la influencia de la edad en el análisis acústico. El análisis de regresión se realiza para estimar la edad de una persona utilizando las características de fonación, articulación, prosodia y fonética. También, en esta tesis se considera el uso de smartphones para aplicaciones en el sector médico.

Contents

Chapter 1

Introduction

1.1 Motivation

Oral communication of adults and children can be affected by developmental or acquired speech disorders resulting from motor/neurological impairments (e.g., brain injuries, Parkinson's disease) or sensory/perceptual disorders (e.g., hearing loss)[1]. On the one hand, neurological diseases such as Parkinson's disease (PD) affect certain regions in the brain and the muscles involved in the speech production process, leading to different motor speech-based impairments such as imprecise articulation, slower speaking rate, monotonous speech, hoarse quality of voice, among others (Ho et al., 1999; Trail et al., 2005). On the other hand, perceptual disorders such as sensorineural hearing loss cause decreased speech intelligibility, changes in terms of phoneme articulation, abnormal nasalization, slower speaking rate, and decreased variability in fundamental frequency (Hudgins and Numbers, 1942; Langereis et al., 1997; Leder et al., 1987). One of the aims of pathological speech processing is the development of technology to support the diagnosis and monitoring of different medical conditions through speech (Gupta et al., 2016). This thesis focuses on the automatic acoustic analysis of speech signals captured from PD patients and people with hearing loss. Furthermore, as the speech of elderly people

---

[1]www.asha.org/Practice-Portal/Clinical-Topics/Articulation-and-Phonology

1

changes due to the aging process, a clinical condition, or both, the description of acoustic cues in the speech that reflect such differences is a topic that deserves special attention.

PD is a neurodegenerative disease characterized by the progressive loss of dopaminergic neurons in the substantia nigra of the midbrain (Hornykiewicz, 1998). The primary motor symptoms of PD include tremor, slowness, rigidity of the limbs and trunk, postural instability, swallowing disorders, and speech impairments. Many of the symptoms are controlled with medication, however, there is no clear evidence indicating positive effects of those treatments on the speech impairments (Skodda et al., 2010), but there is evidence showing that speech therapy combined with the pharmacological treatment improves the communication ability of PD patients (Schultz and Grant, 2000). The evaluation of PD requires the patient to be present at the clinic, which is time-consuming and expensive for both, the patient and healthcare system (Yang et al., 2020), however, the continuous monitoring of PD patients could help to make timely decisions regarding their medication and therapy.

In the case of hearing loss, there are different treatments available for different types and degrees of deafness. A Cochlear implant (CI) is the most suitable device for severe and profound deafness when hearing aids do not improve sufficiently speech perception. A CI uses a sound processor to capture audio signals and send them to a receiver implanted under the skin behind the ear. The receiver transforms the signal into electrical impulses which are sent to electrodes implanted in the cochlea. However, CI users often present altered speech production and limited understanding even after hearing rehabilitation. Thus, if the deficits of speech would be better known the rehabilitation might be properly addressed (Pomaville and Kladopoulos, 2013). CI users require assistance before, during, and after surgery from audiologists, medical specialists in Otorhinolaryngology, and speech-language pathologists [2]; however, speech production quality is seldom assessed in outcome evaluations, thus including speech technology could lead to a reliable outcome evaluation

---

[2]www.asha.org/Practice-Portal/Professional-Issues/Cochlear-Implants/

contributing to the rehabilitation success.

This thesis addresses the automatic evaluation of speech production from PD patients and CI users by combining signal processing techniques with machine learning methods. Such methods are also considered to analyze the effect of age as another possible source of changes in speech production. Additionally, since the use of smartphones for health care has become more frequent, some of the speech processing techniques addressed in this thesis are implemented in Android-based applications.

1.2 Speech disorders in selected populations

1.2.1 Parkinson's disease

Clinical diagnosis

Parkinson's disease is characterized by a combination of some symptoms regarding motor control. Moreover, next to motor control, other symptoms such as mood changes, cognitive decline, and sleep disorders might occur (Poewe, 2008). There is no standard method to diagnose PD. Doctors rely on the clinical history and physical examination to assess the patients. Additionally, the severity of the disease is evaluated by neurologist experts using different scales such as the Movement Disorder Society–Unified Parkinson Disease Rating Scale (MDS-UPDRS) (Goetz et al., 2008). This is a perceptual scale used to assess motor and non-motor abilities of the patients with 65 items distributed in four sections:

- Section 1 (MDS-UPDRS-I, 13 items) concerns the non-motor experiences of daily living such as cognitive impairment, depressed mood, and fatigue.

- Section 2 (MDS-UPDRS-II, 13 items) considers motor experiences of daily living such as eating, dressing, handwriting, and tremor.

3

- Section 3 (MDS-UPDRS-III, 33 items) is used to evaluate the motor capabilities of the patient including speech production, upper/lower limbs movement, postural stability, and gait.

- Section 4 (MDS-UPDRS-IV, 6 items) concerns motor complications such as time spent without medication (OFF state), time spent with dyskinesia (involuntary movements), among others.

Speech production is evaluated by the neurologist during the patient's visit to the clinic. The patients are asked to talk about different subjects in order to assess several aspects including speech's volume, intelligibility, modulation of words, among others. The speech item of the MDS-UPDRS scale considers the following categories for the evaluation (Table 1.1):

Table 1.1: Speech scoring system from the MDS-UPDRS-III.

Score	Category	Definition
0	Normal	No speech problems
1	Slight	Loss of voice intensity or modulation
2	Mild	Some words are unclear
3	Moderate	Speech is difficult to understand
4	Severe	Speech is unintelligible

The MDS-UPDRS-III also includes the Hoehn & Yahr (H&Y) scale, which comprises a set of five severity levels where 1 is associated with a minimal or no functional disability and 5 is assigned to patients who are confined in bed or wheelchair unless aided. There are two variants of the scale, the original one with integer values for the stages from 1 to 5, and a modified one with the addition of stages 1.5 and 2.5 for a total of 7 severity levels (Hoehn et al., 1998).

The MDS-UPDRS scale is suitable to assess the neurological state of the patients. However, speech production is evaluated only in one item. Regarding the complexity of speech, a single item summarizing different aspects such as voice, articulation, fluency, intonation, speaking rate, and intelligibility is not sufficient. The symptoms of motor speech disorders caused by PD are often associated with hypokinetic dysarthria, resulting from problems controlling the muscles and articulators involved in the speech production process. A more suitable clinical scale to evaluate speech impairments is the Frenchay Dysarthria Assessment–2 (FDA–2) (Enderby and Palmer, 2008), which is a perceptual scale used to evaluate dysarthria considering 34 items distributed in eight sections. Table 1.2 shows the aspects considered in the FDA–2 scale. The patients are asked to perform different tasks in each section. The category *complementary* refers to factors that might influence speech production. All sections (excluding *Complementary*) are rated on a 9-point scale.

Table 1.2: List of items evaluated in the FDA–2 scale.

Category	Item
Reflexes	Cough, swallow, dribble/drool
Respiration	At rest, in speech
Lips	At rest, spread, seal, alternate, in speech
Palate	Fluids, maintenance, in speech
Laryngeal	Time, pitch, volume, in speech
Tongue	At rest, protrusion, elevation, lateral, alternate, in speech
Intelligibility	Producing words, sentences, conversation
Complementary	Hearing, sight, teeth, language, mood, posture, speech rate, sensation (upper lip and tongue tip)

A modified version of the FDA–2 scale, i.e., the mFDA, was proposed by Orozco-Arroyave et al. (2018) and was designed to be applied considering only the speech recordings of the patient; therefore, the patient is not required to visit the clinic for assessment. The mFDA is administered considering different speech tasks including sustained phonation of the vowel /a/, reading, monologues, and the alternating and sequential production of the syllables

5

/pa-ta-ka/, /pa-ka-ta/, /pe-ta-ka/, /pa/, /ta/, and /ka/. The scale has a total of 13 items and each one of them ranges from 0 (normal or completely healthy) to 4 (very impaired), thus the total score of the mFDA ranges from 0 to 52. Table 1.3 shows the details of the mFDA scale. The main limitation of the MDS-UPDRS

Table 1.3: List of items evaluated in the mFDA scale.

Category	Item	Speech task
Respiration	Duration of the recording	Sustained phonation of the vowel /a/
	Breathing capacity	Multiple repetition of /pa-ta-ka/, /pa-ka-ta/, /pe-ta-ka/
Lips	Strength of lip closure	Multiple repetitions of the syllable /pa/
	Lips control	Reading, monologue
Palate	Nasality	Reading, monologue
	Velar movement	Multiple repetitions of the syllable /ka/
Larinx	Phonatory capability 1	Sustained phonation of the vowel /a/
	Phonatory capability 2	Reading, monologue
	Monotonicity	Reading, monologue
	Effort to produce speech	Reading, monologue
Tongue	Velocity to move the tongue 1	Multiple repetition of /pa-ta-ka/ and /pa-ka-ta/
	Velocity to move the tongue 2	Multiple repetitions of the syllable /ta/
Intelligibility	Speech intelligibility	Reading, monologue

or mFDA is the lack of precision, since the severity of the disease is evaluated based on a perceptual score which depends on the experience of the clinician.

Speech production

PD affects the speech of the patients in different ways. For instance, stability and periodicity problems are caused by an inadequate closing of the vocal folds, which is related to rigidity in the muscle (Hanson et al., 1984). Thus, perturbations in the vibration of vocal folds can be measured by estimating fundamental frequency (F0) based features from the sustained phonation of vowels (Almeida et al., 2019; Skodda et al., 2013; Tsanas et al., 2010). Articulation-based deficits are mainly related with reduced amplitude and velocity of lip, tongue, and jaw movements causing a reduced articulatory capability in PD patients to produce vowels and continuous speech (Ackermann and Ziegler, 1991; Skodda et al., 2011). Such reduction can be measured by computing the triangular Vowel Space Area (tVSA) formed with the formant frequencies F_1 and F_2 extracted from the vowels /a/, /i/, and /u/, while articulation-based problems in continuous speech can be detected by analyzing the transitions from voiced-to-voiceless sounds (and vice versa) and computing spectral-based fratures such as the Mel-Frequency Cepstral Coefficients (MFCCs) (Orozco-Arroyave, 2016; Skodda et al., 2011). PD can also influence speech at the segmental (individual sounds/phonemes) and suprasegmental level (speech prosody). For instance at the segmental level, some studies have found that the difficulties of PD patients to control laryngeal movements affects the production of stop consonants e.g., /p/, /t/, /k/, /b/, /d/, /g/ (Fischer and Goberman, 2010). Such difficulties are typically measured by means of the Voice Onset Time (VOT), which is defined as the time interval between the initial burst of a stop consonant and the onset of voicing for the following vowel. The changes in the duration of the VOT produced by patients often differs when compared with respect to a group of age-matched healthy speakers (Argüello-Vélez et al., 2020; Montaña et al., 2018; Novotný et al., 2015; Tykalova et al., 2017). Speech deficits at the segmental level can also be detected by estimating the probability of occurrence of phonemes in a speech sequence (phoneme posterior probabilities), which can be achieved by training a deep neural network to learn the representation of several phoneme classes grouped according to different phonological rules (Cernak et al., 2015; Vásquez-Correa et al., 2019). Suprasegmental speech deficits include variation in intonation, reduced loudness, variable speech rate, among others (Jones, 2009). These deficits can be measured by means of the F0 contour, energy content of the signal, and the amount of speech units (words, voiced segments) produced by the speakers. Chapter 2 contains more details about the relationship between PD and the speech production system.

1.2.2   Hearing loss

Clinical diagnosis

Hearing loss can appear due to various reasons such as senescence, trauma, inflammation, aging, and others, and often without a known cause. Hearing loss can be acquired or it can be congenital, e.g. because of genetic alterations,

7

intrauterine infections or malformations. The treatment for hearing loss depends on the severity and cause. The grade of the impairment can be categorized as normal, mild, moderate, severe, or profound depending on audiometry descriptors. Such descriptors are usually obtained by a pure-tone audiometry test which consists of a threshold search by reproducing sinusoidal waveforms (through speakers or headphones) at different frequencies (125 Hz, 250 Hz, 500 Hz, and from 1000 Hz to 8000 Hz in steps of 1000 Hz) and intensity levels. The patient is asked to indicate whether the sounds are perceived by raising a hand or pressing a button. Figure 1.1 shows an audiogram indicating the degree of hearing loss for different loudness and frequency values. For instance, a person that can only hear sounds between 40 dB and 60 dB might suffer from moderate hearing loss.

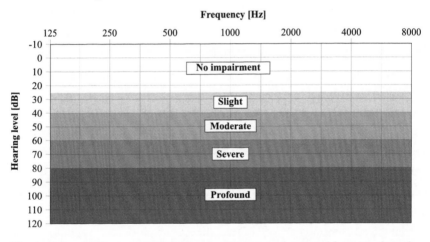

Figure 1.1: *Audiogram indicating the degree and type of hearing loss for different loudness and frequency values. The hearing thresholds correspond to the range of values adopted by the World Health Organization (Olusanya et al., 2019).*

Although, the pure-tone audiometry test provides useful information about the hearing status of a person, expert clinicians do not rely solely on such a test to determine the adequate treatment of the patient. Treatment options are provided to the patient depending on the type of hearing loss which can be conductive, sensorineural, or a mixture of both (Weber and Klein, 1999). On the one hand, conductive hearing loss occurs due to a damage produced in the outer or middle ear or by a malformation (e.g. ear canal, middle ear), causing the person to perceive sounds with low intensity levels. Usually, hearing aids can be used as a treatment option because it amplifies the sounds to improve audio perception. There are types of conductive hearing loss that can be treated with medication or surgery. On the other hand, sensorineural hearing loss is related to disorders in the inner ear (cochlea) or the auditory nerve system resulting in disabling hearing impairment. Usually, therapy consists of the amplification of sounds by hearing aids which are adapted to the hearing loss at different frequencies in the hearing range. In more profound hearing loss and deafness (in the following summarized as deafness), amplification of sounds is not enough to provide sufficient hearing for speech perception. In this case, CIs are the most suitable devices for treatment. Contrary to hearing aids, a CI bypasses the damaged portions of the ear and directly stimulate the auditory nerve. In the cochlea, frequencies are arranged from high frequencies at the base to the deep frequencies at the top. The inserted implant in the cochlea follows this natural representation of the sounds called "tonotopy" and stimulates the nerves that correspond to the region of excitation. Although hearing with a CI is quite different from normal hearing, speech understanding can be restored (Lenarz, 2017; Pisoni et al., 2017). Regarding the outcome after cochlear implantation, some aspects need to be considered. The time of occurrence of sensorineural hearing loss also affects the speech perception and production of the CI users. On the one hand, prelingual onset of deafness refers to people who lost their hearing capability before the acquisition of spoken language, their speech production is affected because they have never monitored their own speech (Smith, 1975). On the other hand, postlingual onset of deafness refers to people who lost their hearing after speech acquisition, however, their speech production might be affected by the lack of sufficient and stable auditory feedback (Leder and Spitzer, 1990).

9

Speech production

People suffering from severe/profound deafness may experience different speech production disorders. At a segmental level, such disorders include voicing errors, phoneme misarticulation, vowel errors, among others (Gold, 1980; Waldstein, 1990). Voicing errors might be caused due to failed attempts to coordinate respiration, phonation (voicing), and articulation resulting in a confusion of the voiced-voiceless distinction. Thus, similar to the PD patients, voicing errors can be detected by automatic extraction of voiced sounds, i.e., speech segments with F0 values different than zero. Phoneme production errors are caused by different reasons. For instance, the studies reviewed by Osberger and McGarr (1982) revealed that there was a general trend of hearing impaired people to better produce the most *visible* phonemes, e.g., phonemes produced with the lips or/and teeth. Consonant errors can also occur due to incorrect timing of the articulators e.g., causing nasalization of non-nasal speech sounds due to improper velar control (Kato and Yoshino, 1988; Stevens et al., 1976). Such phoneme articulation errors might cause a decreased speech intelligibility, which can be evaluated with Automatic Speech Recognition (ASR) systems, phoneme posterior probabilities, among others. At suprasegmental level, the speech of severely and profoundly hearing impaired speakers also exhibits deviation from *normal* speech in timing and voice quality. On the one hand, people suffering from hearing loss have been reported to speak slower than healthy people due to the prolongation of speech and non-speech segments (consonants, vowels, pauses), and the insertion of pauses within sentences (Oster, 1990). On the other hand, voice quality problems include abnormally high F0 values (particularly in adolescent and adult males) and insufficient or excessive variations of F0 within a sentence (Gold, 1980). Thus, similar to the speech of PD patients, some of the suprasegmental aspects of speech can be evaluated by computing F0-related features, duration, speech rate, energy, among others. Chapter 2 contains more details about the role of auditory feedback on the speech production system.

1.2.3 Aging

Speech of the elderly sometimes can be called "slurred" with comprises slight changes in voicing, articulation and prosody. The changes in organs and tissues involved in voice production which are associated with the aging process include facial skeleton growth (Israel, 1973), pharyngeal muscle atrophy (Zaino and Benventano, 1977), tooth loss (Adams, 1991), reduced mobility of the jaw (Kahane, 1981), tongue musculature atrophy, and weakening of pharyngeal musculature. The precise nature of vocal resonance is unclear, however a consistent pattern seems to be a vocal tract lengthening with age (Linville, 1996). These changes alter the phonation and articulation dimensions of speech, for instance elderly people exhibit a significantly greater frequency perturbation than the young speakers (Benjamin, 1981). There are also differences in the stability of F0 and amplitude of vocal fold vibration relative to young and middle-aged adults (Xue and Deliyski, 2001). Changes in F0 and the formant frequencies have been also observed in longitudinal analyses. Particularly, changes in the first formant frequency are believed to compensate the decline of F0 in order to maintain the auditory distance between F0 and F1 (Reubold et al., 2010). The influence of some of these parameters on speech assessment have been addressed before when measuring speech intelligibility by considering an Automatic Speech Recognition (ASR) system. In the experiments performed by Vipperla et al. (2010) on adult and older voices, the authors found that elderly people show increased jitter and shimmer and these variations have an impact on average phoneme recognition.

1.3 Hypotheses

Since different factors influencing speech production are considered in this thesis, the following hypotheses are investigated:

- It is possible to evaluate the speech production of PD patients, CI users, and elderly speakers using similar signal processing techniques.

- Since PD is a progressive disease that also affects speech, it is possible to assess the progression per patient from speech signals captured in different recording sessions.

- The duration and onset of deafness influences speech production of CI users in different ways, thus, automatic acoustic analysis can be used to detect these changes.

- It is possible to use smartphone applications to evaluate the speech production of PD patients and CI users.

- Aging affects different aspects of speech production and such changes can be captured by most of the features considered to analyze pathological speech.

1.4 Objectives

1.4.1 General objective

To propose a methodology for the monitoring of pathological speech signals combining different signal processing techniques and machine learning methods.

1.4.2 Specific objectives

- To identify the contribution of different speech dimensions for the automatic assessment of pathological speech signals.

- To analyze and select the most suitable features to detect changes in pathological speech signals.

- To combine different speech processing techniques and machine learning methods for the automatic assessment of pathological speech signals.

1.5 Contribution of this thesis

- Collection of a speech corpus from PD patients and CI users. The recordings were captured in clinical settings and at-home of the patients using smartphones.

- A methodology for the automatic detection of VOT in voiceless stop sounds using a deep neural network approach.

- A methodology to monitor the progression of PD patients over time using automatic acoustic analysis.

- A methodology to quantify the phoneme production of CI users using a deep neural network approach.

- A methodology to evaluate the impact of age on different acoustic measurements.

- Implementation of signal processing techniques on smartphones to evaluate speech production of PD patients and CI users.

- Participation in the development of the mobile application $Apkinson$, used to collect speech and movement data from PD patients.

- Participation in the the development of the mobile application $CITA$ (Cochlear Implant Testing App), which is intended to collect data from CI users in order to evaluate the speech perception and production of the patients. The source code of $CITA$ is based on $Apkinson$.

1.6 Structure of the thesis

Chapter 2 includes information about the physiological processes of speech production, the influence of PD in speech motor control and speech disorders associated with the disease. This chapter also gives an overview of the auditory system, cochlear implants, and the role of auditory feedback in speech motor control.

Chapter 3 includes information about the contributions in the state-of-the-art methods related to predicting the severity of PD from speech signals, automatic methods used for analysis of speech production in CI users, and smartphone-based applications developed to evaluate PD and hearing loss.

Chapter 4 describes the speech processing techniques and acoustic features used to model speech disorders. Additionally, this chapter includes the machine learning methods used in this thesis for classification, regression analysis, and speaker models.

Chapter 5 includes details about the PD patients, CI users, and healthy speakers considered in this thesis. Additional databases used to support the training of models used for automatic speech analysis are also described.

Chapter 6 includes the experiments and results obtained for the automatic analysis of PD patients and CI users from speech signals, and the effect of aging in speech production.

Chapter 7 summarizes the addressed aspects about pathological speech analysis.

Chapter 2

Speech production process

2.1 Speech chain

In the speech chain model described by Denes and Pinson (1993), oral communication consists of a sequence of events happening on three levels: linguistic, physiological, and acoustic. The process to produce intelligible speech starts in the speaker's brain, at the linguistic level (Figure 2.1). First, the speaker collects his/her thoughts, decides what words to say, and places these words to form sentences according to language dependent rules. The speech production process continues at the physiological level, with the neural activity inside the brain sending the necessary instructions to activate the muscles that control the vocal folds, tongue, lips, jaw, among others. The speech production is completed at the acoustic level, where the movements of the vocal muscles (combined with the air coming from the lungs) generates speech sound waves. Once the speech is produced it travels through the air activating the hearing mechanism of the listeners. The auditory feedback plays a key role in oral communication because it helps the speakers to continuously monitor the quality and intelligibility of their own speech.

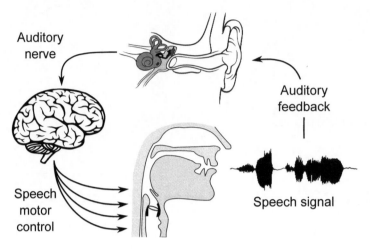

Figure 2.1: *The speech production process starts in the brain, at the linguistic level, continues with the neural and motor activity at the physiological level, and its completed with the generation and transmission of sound waves at the acoustic level. The auditory feedback allows the speaker to monitor its own speech. Based on Denes and Pinson (1993).*

2.1.1 Physiological processes of speech production

In general, the speech production process involves the complex coordination and activation of different muscles and limbs in the respiratory, laryngeal, and oral motor system. The respiratory system is essential to produce speech by generating air pressure from the lungs during the expiratory and inspiratory phases. The airflow passes a small valve, the glottis, which is formed by the two vocal folds. During respiration, the vocal folds are in a lateral position. During phonation, the vocal folds are closing resulting in vibrations of the soft mucosal tissue as a result of the subglottal pressure and the airflow passing through the glottis (Van den Berg, 1958). During oscillation, the vocal folds convert the air into a rapid sequence of airflow pulses generating audible sounds (voice source sounds), which are perceived as a *buzz* whose frequency is proportional to the vibration rate. During the production of the airflow pulses, the vocal folds have four main stages: closed, opening, open, and closing (Figure 2.2).

Speech sounds produced in this way are commonly known as voiced sounds. If the vocal folds remain open, then the source of energy for speech production is a stable stream of air coming from the lungs which is made audible by other articulator (s) at some place in the vocal tract. The speech sounds that are not produced by vibration of the vocal folds are commonly known as unvoiced sounds.

The oral motor system includes the articulatory mechanism necessary to modulate the voice source which allows us to produce speech sounds with different acoustic properties. Such properties depend on the shape of the vocal tract, which can be modified by moving the principal articulators namely the tongue, lower jaw, lips, and velum. The oral motor system also includes nasal, oral, and pharyngeal cavities which act as resonance chambers to transform the stream of air into sounds with an additional acoustic characteristic (Benesty et al., 2007; Denes and Pinson, 1993; Fant, 1980). Figure 2.2 shows a diagram of the main articulators and resonators (oral, nasal pharyngeal cavities) involved in the speech production process. The air coming from the lungs is the source to generate speech sounds. The muscles in the larynx act as a valve to control the air stream coming from the lungs. The coordination and movements of the different articulators together with the nasal, oral, and pharyngeal cavities provide the acoustic properties necessary to generate different speech sounds. For instance, the vowel /a/ is commonly produced by a combination of tongue, jaw, and vocal folds movements. The vibration of the vocal folds creates the voice source sound, which is then modulated by opening the mouth (lowering of the jaw) and holding the tongue in a low position. Another example is the production of plosive sounds such as /p/, which is produced by blocking (for a short period of time) the air stream with the lips building enough air pressure to produce the sound when the closure is released. Generally, the vocal folds remain open when producing the consonant /p/. Nasal cavities are also used to generate speech sounds. For instance the nasal consonants /n/ and /m/ are produced during vibration of the vocal folds and by blocking the air stream in the oral cavity with the lips (in the case of /m/) or the tip of the tongue (in the

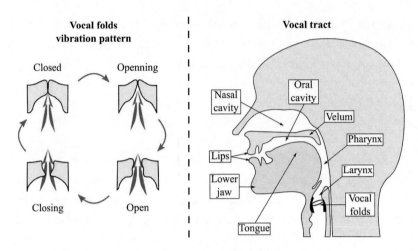

Figure 2.2: *Schematic views of the speech production system. (Left) Vocal folds vibration pattern during the production of voiced speech segments. (Right) Components of the vocal tract used to produce speech sounds. Based on Benesty et al. (2007) and Denes and Pinson (1993)*

case of /n/). Additionally, the velum partially blocks the air to the vocal cavity and routes it to the nasal cavity.

2.2   Impact of Parkinson's disease on speech motor control

2.2.1   Neuropathophysiology of motor control related to Parkinson's disease

Motor deficits in PD can be analyzed by considering the interaction of the basal ganglia, the motor cortex, and the thalamus (Figure 2.3[1]). The basal ganglia are a group of neural formations (subcortical structures) including the striatum

---

[1]These figures are adapted versions of `https://commons.wikimedia.org/wiki/File:Basal_ganglia_circuits.svg` and `https://commons.wikimedia.org/wiki/File:Midbrainsection.svg`
Last retrieved 02/02/2021; under the Creative Commons Attribution-Share Alike 3.0 Unported license.

(putamen and caudate nucleus), the Globus Pallidus and its internal (Gpi) and external (Gpe) segments, the subthalamic nucleus (STN), and the substantia nigra pars compacta (SNpc) and pars reticulata (SNpr). Anatomically, the STN belongs to the subthalamus and the substantia nigra to the midbrain, however, they play a key role in the functioning of the basal ganglia. Motor impairments in PD are mainly caused due to a degeneration of dopaminergic neurons in the SNpc located in the midbrain.

The main function of the subcortical structures in the basal ganglia is to send signals to the thalamus which then influence the activity in the motor cortex. This interaction can be analyzed considering the most basic circuit model of the basal ganglia proposed by Albin et al. (1989) more than 30 years ago. Although, more complex connections in the basal ganglia have been discovered since then (Bostan and Strick, 2018; Redgrave et al., 2010), the basic model proposed in the late 80s is still valid to understand some of the most important aspects of motor control related to PD (Milardi et al., 2019). Figure 2.4 shows a diagram of the neural circuits and neurotransmission mechanism involved in the communication between cerebral cortex and basal ganglia. Basically, the circuit model involves two main parallel *loops*:

1. The first loop is a cortex-to-cortex circuit in which the motor cortex sends signals to the striatum, from which neural projections travel to the globus pallidus and then continue to the thalamus which in turn sends information to the motor cortex.

2. The second loop involves activity from the substantia nigra, which projects dopaminergic neurons to the striatum causing two opposite effects on two different receptors, the D1 and D2 dopamine receptors: excitation (in D1) and inhibition (in D2).

The excitation and inhibition of movements are regulated by the dopaminergic input to the striatum (from the SNpc) and go to the basal ganglia via the *direct* and *indirect* pathways:

- **Direct pathway:** The main function of the direct pathway is to excite

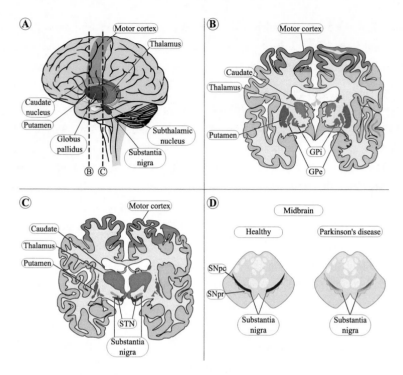

Figure 2.3: *Schematic views of the motor cortex, the thalamus, and components of the basal ganglia. (A) shows a lateral view of the left hemisphere of the human brain. The dashed vertical lines represent two coronal cuts (B and C) of posterior sections of the brain. (D) shows a superior view of the midbrain signaling the substantia nigra (with SNpc and SNpr) in a healthy (left) and Parkinson's disease (right) brain.* **GPi:** *Globus pallidus internal segment;* **GPe:** *Globus pallidus external segment;* **STN:** *Subthalamic nucleus;* **SNpc:** *substantia nigra pars compacta;* **SNpr:** *substantia nigra pars reticulata. Adapted from Häggström (2021) and Madhero (2021)*

the motor cortex and to facilitate movement. This pathway begins in the motor cortex, where the neural impulses enter the basal ganglia through the striatum via glutamatergic neurons, which produce an excitatory neurotransmitter called glutamate. Then, the neurons from the striatum send their axons to the GPi and SNpr via GABAergic inhibitory projections.

The neurons from the Gpi/SNpr communicate with the thalamus, also via inhibitory projections. Then, the thalamus excitatory pathways go to the motor cortex resulting in an increased motor activity.

• **Indirect pathway:** The main function is to inhibit motor activity by suppressing involuntary movement. The pathway begins in the motor cortex by projecting glutamate to the striatum. The neurons in the striatum send their axons to the GPe, then continue to the STN and the Gpi/SNpr, which in turn, suppress the activity of the thalamus on the motor cortex.

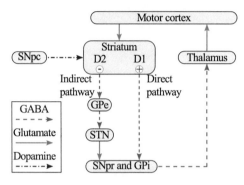

Figure 2.4: *Diagram of the internal connections between motor cortex and basal ganglia. The dashed red lines indicate inhibitory projections and the green lines indicate excitatory projections. In the direct pathway the striatum communicates directly to the GPi and SNpr. In the indirect pathway, the striatum communicates to the GPi and SNpr through the GPe and the STN. The dopamine projected from the SNpc to the striatum causes excitatory and inhibitory effects on D1 and D2 receptors, respectively. **GABA**: γ-aminobutyric acid; **GPi**: Globus pallidus internal segment; **GPe**: Globus pallidus external segment; **STN**: Subthalamic nucleus; **SNpc**: substantia nigra pars compacta; **SNpr**: substantia nigra pars reticulata. Based on Obeso et al. (2000)*

In summary, dopamine helps to regulate the excitability of the neurons in the striatum, which is involved in the body movement. In a healthy brain, the signal that is forwarded from the motor cortex (and continues to the body) is the result (in part) of a balanced activation of neurons in the direct and indirect pathways. In PD patients, decreased dopamine levels cause an *increased* inhibition in the Gpe in the indirect pathway. In parallel, there is a *decreased* inhibition of the GPi activity in the direct pathway. The result is an increased activity in the GPi/SNpr output of the basal ganglia, which makes it difficult to the patients to control their movements (Obeso et al., 2000).

2.2.2 Motor speech disorders in Parkinson's disease

The speech production disorders often associated with PD are known as hypokinetic dysarthria, which is the result of a dysfunction in the basal ganglia internal pathways. As described by Duffy (2000), hypokinetic dysarthria is characterized by a reduction in the range of movements, rigidity, and slow repetitive movements affecting different dimensions of speech such as phonation, articulation, and prosody. Phonation problems include tight breathiness, hoarse speech, voice tremor, and bowing of the vocal cords. Phonatory deviations are usually evaluated during sustained phonation of vowels. In the case of articulation, the reduced range of movements of jaw, lips, and tongue results in prolongation of speech sounds, problems to initiate speech, and imprecise articulation of sounds, which can be evident during speech tasks including conversations, reading, alternating and sequential production of syllables (/pa/, /ta/, /ka/, and /pa-ta-ka/). In the case of prosody, the most common speech disorders include a reduction in the variability of pitch (monopitch) and loudness (monoloudness), rapid speech rate, reduced loudness. Prosodic deviations are mainly detected during conversational and read speech tasks.

2.3 Auditory system and speech control

2.3.1 Overview of the auditory system

The auditory system is composed of the outer, middle, and inner ear (cochlea) and regions in the brain including the auditory cortex. Figure 2.5[2] shows a

---

[2]This figure is an adapted version of https://en.wikipedia.org/wiki/File:Anatomy_of_the_Human_Ear_cs.svg

diagram of the components in the ear. Sound waves travel through the ear canal (an air-filled path) setting the eardrum into vibration. The middle ear (an air-filled chamber) acts as a mechanical bridge between the eardrum and the inner ear by means of three small bones (*malleus*, *incus*, and *stapes*). The movements of the eardrum are transmitted by these bones to the *oval window*, which is the entrance to the inner ear: the cochlea is a fluid-filled cavity (*perilymphatic* fluid) with three scales formed as a snake. In the middle scale is the Corti organ on the basilar membrane which contains the hair cells. The mechanical vibrations produced in the middle ear are transformed into electrical signals by hair cells found in the *basilar membrane* within the cochlea (Figure 2.5[3]). Specifically, when the *oval window* is being push-in by the *stapes*, the fluids in the cochlea are moved towards the apex, generating pressure waves at different points in the *basilar membrane*, which in turn, bends the hair cells releasing a neurotransmitter that fires *auditory* neurons that connect the ear with the brain. There are two different hair cells - the inner hair cell that functions as a receptor and the outer hair cell that amplify the incoming signal. A deviation of the *basilar membrane* leads to a bending of the tiny hairs on the top of these cells that results in rhythmic elongation and shortening of the outer cells according to the frequency representation at their location and by that to an increased *basilar membrane* vibration. The flow of fluid inside the cochlea produced by the inward movement of the *oval window* is accommodated by the *round window* at the other end of the cochlea (Denes and Pinson, 1993).

The information about frequencies of the acoustic signals are encoded by the auditory system by locating the places of the *basilar membrane* in which the pressure waves produce the maximum displacement (vibration) amplitude. For instance, the place of maximum displacement for high frequencies occurs near the base (stiffest part), while for lower frequencies, the place of maximum

[3]This figure is an adapted version of `https://medienportal.siemens-stiftung.org/en/cochlea-transparent-uncoiled-101976`

vibration displacement occurs towards the apex (Loizou, 1999). After the sound waves are transmitted and transformed into electrical impulses in the inner ear, the receptor neurons transmit the signals over a pathway of nerves (passing through regions of the medulla and the midbrain) connected to the auditory cortex. The phenomenon of frequency-localization-organization called "tonotopy" persists from the cochlea over the neurons to the cortex.

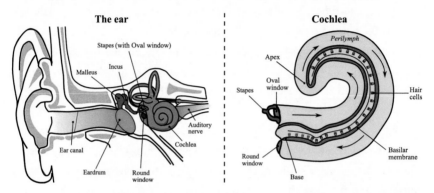

Figure 2.5: *(Left). Schematic view of the outer, middle, and inner ear. (Right). portion of the cochlea in the inner ear. Sound waves are transformed into electrical signals by the bending of the hair cells inside the basilar membrane. Adapted from Brockmann (2021).*

2.3.2 Cochlear implants (CIs)

As described in Section 1.2.2, sensorineural hearing loss is caused by disorders in the inner ear occurring at birth, due to a disease, as the result of an infection, among others. For instance, Meningitis is an infection that can destroy the hair cells within the cochlea. Thus, without the hair cells, the connection between the ear and the central nervous system is broken (Weber and Klein, 1999). CIs bypass the damaged parts by triggering the hearing nerves via a direct electrical stimulation through electrodes inserted in the cochlea (Figure 2.6[4]). In general,

---

[4]This figure is an adapted version of `https://www.embopress.org/doi/full/10.15252/emmm.201911618`
Last retrieved 02/02/2021; under the Creative Commons Attribution 4.0 license

a CI consists of an external speech processor, which captures, preprocesses, and transforms the speech signals into electrical impulses which are sent to an array of electrodes implanted inside the cochlea of the patient. Commonly, the insertion of the electrodes is performed through the *round window*. The insertion depth depends on the size of the cochlea and can reach distances close to the apex (Carlson, 2020; Lenarz, 2017). The implants may have 12 or 22 (only half of them are active) electrodes along the cochlea. There are a number of factors that can influence the frequency resolution of the sounds perceived with help of a CI (Brant and Eliades, 2020; Loizou, 1999). Some factors are:

1. The distance between the electrode contacts and the auditory neurons. Neural activation decreases as the result of a decreased strength of the electrical stimulation in the targeted neuron region.

2. The spread of the electrical stimulation. The propagation of the electrical current in the electrodes, is spread by the *perilymphatic* fluid along the cochlea; thus, the electrical excitation is not focused on a single region and might excite the surrounding neurons.

3. The number of *auditory* neurons available for electrical stimulation is limited. In order for the CI to work properly, there has to be neural tissue left to receive electrical current.

4. The insertion by the surgeon sometimes is difficult resulting in a diminished number of activated electrodes.

Considering what is mentioned above, it is clear why a CI user may notice differences between the sounds perceived and the sounds produced, even after cochlear implantation (Lane et al., 1995).

2.3.3 Auditory feedback and speech control

Auditory feedback is the precondition of constant survey and correction of our own speech and by that for the development and maintenance of speech

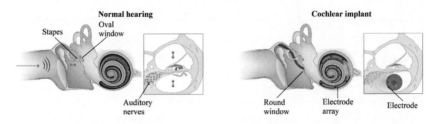

Figure 2.6: *(Left). Schematic view of a cochlea (and cross-section) with normal hearing. (Right). Schematic view of a cochlea (and cross-section) with an implant. Commonly, the electrode array is implanted through the round window. The electrical stimulation of the electrode contact is spread in a region of the target neurons. Adapted from Dieter et al. (2020).*

movements. As described by Tourville et al. (2008), speech motor control is characterized by $feedback$ and $feedforward$ control. On the one hand, in $feedback\ control$ the performance of the movements is evaluated during execution and any deviation is corrected according to sensory information. On the other hand, in $feedforward\ control$ the performance of the movements depends on previously learned commands without relying on sensory information. These mechanisms of speech control are often examined and include different aspects. Some examples of the impact of auditory feedback on these two processes include:

- Voice control, when a speaker raises his/her voice because the self-perceived loudness is too low or simply to overcome background noise (Lombard effect; Lombard (1911)).

- Speech disfluency caused by delayed auditory feedback (Stuart et al., 2002)

- Adaptation of formant frequencies when a speaker hears persistent shift of formants of their own speech (Purcell and Munhall, 2006; Tourville et al., 2008).

Normally, speech production is constantly monitored and compared to an internal speech model in the brain which is acquired and maintained with the use of auditory feedback (Perkell et al., 2000). In the Directions Into Velocities of Articulators (DIVA) model of speech production proposed by Guenther (1994), the speech movements are planned considering a speech sound map (in the motor cortex) that is activated to: (1) learn speech sound targets and (2) to control the necessary articulatory movements to achieve different acoustic goals (Guenther and Hickok, 2016). With ongoing hearing loss the speech sound map can slightly change, but moreover, the sensory-motor control is decreasing as one tends to use only as much force and effort for all movements as necessary (Guenther et al., 2004; Perkell et al., 2007). This has a considerable impact on speech of people with hearing impairment. For instance, when hearing loss occurs after speech acquisition (post-lingual onset of deafness), at first somatosensory feedback maintains precise speech production. If there is a persistent lack of auditory feedback, speech production may eventually deteriorate due to a diminished precision of articulation.

Summary

The speech production process requires the complex coordination of regions in the brain, vocal tract, and auditory system. Depending on the clinical condition, different aspects of speech can be affected, and thus, it is possible to detect these changes using automatic acoustic analysis. The following chapter describes the techniques and methods used to model pathological speech signals and detect speech production changes by analyzing aspects related to phonation, articulation, and prosody.

Chapter 3

State-of-the-art

3.1 Severity estimation of Parkinson's disease from speech

Typically, the assessment of the neurological state of PD patients from the speech is performed using regression analysis, which consists of training a model to learn the relationship between acoustic features (extracted from the speech signals) and the clinical score of the patient.

Several studies have addressed the prediction of clinical scores of PD patients. Asgari and Shafran (2010) proposed a methodology to predict the UPDRS-III score (motor sub-score) from speech recordings of 61 PD patients and 21 Healthy Controls (HC). Phonation, articulation, and prosody analyses were performed by extracting acoustic features from the sustained phonation of the vowel /a/, the rapid repetition of /pa-ta-ka/, and the reading of three standard texts. The set of features considered are F0, jitter (cycle-to-cycle variation of pitch), shimmer (cycle-to-cycle variation of the glottal waveform), spectral entropy (entropy of the log power spectrum), cepstral coefficients (shape of the spectral envelope), the number and duration of voiced and unvoiced frames, among others. A feature vector was formed for each speaker, and a Support Vector Regressor (SVR) was trained to predict the patients' UPDRS scores. The authors reported that it is possible to estimate the UPDRS-III with a Mean

Absolute Error (MAE) of 5.66 using an ε-SVR with a cubic polynomial kernel. Tsanas et al. (2010) performed regression analysis to estimate the UPDRS scores from 42 PD patients (28 male, 14 female). Speech recordings with the sustained phonation of vowels were captured once per week for six months. However, the neurological state of the patients was assessed only three times during that period: at the beginning, three months later, and at the end. Thus, the authors used a piece-wise linear interpolation in order to obtain the missing UPDRS scores. Speech signals were modeled considering acoustic features based on pitch/amplitude perturbation, noise, and entropy. Regression analysis was performed using least squares, Least Absolute Shrinkage and Selection Operator (LASSO), and Classification And Regression Trees (CARTs). Additionally, the MAE was used to evaluate the proposed approach's performance to estimate the total UPDRS and the scores from the motor section (UPDRS-III). The authors reported that the CARTs approach was the best approach with an MAE of 7.5 points in the evaluation of the total value of the UPDRS scale. The scores of the motor section in the UPDRS were estimated with an MAE of 6 points. Skodda et al. (2013) presented a study where the speech deterioration was evaluated over time. The speech of 80 PD patients (48 male, 32 female) was recorded from 2002 to 2012 in two recording sessions. The time between the first and second sessions ranged from 12 to 88 months. A control group of 60 healthy persons (30 male, 30 female) was also considered. The participants were asked to read a text and to produce a sustained phonation of the vowel /a/. In both sessions, the patients were assessed by neurologist experts according to the UPDRS-III. The audio signals were perceptually evaluated considering four aspects of speech: voice, articulation, prosody, and fluency. Acoustic analysis was performed to describe these speech aspects. Voice was modeled with a set of features, including jitter, shimmer, and pitch average. The Vowel Articulation Index (VAI) and the proportion of pauses within polysyllabic words were considered for articulation. Prosody is analyzed with the estimation of the standard deviation of the pitch. In addition, fluency was evaluated considering the speech rate and the pause ratio. To assess the progression of speech and voice impairments, the authors compared the extracted features in the first and the second session. The authors found significant differences for shimmer, speech rate, pause ratio, and VAI when features extracted from the first session were compared to the same features extracted from the second session. However, as the authors stated, the results were not conclusive due to methodological limitations, like a long time between the two recording sessions. Bayestehtashk et al. (2015) considered three regression techniques to predict the UPDRS scores, including ridge regression, LASSO regression, and linear SVR. Speech recordings of 168 patients were collected in a single recording session. Automatic methods for acoustic analysis of PD was also addressed in the Parkinson's Condition sub-challenge, which was part of the INTERSPEECH 2015 Computational Paralinguistic Challenge (Schuller et al., 2015). The challenge consisted on predicting the MDS-UPDRS-III score, using recordings of 50 patients (25 male, 25 female) included in the PC-GITA database (Orozco-Arroyave et al., 2014) were considered to form the train and development subsets. The test set included a total of 11 new patients recorded in non-controlled noise conditions, i.e., not using a sound-proof booth. A total of 42 speech tasks were considered. The neurological state of the patients was assessed by a neurologist expert according to the MDS-UPDRS-III subscale. The winners of the challenge (Grósz et al., 2015) reported a Spearman's correlation of 0.65 between the real MDS-UPDRS-III scores and the predicted values using deep rectifier neural networks and Gaussian processes. Orozco-Arroyave et al. (2016) presented a methodology to estimate the neurological state (MDS-UPDRS-III) of 158 PD patients: 50 Colombian (25 male), 88 Germans (47 male), and 20 Czech (all male). The regression process was performed using a linear ϵ-SVR. The speech tasks considered are reading isolated words, sentences, a standard text, and a monologue. In order to model articulation problems, the authors extracted the energy in the transitions from unvoiced to voiced (onset) and from voiced to unvoiced (offset) segments considering different frequency bands distributed according to the Bark and the Mel scales. Speech intelligibility was evaluated using an automatic speech recognition system. According to the authors, the neurological state of the patients (MDS-UPDRS-III) can be estimated with a Spearman's correlation of up to 0.74 when several speech tasks are modeled considering the fusion of articulation and intelligibility measures. The openSMILE toolkit was considered for feature extraction, which allows computing more than 6000 descriptors (Eyben et al., 2010). The authors reported that the neurological state of the patients could be assessed with an MAE of 5.5. A study for the monitoring of PD progression was also presented by Gómez-Vilda et al. (2017). The authors considered speech recordings from 8 male patients captured twice for four weeks between sessions. Speech recordings of 100 healthy speakers were considered as a baseline. The participants were asked to perform the sustained phonation of the vowels /a/, /e/, /i/, /o/,/u/, and read a short sentence and a standard text. The authors used two methods to estimate the features: (i) vocal tract inversion using an adaptive lattice filter and (ii) biomechanical inversion of a 2-mass model of the vocal folds. The features include jitter, shimmer, harmonicity, vocal fold body mechanical stress, and tremor during vibration of the vocal folds. During the recording sessions, the patients continued their pharmacological treatment and received speech therapy. Each patient was evaluated according to the H&Y scale. The relationship between the neurological scale and the acoustic features was evaluated using hypothesis testing based on Bayesian Likelihood. According to the authors, the tremor and biomechanical features evolve differently with the treatment. The authors suggest defining different time intervals between evaluations to obtain more conclusive results. Sztahó et al. (2017) proposed a method to estimate the severity of PD using rhythm-based features. The authors considered speech recordings of 51 PD patients (25 male) and 27 healthy speakers (14 male) from Hungary. All of the patients were evaluated according to the H&Y scale. The speech tasks consisted of a monologue and the reading of a standard text. The set of rhythm features includes the standard deviation of the duration of consonants and vowels, the average duration of the speech/pauses, the pause ratio, percentage of consonants/vowels, the articulation rate, and the raw and normalized Pairwise Variability Index (rPVI, nPVI) of the consonants and vowels. Regression analysis was performed to estimate the severity of the disease using linear regression, SVR, Artificial Neural Networks (ANN), and Deep Neural Networks (DNN). The authors obtained Spearman's correlation coefficient of up to 0.744 (SVR, reading task) between the predicted and the target H&Y scores. Hemmerling and Wojcik-Pedziwiatr (2020) estimated the severity of PD by extracting acoustic features from the sustained phonation of the vowels /a/, /e/, /i/, /o/, and /u/. The set of features includes average F0, jitter, shimmer, energy, spectral moments, MFCCs, Perceptual Linear Prediction (PLP) coefficients, among others. For this, speech recordings of 27 PD patients from Poland were captured five times for 180 minutes after taking levodopa medication. Additionally, a neurologist expert estimated the UPDRS score of the patients in the five recording sessions. The motor UPDRS scores of the patients were estimated using multiple linear regression, Random Forest (RF) regression, and SVR. The authors reported that the lowest error between predictions and clinical scores was obtained for the vowel /a/ (MAE=1.85) when the regression analysis was performed with RF.

Other studies have also considered regression analysis to estimate the dysarthria level of PD patients. Cernak et al. (2017) evaluated the changes in the voice quality of the speakers by considering the mFDA score related to larynx deficits (Table 1.3). The authors trained an SVR with phoneme posterior probabilities extracted from recordings of 50 PD patients and 50 HC speakers from Colombia. The speech tasks include the rapid repetition of /pa-ta-ka/, the reading of a standard text, and a monologue. The authors reported Spearman's correlation coefficients of up to 0.57 between the predicted scores and the larynx mFDA score. García et al. (2017) predicted the neurological state and dysarthria level of 50 PD patients according to the MDS-UPDRS-III and mFDA scores, respectively. Acoustic analysis was performed by considering different pitch, loudness, duration, and filterbank analysis parameters. These features were extracted from 4 speech tasks, including the rapid repetition of syllables (e.g.,/pa-ta-ka/), a monologue, and reading a text and different

33

sentences. Then, the i–vector approach was considered to obtain the speaker models (or embeddings) of 50 PD patients and 50 HC speakers from Colombia (See Chapter 4). The authors reported that it was possible to predict the MDS-UPDRS-III with a Spearman correlation of 0.63 when phonation and articulation features extracted from the sentences were considered to train the i–vectors. Additionally, the mFDA was predicted with a Spearman correlation of 0.72 when considering the rapid repetition of /pa-ta-ka/ modeled with phonation, articulation, and prosody features. Vásquez-Correa et al. (2018) estimated the dysarthria level of 68 PD patients and 50 HC speakers from Colombia. The set of speech tasks included the sustained phonation of Spanish vowels, the reading of 10 sentences, a standard text, a monologue, and the rapid repetition of /pa-ta-ka/, /pa-ka-ta/, /pe-ta-ka/, /pa/, /ta/, and /ka/. Automatic acoustic analysis was performed with i–vector speaker models obtained from phonation, articulation, prosody, and intelligibility-based features. Additionally, three variations of ridge regression (linear, kernel, bayesian) and two variations of SVR were considered to estimate the mFDA scores of the patients and the HC controls. The authors reported that the higher Spearman's correlation coefficient was 0.69 for articulation features extracted from continuous speech. Karan et al. (2020) combined $F0$ and Hilbert's spectral features to estimate the mFDA score of 70 PD patients. The authors considered speech recordings with the sustained phonation of the vowels /a/, /e/, /i/, /o/, and /u/ and the reading of 10 isolated words. Regression analysis was performed with an ε-SVR. The authors reported Spearman's correlations of 0.75 (for the vowel /o/) and 0.77 (for the word $reina$; "Queen").

Table 3.1 summarizes the studies related to the severity estimation of PD. In general, the sustained phonation of vowels and the reading of a standard text are the most frequently used speech tasks to assess the patient's neurological state. As described in Section 1.2.1, such a task allows detection of speech problems. In the case of the reading task, the acoustic analysis allows evaluating articulation and prosody problems. The most common biomarkers considered to model speech problems include pitch ($F0$, jitter), harmonicity, e.g., harmonics-to-noise ratio, and the spectral energy of the signal. Furthermore, the SVR has been suitable for modeling the relationship between the acoustic features and the clinical score.

Table 3.1: Summary of works related to the severity estimation of PD. Longitudinal analysis refers to studies that consider several speech recordings captured in different sessions from the same patients.

Authors	Subjects	Acoustic parameters	Method (best result)	Clinical scale	Longitudinal analysis
Asgari 2010	61 PD/21 HC	Loudness, duration entropy, harmonicity pitch, spectral energy	SVR	UPDRS-III	No
Tsanas 2010	42 PD	Pitch, harmonicity nonlinear analysis	CART	Total UPDRS UPDRS-III	Yes
Skodda 2013	80 PD	Pitch, articulation fluency, harmonicity	Shapiro-Wilk statistical test	UPDRS-III	Yes
Bayestehtashk. 2015	168 PD	Loudness, duration entropy, harmonicity pitch, spectral energy	SVR	UPDRS-III	No
Grósz 2015[‡]	61 PD/ 50 HC	Articulation	Gaussian processes	MDS-UPDRS-III	No
Orozco-Arroyave 2016	158 PD[*]	Articulation, intelligibility	SVR	MDS-UPDRS-III	No
Gómez-Vilda 2017	8 PD/ 100 HC	Pitch, harmonicity vocal folds tremor, body mass features	Bayesian likelihood	H&Y	Yes
Sztahó 2017	51 PD/27 HC	Speech rate, duration, rhythm	SVR	H&Y	No
Cernak 2017	50 PD/ 50 HC	Phoneme posterior probabilities	SVR	mFDA (Larynx)	No
García-Ospina 2017	50 PD/ 50 HC	Pitch, loudness articulation, duration	i–vectors	mFDA MDS-UPDRS-III	No
Vásquez-Correa 2018	68 PD/ 50 HC	Speaker embeddings with i–vectors	SVR	mFDA	No
Hemmerling 2020	27 PD	Pitch, loudness, spectral energy, filterbank features	SVR	UPDRS-III	No
Karan 2020	70 PD	Pitch, Hilbert spectral features	SVR	mFDA	No

[*] This study includes speakers from Colombia (50), Germany (88), and Czech republic (20)
[‡] Winners of the Parkinson's Condition sub-challenge (Schuller et al., 2015)

3.2 Speech analysis of cochlear implant users

Oral communication skills of severely and profoundly hearing-impaired speakers can be improved by cochlear implantation. Such an improvement has been observed by a better contrast to produce consonants, a decreased production

35

of average F0 values, loudness, and duration of speech segments. Nevertheless, the speech production of CI users is affected even after rehabilitation by cochlear implantation. Plant and Oster (1986) investigated pitch, duration, and articulation changes on the speech of one female speaker recorded in two sessions: before and after cochlear implantation. The speech tasks consisted of the reading of a text and a list of words. Pitch and duration were evaluated from the reading of the text by computing the average and standard deviation of the $F0$ contour, the total phonation time, the average duration of the pauses, and an estimated value of articulation rate (the number of syllables divided by the total phonation time). Articulation was evaluated by extracting the vowels from the list of words and computing the ratio between the first and second formants ($F1/F2$) to detect shifts in the vowel space area. The authors reported that after implantation, the speech parameters from the CI uses moved towards "normality" values, which were obtained by performing the same analysis on the recording of an age-matched typical hearing speaker. As stated by the authors, the main limitation of that study was that only one speaker was considered. Furthermore, the authors believe that speech improvement by the CI users may be the result of training. Perkell et al. (1992) performed acoustic analysis considering speech recordings of four postlingually deafened CI users. The recording sessions were performed pre- and post-activation of the speech processor. Post-activation recordings were captured at different week intervals. The features considered for analysis were $F0$, $F1$, $F2$, Sound Pressure Level (SPL), duration, and amplitude difference between the first two harmonic peaks in the log-magnitude spectrum. The speech tasks consisted of reading nine vowels (included in predefined words) spoken in a carrier sentence. The authors reported that, after activation, many of the acoustic parameters moved toward values reported in previous studies, which considered healthy speakers. However, these results were based on the outcome of only four speakers. Lane et al. (1995) measured the VOT in stop-initial syllables produced by five CI users. Short-term and long-term analyses were performed. For the short-term analysis, the recordings were captured after turning off the speech processor of the patients for 24 hours, then turned on, and then off again. For long-term analysis, speech recordings were captured before and after activation of the speech processor in intervals of 0, 4, 12, 26, 52, 104 weeks. The speech task consisted of the reading of the six English stop consonants embedded in a carrier sentence. The measurements for the VOT were performed manually. The authors examined the effect of processor activation and found increased VOT measurements in the voiced stop consonants for the short-time analysis and increased VOT values for the long-term analysis. The authors suggest that changes in voiced stops are related to concurrent changes in pitch and SPL. For the case of voiceless stops, the changes are linked to auditory valida-tion of phonemic settings. One limitation of this study is the reduced amount of speakers considered for the experiments. Gould et al. (2001) examined speech intelligibility of four postlingually deafened adults before and after 6 and 12 months of activation. The participants were instructed to produce ten repetitions. Speech intelligibility was measured for vowels and consonants individually using a metric called the percentage of transmitted information. The authors reported an overall improvement in word intelligibility; however, such an improvement was not consistent for individual consonants or vowels. Blamey et al. (2001) analyzed the speech production of nine children for six years after implantation. Speech intelligibility was assessed by considering phonetic transcriptions of conversational speech. The transcriptions were used to measure the percentage of correctly produced words. The authors observed an increase in speech intelligibility, length, and phonemic accuracy during the six years. However, the rate of improvement was considerably slower than that observed in normally-hearing children who developed their linguistic skills at a younger age. Hassan et al. (2012) evaluated speech nasalization considering 25 postlingual CI users and 25 age-matched HC from Saudi Arabia. The patients were divided into three groups according to the duration of hearing loss before implantation: (1) less than three years (7 patients), (2) between 3 and 6 years (8 patients), and (3) more than six years (10 patients). For evaluation, percentage scores of nasalance were obtained from two sentences read by participants.

The scores were obtained with a nasometer which measures the acoustic output from the oral and nasal cavities. Nasalance scores were obtained for each patient before implantation and after 6, 12, and 24 months of CI activation. The authors reported that for the three groups of patients, there is a tendency from the nasalance scores to decrease over time; however, the level of nasality was still higher than in the control group. Furthermore, the authors found that the degree of nasality and the improvement over time depend on hearing loss duration. In the study presented by Ubrig et al. (2011) deviations in the phonation of CI users were investigated. For this, the authors considered speech recordings of 40 postlingual CI users and 12 postlingually hearing-impaired adults without implants from Brazil. Two recording sessions were performed for the CI users: before implantation and 6-9 months after activation of the device. Acoustic analysis was performed by computing the average and standard deviation of the F0 contour obtained from the recordings of the sustained phonation of the vowel /a/ and the reading of a standard text. The authors found a significant reduction of F0 variability when comparing the first to the second recording session.

Other works have investigated the impact of the onset of hearing loss in the speech of CI users, i.e., pre-/post-lingual hearing loss. Vowel articulation of pre- and post-lingual deafened CI users was evaluated by Neumeyer et al. (2010). Speech recordings of 10 CI users (5 prelingual) and ten age-matched normal hearing speakers from Germany were considered for the test. Articulation analysis was performed by computing the vowel space of /a/, /e/, /i/, /o/, and /u/ which are extracted from target words included within 20 standard sentences. The acoustic parameters extracted from the vowels include the first and second formant frequencies. The authors reported a reduction of the vowel space area for the CI users compared to normal hearing speakers; particularly, such a reduction is mainly caused by the misarticulation of back vowels (/o/, /u/). One reason the authors give is that such vowels are produced with tongue movements that are not *visible* to the CI users. Additionally, the authors did not report differences between pre- and post-lingual CI users. The authors suggest that

38

since postlingual CI users spent years without sufficient hearing and auditory feedback before implantation, their articulatory capability was diminished. Pre- and post-lingual CI users have been found to have limited production contrast of sibilant sounds, e.g., /s/ and /ʃ/. Todd et al. (2011) analyzed speech recordings from 33 CI children (all prelingual) and 43 age-matched HC English native speakers from the United States. All children were asked to read 18 words with the sibilant sound (/s/ or /ʃ/) in the initial position. The target phonemes were manually transcribed and evaluated by trained native speakers. The acoustic analysis was performed by computing the energy in the Bark scale from a Hamming window of 40 ms located in the middle of the sibilant sound. Then, only the Bark band with the highest energy was selected for evaluation. From the transcription analysis, it was observed that CI children produced the /s/ with less accuracy than /ʃ/. Furthermore, the children produced these two phonemes with less accuracy than the HC. Regarding the acoustic analysis, the authors found that CI children produced the sibilant sounds with less energy than the control group, which results in a reduced contrast between /s/ and /ʃ/. The authors suggest that such a diminished contrast may be caused by a poor frequency resolution in the implant. Similarly, Neumeyer et al. (2015) analyzed the German sibilant sounds /s/ and /ʃ/ produced by 48 CI users (24 prelinguals) and 48 HC speakers. The patients were divided into four groups depending on the onset of hearing loss (pre-/post-lingual) and the time between hearing loss and cochlear implantation (before/after language acquisition). The study participants were asked to read a *carrier* sentence containing two words that differed only in one consonant and with different meanings: *Tasche* (bag) and *Tasse* (cup). Acoustic analysis was performed by manually segmenting the sibilant sounds from the recordings and then computing the first spectral moment. From the results, the authors concluded that the sibilant production of CI users deviates from normal speech, that onset of deafness plays a role in the degree of the deviation, but that the duration between onset of hearing loss and implantation has no significant effect impact on the sibilant production. The authors explained that such deviations might occur because the spectral resolution of the implant is lower in higher frequencies; thus, CI users shift the production of the sibilant sounds into the frequency range perceived by them. The speech intelligibility of pre- and post-lingual CI users can also be affected in different ways. Ruff et al. (2017) performed the automatic evaluation of the speech production intelligibility using an ASR system. The authors considered recordings of 50 CI users (14 prelingual, 36 postlingual) and 50 HC German native speakers for the experiments. The patients were divided into three groups: (1) prelingually deafened CI users with more than two years before surgery, (2) postlingually deafened CI users with **less** than two years before surgery, and (3) postlingually deafened CI users with **more** than two years before surgery. The study participants were asked to read a total of 97 words that contain every phoneme of the German language in different positions within the words. Then, the Word Recognition Rate (WR) was computed from the automatic transcriptions obtained from the ASR. The system was trained with 27 hours of speech recordings using the 97 words from the test as the vocabulary. The authors found that CI users with the postlingual onset of hearing loss and short duration of deafness (< 2 years before surgery) have higher WR than postlingual with a long duration of deafness and prelingual. Furthermore, the postlingual CI users with a short duration of deafness showed WR similar to the HC speakers. Gautam et al. (2019) presented a review of more than 25 studies (from 1983 to 2017) related to speech and voice changes due to hearing loss and the effect of CI in adults and children. The acoustic parameters evaluated in those works include pitch, loudness, consonant contrast, speech duration/rate, vowel articulation (VSA), and VOT. Changes in speech and voice due to hearing loss include: (1) increased pitch, loudness, and duration of speech, (2) reduced VSA and VOT, and (3) slower speech rate. The studies in the literature have reported that most of these parameters move towards normality after cochlear implantation; however, speech and voice deviations are still present.

Table 3.2 shows a summary of the works reviewed in this section. Although speech production of CI users has been addressed before, the number of studies considering automatic methods for acoustic analysis is limited. From the works reviewed, it can be observed that speech and voice parameters such as pitch and loudness deviate from *normality* values even after implantation. Furthermore, poor contrast to produce some phonemes such as /s/ and /ʃ/ has been associated with the limited resolution of the CI to provided good perception to the patients.

Table 3.2: Summary of works related to acoustic analysis of speech production of CI users.

Authors	Subjects	Acoustic parameters	Method	Effect of hearing loss	Automatic analysis
Plant 1986	1 CI/1 HC	Pitch	Mean and variation of $F0$	Reduced $F0$	No
		Duration	Voiced segments	Longer duration	
		Vowel articulation	Formant frequencies	Reduced VSA	
Perkell 1992	4 CI	Pitch	Mean $F0$	Reduced $F0$	No
		Duration	Vowel duration	Longer duration	
		Loudness	Mean SPL	Reduced loudness	
		Vowel articulation	Formant frequencies	Reduced VSA	
Lane 1995	5 CI	Duration	Voiced and voiceless VOT	Reduced VOT	No
Gould 2001	4 CI	Intelligibility	Percentage of information transmitted	Poor speech intelligibility	No
Blamey 2001	9 CI	Intelligibility words	Percentage of correct intelligibility	Poor speech	No
Neumeyer 2010	10 CI	Vowel articulation	Formant frequencies to estimate the VSA	Reduced VSA	No
Todd 2011	33 CI	Consonant articulation	Bark energies to evaluate the production contrast between the phonemes /s/ and /ʃ/	Poor contrast	No
Ubrig 2011	40 CI/12 HI*	Pitch	Mean and standard deviation of $F0$	Higher variation of $F0$	No
					No
Hassan 2012	25 CI/ 25 HC	Nasality	Nasometer to estimate the nasality level	Higher level of nasality	No
Neumeyer 2015	48 CI	Consonant articulation	Spectral moment to evaluate the production contrast between the phonemes /s/ and /ʃ/	Poor contrast	No
Ruff 2017	50 CI/ 50 HC	Intelligibility using an ASR system	Word recognition rate recognition rate	Lower word	Yes
Gautam 2019	NA†	Pitch	Mean $F0$ and jitter	Increased pitch	-
		Loudness	Mean SPL and shimmer	Increased loudness	
		Duration	Word/syllable duration, VOT	Longer durations	
		Speech rate	Speaking rate	Slower rate	
		Vowel articulation	Formant frequencies, VSA	Reduced VSA	
		Consonant articulation	/s/ vs /ʃ/; /r/ vs /l/	Poor contrast	

*HI: Hearing impaired.
†Information about the number of speakers not available.

3.3   Aging and speech

Some studies have analyzed the impact of aging in speech. Xue and Deliyski (2001) considered sustained phonations of the English vowel /a/ and computed fifteen phonation measures of the Multi-Dimensional Voice Program. The set of measures includes F0, jitter, Pitch Perturbation Quotient (PPQ), Relative Average Perturbation (RAP), variability of F0, Amplitude Perturbation Quotient (APQ), shimmer, Noise to Harmonics Ratio (NHR), among others. A total of 44 speakers (21 male and 23 female) aged between 70 and 80 years were considered and compared with respect to the norms for young and middle-aged adults published by Deliyski and Gress (1998). The authors performed statistical analyses and reported that the voice of elderly people is significantly different (usually poorer) than the voice of young and middle-aged adults. Goy et al. (2013) considered several phonation measures to assess the stability of vocal fold vibration and to quantify the noise in the voice of 159 younger speakers at ages between 18 and 28 years, and 133 older adults with ages between 63 and 86 years. The authors concluded that the instability of the vocal fold vibration increases with age. The dysphonia severity index was also measured and only older females exhibited higher values than those in younger females. No statistical differences were observed between younger and older males. Another study that evaluates the influence of aging in the speech of elderly people considering phonation and articulation analyses is presented by Torre and Barlow (2009). A total of 27 young speakers with mean age of 25.6 years and 59 older people with mean age of 75.2 years were considered. Each participant was asked to read a set of 22 consonant-vowel-consonant words. The vowels and oral stops of each word where extracted and analyzed using Praat (Boersma and Weenink, 2001). The authors analyzed several acoustic properties including F0, the first three formant frequencies and the VOT. According to the results, there was a decrease of F0 with age for women and a increase of F0 with age for men. This finding is consistent with the results reported by Benjamin (1981). The authors highlighted also that older men showed shorter VOTs than both younger men and younger women, which is also reported by

Benjamin (1982). A greater variability in F0, the three formants, and the VOT is systematically observed in the speech productions by older adults compared to their younger same-sex counterparts. As the natural aging process in humans carries several alterations in speech production and perception, the impact of aging in the detection of voice disorders is still an open problem and its relevance in the clinical practice was studied by Pernambuco et al. (2017). The relationship between age and speech production was investigated by Tremblay et al. (2018). Speech recordings of 60 adults at ages ranging from 18 to 83 years were considered for the experiments. The participants were asked to read meaningless non-words aloud as quickly and accurately as possible. Acoustic parameters included the error rate, vocal reaction time, vocal raction time variability, vocal response duration, and vocal response duration variability. The authors reported an overall increase in error rate, vocal response duration, and in duration variability with age. The authors concluded that there is an age-related decline in the planning and execution of speech movements of cognitively healthy adults. Gollan and Goldrick (2019) investigated the influence of the aging process in the production and self-correction of errors during connected speech. Speech recordings of 35 cognitively healthy adults and 56 younger speakers were considered for the tests. The speech task consisted of the reading of 6 paragraphs in three conditions with increasing difficulty: normal, nouns-swapped, and reversing the order of adjacent words every two sentences. Reading times and errors increased with task difficulty, but self-correction rates were lowest in the nouns-swapped condition. The authors observed that elderly speakers read aloud more slowly, produced more speech errors, and self-corrected their errors less often than the young speakers. The authors concluded that aging speakers can compensate for aging-related decline in control over speech production with their vocabulary knowledge and attention to speech planning in more difficult speaking conditions, which suggest that a there is a model of speech production in which planning of speech is relatively automatic, whereas monitoring and self-correction are more attention-demanding, which keeps the speech production relatively intact in aging. Differences in speech and voice were examined by Taylor et al. (2020) which considered speech recordings from 169 speakers across 18 families, with ages ranging from 17 to 89 years. Acoustic analysis was performed by computing pitch, duration, and spectral features including fricative spectral moments, the proportion of time spent speaking, mean speaking fundamental frequency, semitone standard deviation, and cepstral peak prominence. The speech task consisted of the reading of two passages. The authors found significant age effect for fricative spectral center of gravity, spectral skewness, and speaking semitone standard deviation.

3.4 Smartphone-based applications for health care

3.4.1 Applications for Parkinson's disease

Linares-Del Rey et al. (2019) reviewed 125 mobile phone applications reported in the literature between 2011 and 2016. However, only 29 of those apps were identified as assessment apps specifically developed to evaluate PD, and only 2 of those considered speech. Dubey et al. (2015) presented a smartwatch-based system to monitor speech and voice impairments of PD patients. The system consists of a tablet and a smartwatch to perform the data collection. Speech impairments were analyzed considering the sustained phonation of vowel /a/. The speech recordings were sent to a cloud-based server to store and perform the speech analyses; however, those analyses were limited to only phonation measures. Tao et al. (2016) presented a portable system for the automatic recognition of the syllables /pa-ta-ka/. The proposed approach consists of a tablet and a headset to capture the speech signals. The system was trained using speech recordings from two groups of speakers: patients with traumatic brain injuries and PD patients. The automatic recognition of /pa-ta-ka/ was performed in the mobile device using an ASR system. Speech impairments were assessed using a single metric, which consists of the syllable error rate. Another platform to monitor PD using a smartphone was presented by Zhan et al. (2016). The application includes several tests to evaluate different PD symptoms related to dysphonia, postural instability, bradykinesia, and tremor. The monitoring and assessment of PD symptoms were performed with a defined protocol to measure different motor impairments in voice, gait, dexterity, and balance. Later, Zhan et al. (2018) used the same app to collect data from 129 PD patients over the internet and used a ranking algorithm (Dyagilev and Saria, 2016) to assess the severity of the disease. However, only one aspect of speech (phonation) was considered to evaluate the patients.

3.4.2 Applications for hearing loss

To the best of my knowledge, there are no smartphone applications reported in the literature that consider both speech perception and production to assess hearing-impaired people. There are, however, some applications developed to assess hearing perception. There are two types of mobile phone-based applications for hearing screening: tone-based audiometry test and speech-in-noise tests (De De Wet Swanepoel et al., 2019). In a clinical setting, pure-tone testing is performed by reproducing sinusoidal waveforms (tones) at different frequencies through speakers or headphones. One of the main difficulties in adapting this kind of test to mobile phones is that the hardware has to be calibrated. For instance, the mobile phone application presented by Abu-Ghanem et al. (2016), was developed to evaluate hearing loss using pure-tone testing. The app, called $uHear$ (only available on iOS), was validated with a standard audiometric in a clinical setting. For the experiments, the authors considered 26 healthy controls older than 65 years. The patients were asked to put on earphones in order to perform the experiments. The results obtained from $uHear$ and the standard audiometric evaluation agreed to 24 out of 26 subjects; however, the hearing thresholds obtained with the app were less accurate than the standard pure-tone test. The authors suggest that the quality of the earphones influences the obtained results. The multinational technology company Apple Inc. released the app $hearingOS$, which includes a standardized audiometry test module. Since Apple has standard hardware embedded in its devices, the application comes with calibration values. However, due to the high costs of Apple devices, such an app has low usability in low-income countries. The Speech-in-noise test assesses speech perception and understanding of hearing-impaired people in noisy environments. Contrary to the pure-tone test, speech-in-noise does not require device calibration, which allows adapting such tests to different mobile phones and headphones. In 2019, the World Health Organization developed a mobile (iOS and Android) application for hearing screening called $hearWHO$[1]. The app includes a digits-in-noise test which plays pre-recorded digit triplets reproduced only through headphones. The recordings are played with background noise (white noise) to determine the signal-to-noise ratio where a person can identify 50% of triplets correctly (Potgieter et al., 2016).

Table 3.3: Mobile-based applications considering the assessment of PD and hearing loss

Author	Operative system	Description	Speech analysis	Target users
Dubey 2015	Android	Smartwatch and tablet to collect speech data	No	PD patients
Tao 2016	Android	ASR to compute the syllable error rate	Yes	PD patients
Zhan 2018	Android	Evaluation of voice, gait dexterity, and balance	Yes	PD patients
Abu 2016	iOS	Pure-tone audiometry test	No	Hearing impaired
Apple Inc.	iOS	Pure-tone audiometry test	No	Hearing impaired
WHO 2019	iOS/Android	Digits-in-noise test	No	Everyone

Table 3.3 shows a summary of iOS and Android based applications to evaluate PD and hearing loss. In the case of PD, the evaluation of speech production only focuses on one dimension (mostly the sustained phonation). In the case of hearing loss, there is a limited number of mobile applications used to evaluate the hearing status. The pure-tone audiometry test is generally used to have an initial evaluation of the hearing status, however, the equipment necessary to perform the test must be properly calibrated.

---

[1] https://www.who.int/health-topics/hearing-loss/hearwho

Summary

Several contributions in the literature have provided evidence that it is possible to detect changes in speech due to PD. Furthermore, those studies have addressed the prediction of the neurological state or dysarthria level of PD patients using speech signals; however, a limited amount of works have considered monitoring the disease over time, which is essential to have more control over the disease progression. Regarding the speech production of CI users, analysis has been focused on articulation, prosody, and intelligibility distortions caused by hearing loss; however, a limited amount of those works have considered automatic methods for acoustic analysis, which in the long term may help the patient to have a personalized rehabilitation. Additionally, in the design of automatic systems for speech analysis, it is also essential to consider that speech changes may occur due to the natural aging process. Finally, integrating acoustic analysis into smartphone devices can increase the individual monitoring of the patients.

Chapter 4

Automatic analysis of pathological speech signals

4.1 Speech processing techniques-an overview

4.1.1 Short-time analysis

Speech sounds result from fast interactions of different areas in the brain, the respiratory system, and several elements of the vocal tract. During speech production, sudden changes in the vocal tract lead to abrupt variations in the temporal structure of the signal. The standard approach to detect and analyze these fast changes is to split a speech signal into a sequence of frames $S_t = \{s_0, s_1, ..., s_T\}$ with $t = 0, 1, 2, ... T - 1$, where T is the number of frames extracted from the speech recording.

Usually, the frame length K is short enough to keep constant measurements within speech segments (e.g., vowels, consonants) and long enough to guarantee measurable parameters (e.g., pitch, energy). Typical values for K are 25 ms and 40 ms, but these values may change depending on the application. The influence of the frame duration will be examined in Section 4.1.2. The distance between consecutive frames Q (frame rate or hop size) is chosen to ensure that abrupt changes in speech can be detected. In general, a value of $Q = 10$ ms is used. For any speech recording, the number of frames T can be estimated as:

$$T = \frac{(D - K)}{Q} \tag{4.1}$$

where D is the duration (in seconds) of the recording. T is approximated to the closest integer value. In order to handle discrete-time signals (e.g., speech recordings), the length of the frame in samples is defined as $N = K f_s$, where f_s is the sampling frequency of the speech recording. Figure 4.1 shows an example of a short-time transformation of a speech signal. One problem with

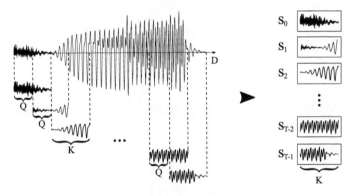

Figure 4.1: *Short-time transformation of a speech signal. The sequence of speech frames "S" are formed with segments of duration "K", which are taken every "Q" time steps.*

the short-time analysis is that splitting a speech signal into frames results in discontinuities at the borders of each frame. A common approach to reduce the impact of such discontinuities is to apply a window function to each frame. For instance, by multiplying a Hann window with each speech frame, the discontinuity goes to zero. The Hann window is defined as

$$w[n] = 0.5 \left(1 - \cos \left(\frac{2\pi n}{N - 1} \right) \right), \text{with } n = 1, 2, \ldots, N \tag{4.2}$$

where N is the number of samples in s_t. Figure 4.2 shows the result of applying a Hann window to a speech frame. In general, the final sequence of frames can

50

be expressed as

$$s_t[n] = w[n]s[n + tH], \text{ with } n = 1, 2, \ldots, N \tag{4.3}$$

where $H = Qf_s$ is the hop size measured in samples.

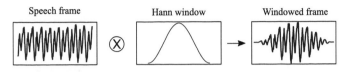

Figure 4.2: *Example of a windowed speech frame s_t using the Hann window. The "×" represents a point-wise multiplication.*

4.1.2 Time-frequency analysis

Short-Time Fourier Transform

In many speech and audio applications, the most common time-frequency analysis is performed by means of the Short-Time Fourier Transform (STFT) due to its simplicity and low computational cost. The reason is that the spectrogram (time-frequency representation) of an audio signal describes how the energy of the signal is distributed in the frequency domain and how it changes over the time. The STFT is obtained by computing the Discrete Fourier Transform (DFT) from sliding windows. For each speech frame s_t with size N, the STFT is computed as

$$F(t, b) = \sum_{n=0}^{N-1} s_t[n]e^{-i2\pi nb/N} \tag{4.4}$$

where $s_t[n]$ is calculated using Equation 4.3, b is the frequency or bin index (Benesty et al., 2007). The frequency at the b-th index is defined as

$$f = \frac{b}{N}f_{\text{nyquist}} \tag{4.5}$$

51

where $f_{\text{nyquist}} = f_s/2$ is the Nyquist frequency. The result of the DFT is an array of complex numbers. Commonly, the logarithm of the power spectrum $\log(|F(t,b)|^2)$ is used for time-frequency analysis. Figure 4.3 shows the result of computing the power spectrum and the log-power spectrum of a windowed speech frame. Note that calculating the STFT with Equation 4.4 results in N^2

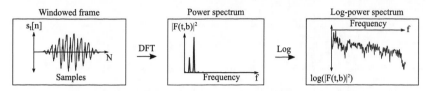

Figure 4.3: *Power spectrum and log-power spectrum of a windowed speech frame. The two peaks in the power spectrum indicate that there are two components in $s_t[n]$ with high energy in two different frequency points.*

operations. In practice, the Fast Fourier Transform (FFT) algorithm, proposed by Cooley and Tukey (1965), is used to reduce the number of operations from N^2 to $N \log_2 N$ by exploiting symmetries and dividing the DFT operations into two smaller pieces of size $N/2$ at each step: One piece to compute even-numbered samples and the other for odd-numbered samples. Using the FFT algorithm, Equation 4.4 becomes

$$F(t,b) = \underbrace{\sum_{m=0}^{N/2-1} s_t[2m]e^{-i2\pi mb/(N/2)}}_{\text{Even values}} + e^{-i2\pi b/N} \underbrace{\sum_{m=0}^{N/2-1} s_t[2m+1]e^{-i2\pi mb/(N/2)}}_{\text{Odd values}}$$

(4.6)

Thus, with the FFT algorithm only half of the operations are computed for the even and odd values, resulting in a faster computation of the STFT. Note also that splitting the DFT into two pieces limits N to be a power of two. In order to meet this condition, the speech frame s_t is usually padded with zeros such that the number of samples in the frame is a power of two.

Figure 4.4 shows a schematic of the process to compute the power spectrum of the sentence "*it's impossible to deal with bureaucracy*" uttered by an English

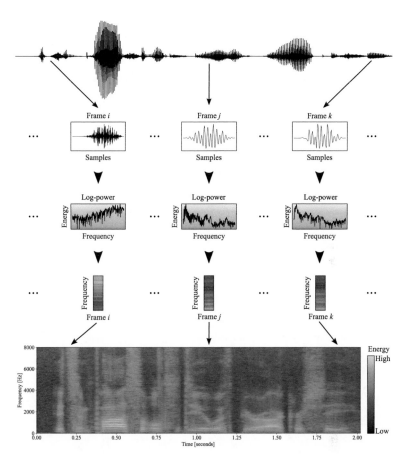

Figure 4.4: *Power spectrum for the sentence "it's impossible to deal with bureaucracy". The energy is represented by the color scale: yellow for high energy and blue for low energy.*

native speaker. In the final STFT, the **time** is given in the horizontal axis, the **frequency** in the vertical axis, and the **energy** of the signal (given by $\log(|F(t, b)|^2)$) is represented by the color scale. High energy values are represented by yellow and low energy values are represented by blue.

Wide-band and narrow-band spectrograms

The resolution of the STFT is a trade-off between time and frequency. On the one hand, in a wide-band spectrogram the temporal resolution is higher at the expense of a lower frequency resolution. On the other hand, in a narrow-band spectrogram the frequency resolution is higher at the expense of a lower temporal resolution. Whether a spectrogram is wide- or narrow-band can be controlled with the length of the selected speech frame. Figure 4.5 shows the power spectrograms of a speech recording windowed with speech frames with selected lengths of $K = \{40\,\text{ms}, 25\,\text{ms}, 15\,\text{ms}\}$. The signal has a sampling frequency of $f_s = 16\,\text{kHz}$ and a hop size of $Q = 10\,\text{ms}$. Furthermore, in order to have a better comparison, the resolution of the STFT is set to $N = 1024$ for all K. The distribution of energy in the frequency domain is more detailed in the narrow-band spectrogram ($K = 40\,\text{ms}$). The transition from one speech segment to another is more clear in the wide-band spectrogram ($K = 15\,\text{ms}$). For the spectrogram with $K = 25\,\text{ms}$, the trade-off between temporal and frequency resolution is more balanced.

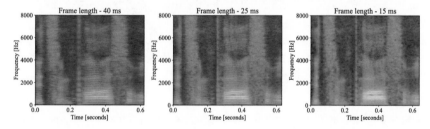

Figure 4.5: *Wide-band and narrow-band spectrograms of a speech recording with $K = \{40\,ms, 25\,ms, 15\,ms\}$*

4.1.3 Filterbank analysis

As described in Section 2.3.1, the human ear can decompose an audio signal into several frequencies by locating the places of maximum displacement in the basilar membrane produced by pressure waves. However, rather than localized points, the basilar membrane is divided into regions or *bands* that encode the frequency information non-linearly across the audio spectrum (from 20 Hz to 20 kHz). This non-linearity is produced because the bandwidth of these bands (and the space between them) increases non-uniformly as the frequency increases. Figure 4.6[1] shows a diagram of the basilar membrane indicating the base, the apex, and the *bands* of maximum displacement in response to sinusoidal waves with different frequencies. As shown in the figure, low

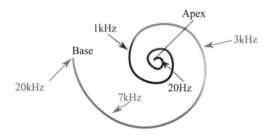

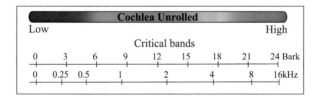

Figure 4.6: *Basilar membrane and the position of maximum displacement in response to sinusoidal waves with different frequencies.*

frequency tones are detected near the apex, where the basilar membrane is wider and more flexible than at the base (which is narrow and stiff), where high frequency tones are detected. The sensitivity of the basilar membrane

---

[1]This figure is an adapted version of http://bibliotecadigital.udea.edu.co/bitstream/10495/18789/4/PerezPaula_2021_SpeechNaturalLanguage.pdf
Last retrieved 05/04/2021; under the Creative Commons Attribution-ShareAlike 4.0 license

to detect different tones can be modeled as an array of overlapping band-pass filters and the bandwidth of these filters is commonly known as *critical bands* (Fletcher, 1940; Havelock et al., 2008). The critical band scale is divided into 24 bands known as Bark scale, which is a psycho-acoustic scale proposed by Zwicker (1961). The aim of filterbank analysis is to provide a time-frequency representation of speech that encodes the frequency components in a similar way to the basilar membrane in the human ear.

Mel-scale filterbank

Mel is a perceptual scale proposed by Volkmann et al. (1937) to measure how different tones are perceived by the human ear. In the Mel-scale, a set of triangular filters is applied to the log-power spectrum in order to obtain the Mel-spectrum, a "compressed" and nonlinear representation of the STFT. It can be considered as a compressed time-frequency representation, because it reduces the size of the STFT from N frequency bins to M filters. It is also non-linear, because the bandwidth and the spacing between the filters increases non-uniformly as the frequency increases. Center frequencies (in the Mel scale) of the filters are obtained by using

$$m = 1125 \ln(1 + f_{\mathrm{Hz}}/700) \tag{4.7}$$

where f_{Hz} is the frequency in Hertz. Converting from Mel back to Hertz

$$h(m) = 700(e^{m/1125} - 1) \tag{4.8}$$

The process to obtain a Mel-spectrum is as follows:

- Compute the STFT of a speech signal as described in Section 4.1.2.

- Select the number of filters M. Typical values are $M = \{32, 64, 128\}$. This parameter also controls the frequency resolution of the Mel-spectrum i.e., the higher the number of filters, the higher the resolution.

- Choose a lower and upper frequency. For speech recordings with $f_s \geq$ 16 kHz, a value of 8 kHz is preferred for the upper value. Speech signals with $f_s = 8$ kHz are limited to an upper frequency of 4 kHz. A typical value for the lower frequency is 50 Hz.

- Construct the triangular filter bank with

$$
FB(k) = \begin{cases} 0 & k < f(m-1) \\ \\ \dfrac{k - f(m-1)}{f(m) - f(m-1)} & f(m-1) \leq k < f(m) \\ \\ \dfrac{f(m+1) - k}{f(m+1) - f(m)} & f(m) \leq k \leq f(m+1) \\ \\ 0 & k > f(m+1) \end{cases} \tag{4.9}
$$

where $k = 1, 2, \ldots M$, $f(m) = (N+1)h(m)/f_s$, and N is the number of frequency bins of the STFT.

- Apply the triangular filterbank to the STFT.

Figure 4.7 shows the power spectrum of a speech signal with $N = 512$ frequency bins, 32 triangular filters, and the resulting Mel-spectrum. The output of each triangular filter represents the log-energy distribution in the frequency domain scaled according to Mel (Equation 4.7).

Gammatone filterbank

Similar to Mel, the Gammatone filterbank can be considered as a nonlinear and compressed time-frequency representation of the STFT. However, there are two main differences with respect to Mel: (1) the frequency scale is based on the Equivalent Rectangular Bandwidth (ERB), which is related to the critical

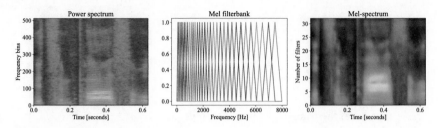

Figure 4.7: *Mel-spectrum of a speech recording resulting from applying a 32 triangular filterbank to the STFT of the signal with a frequency resolution of 512 points (frequency bins).*

bands and (2) the shape of the filterbank is obtained as the multiplication of sine and gamma functions, instead of triangular filters.

The Gammatone filterbank is based on the cochlear model proposed by Holdsworth et al. (1992). The time-frequency representation that results from applying a Gammatone filterbank to the STFT is often called a *Cochleagram*. As defined by Glasberg and Moore (1990), the center frequencies f_c in the ERB scale can be obtained as

$$ERB(f_c) = 24.7 + 0.180 f_c \qquad (4.10)$$

If the number of filters M is known (e.g. $M = 128$), the center frequencies can be calculated as proposed by Slaney et al. (1993):

$$f_c = -\alpha + (f_H + \alpha) e^{m(-\log(f_H + \alpha) + \log(f_L + \alpha))/M}, \text{ with } \alpha = \text{EarQ*minBW}$$
$$(4.11)$$

where m is an M-dimensional array of integer values $m = \{1, 2, 3 \dots M\}$, f_L is the lower frequency (e.g. $f_L = 50$ Hz), f_H is the upper frequency (e.g. $f_H = 8$ kHz), and the parameters EarQ $= 9.26449$ and minBW $= 24.7$ can be changed if another ERB scale is desired (Glasberg and Moore, 1990). The

58

shape of the filters is defined as

$$g(t) = at^{p-1} \exp(-2\pi bt) \cos(2\pi f_c t + \phi) \qquad (4.12)$$

$$\text{with } a = \frac{\pi(2p-2)!\,2^{-(2p-2)}}{(p-1)!^2} \qquad (4.13)$$

$$\text{and } b = \frac{ERB(f_c)}{a} \qquad (4.14)$$

where ϕ is the phase of the carrier in radians, a is the amplitude, p is the order of the filter (typically $p = 4$), b is the bandwidth in Hz, and t is the time.

Figure 4.8 shows the log-power spectrum of a speech signal with $N = 512$ frequency bins, $M = 32$ Gammatone filters, and the Cochleagram. The output of each Gammatone filter represents the log-energy distribution in the frequency domain scaled according to the ERB.

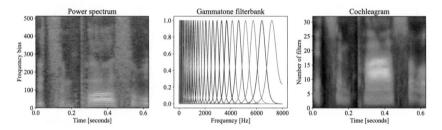

Figure 4.8: *Cochleagram of a speech recording resulting from applying a 32 Gammatone filterbank to the STFT of the signal with a frequency resolution of 512 points (frequency bins).*

Discrete Cosine Transform: The cepstral coefficients

In many speech and machine learning applications it is not always suitable to use the complete Mel-spectrum/Cochleagram. For instance, in some cases the classification method has to be implemented with a reduced number of features in order to reduce the computational complexity or to eliminate redundant features.

The Discrete Cosine Transform (DCT) is a technique that allows decomposing a signal into its more fundamental components. Formally, when using the DCT, the input signal (e.g. filterbank log-energies) is represented as a linear combination of weighted basis functions that are related to the frequency components (Ahmed et al., 1974). The motivation of the DCT is to provide a good approximation to an orthogonal transformation of the input signal, i.e., to transform X in order to have a compressed representation of the signal and to reduce feature redundancy. There are different versions and types of DCT. In this work the normalized version of the DCT-II is considered [2]:

$$\text{DCT}[t, c] = 2\alpha \sum_{m=0}^{M-1} X[t, m] \cos\left(\frac{\pi(2m + 1)c}{2M}\right) \qquad (4.15)$$

where $c = 0, 1, 2, 3, \ldots C$ are the desired coefficients, X is the Mel-spectrum/Cochleagra M is the number of filters, t is the t-th speech frame, and α is a scaling factor that makes the DCT orthonormal

$$\alpha = \begin{cases} \sqrt{1/(4M)} & \text{if } c = 0 \\ \sqrt{1/(2M)} & \text{otherwise} \end{cases}$$

Typically, the number of coefficients ranges from $C = 12$ to $C = 24$. When the DCT is applied on the Mel-spectrum, the resulting feature space is commonly known as Mel-Frequency Cepstral Coefficients (MFCCs) (Davis and Mermelstein, 1980; Mermelstein, 1976). Similarly, Equation 4.15 can be used on the Cochleagram to obtain Gammatone-Frequency Cepstral Coefficients (GFCCs). Applying the DCT to the filterbank log-energies has some advantages:

1. From Figures 4.7 and 4.8 it can be observed that the filters are overlapped. This means that there are frequency components that are considered more than once when computing the log-energies. Thus, according to the motivation of the DCT, using MFCCs or GFCCs helps to reduce feature redundancy.

---

[2]https://docs.scipy.org/doc/scipy/reference/generated/scipy.fftpack.dct.html

2. Since the cepstral coefficients are a compressed representation of the filterbank spectrogram, then the computational cost and processing time is lower than using the completed log-energy space.

Using cepstral coefficients also comes with a cost:

1. The coefficients are a compressed representation of the Mel-spectrum/Cochleagram thus, when using a classification or regression scheme, it is expected to have a lower performance than when the complete spectrogram is used.

2. Interpretation of the feature space is lost due to the DCT transformation. For instance, each MFCC is a linear combination of all the log-energies in the Mel scale.

Nevertheless, the DCT is widely used because it provides a good representation of the feature space and because it helps to reduce the computation cost when the resources are limited. Also, note that the DCT is not restricted only to be used in the Mel-spectrum or Cochleagram decorrelation.

4.1.4 Voice Activity Detection

An energy-based Voice Activity Detection (VAD) algorithm is implemented to automatically detect pauses and to compute some acoustic features (Section 4.2.4). The procedure of the VAD algorithm is as follows:

1. The intensity of the signal is computed from speech frames of 15 ms taken every 1 ms. Short-time frames are used in order to have a better temporal resolution, which is suitable to detect the speech and silence onsets (Section 4.1.2). The intensity of sequence of speech frames $S_t = \{s_0, s_1, ..., s_T\}$ can be computed as

$$E_t = 10 \log_{10} \left(\frac{1}{N} \sum_{n=0}^{N} s_t[n]^2 \right) \text{ dB} \qquad (4.16)$$

where E_t is a sequence of energy values $E_t = \{e_0, e_1, \ldots, e_T\}$ computed for every t-th frame in S_t, $N = 0.015 \times f_s$ is the number of samples in s_t, and f_s is the sampling frequency of the speech recording.

2. The DC level of the sequence E_t is removed:

$$E_t \leftarrow E_t - \frac{1}{T} \sum_{t=0}^{T} e_t$$

3. The new sequence is smoothed by convolving E_t with a Gaussian window of 10 ms. This procedure is performed in order to eliminate "energy spikes" in the signal.

$$E_t \leftarrow E_t \circledast e^{-\frac{1}{2}\left(\frac{W}{\sigma}\right)^2}$$

where $\circledast$ represents the convolution operation, $W = 0.01 \times f_s$ is the length of the Gaussian window, and $\sigma = 0.05 \times W$ is the width of the window, which is set to be 5% of the length in order to ensure that only small portions are smoothed (the energy spikes) and not the speech or silence onsets.

4. After convolution, the sequence E_t is re-scaled to have values between -1 and 1

5. DC removal, smoothing, and re-scaling are performed in order to calculate a threshold that (in theory) will work independent of the signal. The main hypothesis is that even if there is additive noise in the signal, the energy content of the speech segments is still higher than in the silence regions. These silence segments have the lower energy in the signal, which after DC removal should be a negative value; thus, the threshold (E_{THR}) is calculated as the **median** of the **negative** values in E_t. The median is used because it is a measure more robust against outliers than the mean.

6. Finally, the t-th speech frame with energy values higher than $\mathrm{E_{THR}}$ ($e_t >$ $\mathrm{E_{THR}}$) is labeled as a speech segment, and the rest as silence/pauses.

An energy-based VAD is considered due to its simplicity and efficiency when combined with a noise reduction algorithm.

4.2   Pathological speech modeling

The techniques previously described are the foundations for the analysis of pathological speech signals. The acoustic features considered in this section are computed using short-time analysis of the speech signals, i.e., $S_t = \{s_0, s_1, ..., s_{T-1}\}$ where T is the number of frames extracted from the speech recording. Additionally, Hann windowing is applied to such a sequence before feature extraction (Equation 4.3). The acoustic analysis of the pathological speech signals is divided into phonation, articulation, prosody, and phonemic analysis.

4.2.1   Phonation analysis

Voice production problems are mainly associated with abnormal vibration of the vocal folds and disturbances in respiration (Section 2.1.1). Such deviations can be measured by computing pitch, loudness, and perturbation features from the **sustained phonation of vowels**.

Pitch

This parameter is analyzed by means of the fundamental frequency, which is estimated based on the periodicity detector algorithm implemented in the software Praat (Boersma et al., 1993)[3]. The method uses autocorrelation in order to detect periodic-like signals, such as the voiced speech sounds produced by the vibration of the vocal folds (Chapter 2). For every speech recording, the

---

[3]https://www.fon.hum.uva.nl/praat/

pitch is computed from speech frames of duration K. Furthermore, each frame must contain at least 3 pitch periods:

$$K = \frac{3}{\text{minF0}} \tag{4.17}$$

where minF0 is the minimum pitch that can to be detected ($\text{minF0} = 75\,\text{Hz}$). For each speech signal, a sequence of $F0$ values are computed for every t-th speech frame. Figure 4.9 shows the $F0$ contour computed from the sustained phonation of the vowel /a/ produced by a healthy speaker and a PD patient.

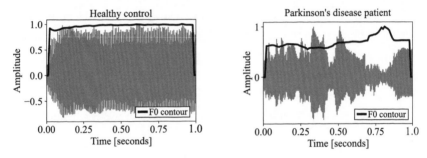

Figure 4.9: *F0 contour (blue lines) computed from the sustained phonation of the vowel /a/ produced by a healthy speaker (left) and a PD patient (right)*

Loudness

The Sound Pressure Level (SPL) is considered to measure the amount of acoustic energy produced by a speaker (Švec and Granqvist, 2018). For every speech frame in S_t, the SPL (measured in dB) is computed as

$$\text{SPL}_t = 20 \log_{10} \left(\frac{p_t}{p_0} \right) \text{ dB} \tag{4.18}$$

where p_0 is the reference sound pressure of the air expressed in Pascal ($p_0 = 20\mu\text{Pa}$) and p_t is the sound pressure computed as the root mean square value of the t-th speech frame:

$$p_t = \sqrt{\frac{\sum_{n=0}^{N} s_t[n]^2}{N}} \qquad (4.19)$$

where N is the number of samples in s_t. Figure 4.10 shows the SPL contour computed from the sustained phonation of the vowel /a/ produced by a healthy speaker and a PD patient.

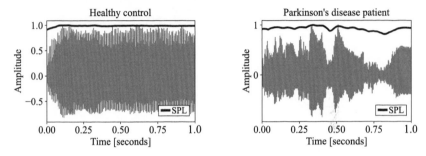

Figure 4.10: SPL *contour (blue lines) computed from the sustained phonation of the vowel /a/ produced by a healthy speaker (left) and a PD patient (right)*

Perturbation measures

Pitch and amplitude variations during phonation are measured considering 6 perturbation features. The Jitter, the PPQ3 and the PPQ5 are considered in order to measure short and long term $F0$ variations (Teixeira and Gonçalves, 2016):

$$\text{Jitt}(\%) = 100 \times \frac{T}{T-1} \frac{\sum_{t=1}^{T-1} |F0_t - F0_{t-1}|}{\sum_{t=1}^{T} F0_t} \qquad (4.20)$$

$$\text{PPQ3}(\%) = 100 \times \frac{T}{T-1} \frac{\sum_{t=1}^{T-1} |F0_t - \left(\frac{1}{3}\sum_{i=t-1}^{t+1} F0_i\right)|}{\sum_{t=1}^{T} F0_t} \qquad (4.21)$$

$$\text{PPQ5}(\%) = 100 \times \frac{T}{T-1} \frac{\sum_{t=1}^{T-1} |F0_t - \left(\frac{1}{5}\sum_{i=t-2}^{t+2} F0_i\right)|}{\sum_{t=1}^{T} F0_t} \qquad (4.22)$$

where T is the total number of speech frames. The short and long term amplitude perturbation measures include the Shimmer, the APQ3, and APQ5:

$$\text{Shim}(\%) = 100 \times \frac{T}{T-1} \frac{\sum_{t=1}^{T-1} |\text{SPL}_t - \text{SPL}_{t-1}|}{\sum_{t=1}^{T} \text{SPL}_t} \qquad (4.23)$$

$$\text{APQ3}(\%) = 100 \times \frac{T}{T-1} \frac{\sum_{t=1}^{T-1} |\text{SPL}_t - \left(\frac{1}{3} \sum_{i=t-1}^{t+1} \text{SPL}_i\right)|}{\sum_{t=1}^{T} \text{SPL}_t} \qquad (4.24)$$

$$\text{APQ5}(\%) = 100 \times \frac{T}{T-1} \frac{\sum_{t=1}^{T-1} |\text{SPL}_t - \left(\frac{1}{5} \sum_{i=t-2}^{t+2} \text{SPL}_i\right)|}{\sum_{t=1}^{T} \text{SPL}_t} \qquad (4.25)$$

where SPL is computed used Equation 4.18.

4.2.2 Articulation analysis

Articulation is defined as the ability to physically move the tongue, lips, teeth and jaw to produce sequences of speech sounds. In this thesis, articulation is analyzed using formant frequencies and the transitions from voiced-to-voiceless sounds and vice-versa.

Vowel formants

Formants are acoustic resonances produced in the vocal tract. The first and second formant frequencies ($F1$ and $F2$) are considered in this thesis, because of their relationship to the position of the tongue when producing front (e.g. /i/), central (e.g. /a/), and back (e.g. /u/) vowels: **Front**: low $F1$ and high $F2$; **Central**: high $F1$ and low $F2$; and **Back**: low $F1$ and low $F2$. Commonly, the location of formants is estimated from the filter coefficients obtained with the Linear Prediction Coding (LPC) analysis, which in this thesis is performed with Burg's algorithm.

Triangular Vowel Space Area

A reduction of the articulation can be measured with the triangular Vowel Space Area (tVSA), which is constructed using the $F1$ and $F2$ of /i/ ($F1_{/i/}$ and $F2_{/i/}$), /a/ ($F1_{/a/}$ and $F2_{/a/}$), and /u/ ($F1_{/u/}$ and $F2_{/u/}$). The tVSA is computed as

$$tVSA = \frac{|F1_{/i/}(F2_{/a/} - F2_{/u/}) + F1_{/a/}(F2_{/u/} - F2_{/i/}) + F1_{/u/}(F2_{/i/} - F2_{/a/})|}{2}$$

(4.26)

A reduction of the tVSA is associated with a reduction of the vowel articulation, which can result from the normal aging process or a speech disorder. Usually, the logarithm of the tVSA (LntVSA) is also considered for analysis.

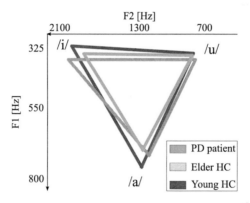

Figure 4.11: *Triangular vowel space from Parkinson's disease patients, elderly healthy controls, and young healthy speakers.*

Formant Centralization Ratio

The Formant Centralization Ratio (FCR) was introduced by Sapir et al. (2010) to analyze changes in the vocal formants with a reduced inter-speaker variability. The FCR was designed so it will increase when the vowel space area decreases.

The FCR is defined as:

$$FCR = \frac{F2_{/u/} + F2_{/a/} + F1_{/i/} + F1_{/u/}}{F2_{/i/} + F1_{/a/}} \qquad (4.27)$$

Onset/offset transitions

The transitions from voiceless-to-voiced sounds (onset) and voiced-to-voiceless sounds (offset) are considered to model difficulties of the speakers to start and stop the vibration of the vocal folds during continuous speech (e.g., reading of a text). The transitions are extracted by detecting voiced segments based on the presence of pitch. Speech segments of 80 ms duration are taken to the left and right of the border between the voiced and voiceless sounds, forming speech segments of 160 ms (Orozco-Arroyave, 2016). Filterbank analysis is applied to the transitions in order to compute MFCCs and GFCCs (Section 4.1.3), which contain information about the changes of energy (in different frequency bands) when moving from a sound to the other (Figure 4.12). It is hypothesized that the transitions can capture the abnormal articulation movements of disordered speech because filterbank analysis can encode the time-frequency information of different sounds.

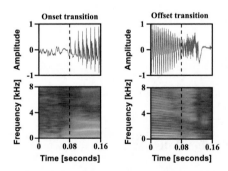

Figure 4.12: *Onset (/k-a/) and offset (/o-s/) transitions extracted from a sentence read by a healthy speaker.*

4.2.3 Phonemic analysis

Phoneme posterior probabilities

The method considered in this thesis to measure phoneme articulation precision consists of converting a sequence of speech frames $S_t = \{s_0, s_1, ..., s_{T-1}\}$ into a sequence of phoneme posterior probabilities $Y_t[z] = \{y_0[z], y_1[z], ..., y_{T-1}[z]\}$, where $z = 1, 2, ..., z, ..., Z$ are all the possible phoneme groups (Cernak et al., 2015); thus, $y_t[z]$ is the probability of occurrence of the z-th phoneme class in the t-th speech frame. In this thesis, phoneme precision is evaluated considering three main dimensions:

1. Manner of articulation: Refers to the way the speech articulators are set so that different consonants and vowels can be produced.

2. Place of articulation: The point of contact where an obstruction occurs in the vocal tract in order to produce different speech sounds

3. Voicing: Activity of the vocal folds, i.e., whether a phoneme is voiced or voiceless

Figure 4.13 shows an example phoneme posterior probabilities computed for the German word "Giesskanne" uttered by a normal hearing speaker and a CI user. If the phonemes are grouped according to manner of articulation, the correct sequence of phoneme is Stop (/G/)-Vowel (/iː/)-Fricative (/s/)-Stop (/k/)-Vowel (/a/)-Nasal (/n/)-Vowel (/e/). Note that for the CI user the system detects a nasal sound in the middle of the emission of the first vowel.

Table 4.1 shows the phoneme groups considered in this thesis. The table is not complete as the phoneme clusters for German, Spanish, and English are different, thus, the phoneme provided in the table are the most representative (and common) for these three languages. Note that a single phone may belong to more than 1 class, e.g., /p/ belong to the class *stop*, *bilabial*, and *voiceless*. Moreover, coarticulatory characteristics are summarized in each phoneme representation; e.g. /i/ as in "Bier" (German word for Beer) and "bitte" (German word for "please") are pronounced slightly different but are both included

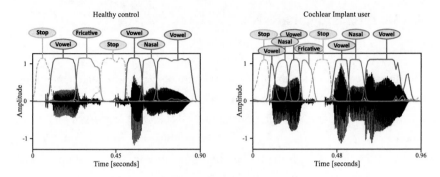

Figure 4.13: *Phoneme posterior probabilities (colored lines) computed from the German word "Giesskanne" uttered by a normal hearing speaker (left) and a cochlear implant user (right).*

in /i/. The posterior probabilities are computed using a multilabel recurrent

Table 4.1: Phoneme classes considered in this study.

c	Dimension	Class	Phonemes	Brief description
0	-	Silence	-	Non-speech segments
1	Manner	Stop	/p/, /t/, /k/, /b/, /d/, /g/	Total oral closure with rapid release
2		Nasal	/n/, /m/, /ŋ/	Airflow through the nasal cavity
3		Trill	/r/, /ɾ/	Turbulent airflow
4		Fricative	/s/, /ʃ/, /z/, /f/	Hissing sounds due to turbulent airflow
5		Approximants	/j/	Hissing sounds without turbulent airflow
6		Lateral	/l/	The air passes at the sides of the tongue
7		Vowel	/a/, /e/, /i/, /o/, /u/	Vibration of the vocal folds
8	Place	Labial	/p/, /b/, /m/, /f/, /v/	Lips and teeth
9		Alveolar	/t/, /d/, /n/	Tip of the tongue and alveolar ridge
10		Velar	/k/, /g/, /ŋ/	Back of the tongue and soft palate
11		Palatal	/j/	Front of the tongue and hard palate
12		Postalveolar	/ʃ/	Blade of the tongue
13		Central	/a/, /aː/	Tongue halfway the mouth
14		Front	/i/, /e/	Tongue on the front of the mouth
15		Back	/u/, /o/	Tongue on the back of the mouth
16	Voicing	Voiceless	/p/, /t/, /k/, /ʃ/, /s/	No vibration of the vocal folds
17		Voiced	/m/, /n/, /b/, /d/, /g/, /a/	Vibration of the vocal folds

network (Sections 4.3.3 and 4.3.5), which can be used for the automatic recognition of phoneme sequences based on probability of phone occurrence. The details about the system trained in this thesis will be discussed in Chapter 6; Section 6.1.1. The phoneme articulation precision is evaluated computing 3 fundamental parameters for each one of the 17 classes in Table 4.1:

- MaxPh: Average of the maximum phoneme posteriors.

- LLRPh: Average posterior log-likelihood ratio computed as

$$\text{LLRPh} = \log\left(\frac{p[c]}{1 - p[c]}\right) \tag{4.28}$$

$$\text{with } p[c] = \frac{1}{T}\sum_{t=0}^{T} \boldsymbol{y}_t[c] \tag{4.29}$$

where $p[c]$ is the average posterior probability of the c-th phoneme group (Diez et al., 2014; Vásquez-Correa et al., 2019).

- durPH: Average phoneme duration.

Voice Onset Time

Voice Onset Time (VOT) is defined as the interval between the initial burst of a stop consonant and the onset of voicing for the following vowel. VOT has been used as an acoustic cue to understand several aspects of speech production and language development. This work considers the VOT segments extracted from the voiceless plosive sounds /p/, /t/, and /k/ produced during the rapid repetition of the syllables /pa-ta-ka/. Figure 4.14 shows an example of the VOT for /p/, /t/, and /k/ extracted from the sequence /pa-ta-ka/. In general, stop consonants are characterized by three stages: closure, release, and aspiration. In the closure stage, a silence region is created due to an obstruction of airflow by the articulators (e.g., the lips to produce the /p/ sound). During the release stage, the articulators move away from each other producing an explosive burst of air with energy spread across the audible spectrum. After the burst, the air pressure (generated by obstruction of the articulators) is decreased, which results in turbulent airflow with energy values no longer spread across the spectrum. In other cases, however, the production of the voiceless stops is affected by different acoustic factors that occur at intermediate positions in an utterance:

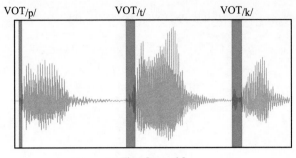

VOT_{/p/}   VOT_{/t/}   VOT_{/k/}

Time [seconds]

Figure 4.14: *VOT labels (blue shadowed segments) of /p/, /t/, and /k/ from the sequence /pa-ta-ka/.*

1. Voicing: Is characterized by the presence of glottal pulses during the closure and release stages. Figure 4.15 shows an example of voicing in a speech segment with the transition from /ka/ to /pa/.

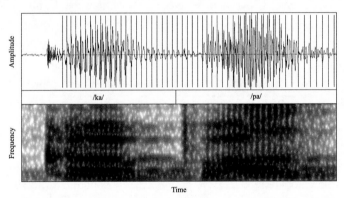

Figure 4.15: *Voicing effect present in the speech transition from /ka/ to /pa/. The vertical lines in the time domain signal (top) are the glottal pulses extracted with Praat.*

2. Partial voicing: It can identified by the presence of glottal pulses during the closure stage of the plosive sound but not in release and aspiration stages. Figure 4.16 shows an example of a partially-voiced /t/ sound.

72

The glottal pulses are present during the closure stage, but not during the VOT.

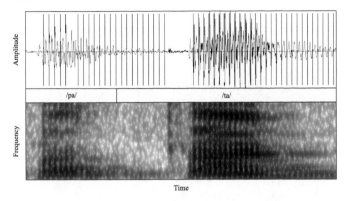

Figure 4.16: *Partially voiced /t/ sound extracted from a transition from /pa/ to /ta/. The vertical lines in the time domain signal (top) are the glottal pulses extracted with Praat.*

3. Consonant weakening: Is characterized by the absence of the burst. As a result, the stop sound is weaker and can be perceived as its voiced counterpart e.g., a /p/ may be perceived as a /b/. Figure 4.17 shows an example of the weakening effect in a /p/ sound.

4.2.4   Prosody analysis

Speech prosody includes the pitch, loudness, and duration that contributes to production and perception of intonation, rhythm, lexical tone, and stress. These parameters are important for the expression of emotions and also to provide linguistic information (Hardcastle et al., 2012).

Pitch and loudness

The $F0$ is computed using the same method as for the phonation analysis. Additionally, the mean (meanF0) and standard deviation (stdF0) are computed in order to measure voice quality and monotonous speech during the reading

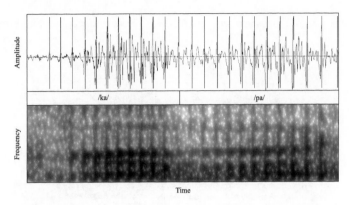

Figure 4.17: *Consonant weakening of the /p/ sound in an intermediate position. The vertical lines in the time domain signal (top) are the glottal pulses extracted with Praat. Note the absence of the burst in /p/.*

of a standard text. Loudness is measured only on speech segments (VAD algorithm; Section 4.1.4) by computing the mean (meanSPL) and standard deviation (stdSPL) of the SPL (Equation 4.18).

Duration

Duration and ratio of speech are modeled by considering speech, segments, *voiced* sounds and pauses. The speech rate (rSpeech) is measured as the number of non-silence segments (VAD algorithm; Section 4.1.4) produced per second. The average duration of the detected speech segments is also considered (dSpeech). The voiced sounds are extracted by selecting the speech frames with $F0 \neq 0$. The sequence of pitch values is computed using speech frames of 40 ms duration. Then only voiced segments longer than 40 ms are considered for feature extraction. The set of voiced features includes the number of voiced segments per second (rVoiced) and the average duration of voiced segments (dVoiced).

The set of pause features includes the number of pauses per second (rPause) and the average duration of pauses (dPause) within the speech recording. The silence regions at the start and end of the signal are not considered for feature extraction. Note that **voiceless** sounds can be derived by selecting the segments of the signal that are not labeled as voiced nor pause segments.

Figure 4.18 shows the pitch, loudness, and duration parameters computed for a speech recording.

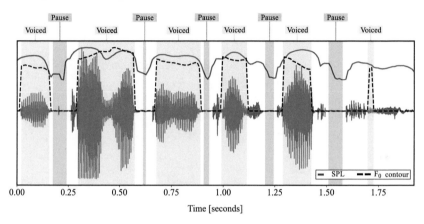

Figure 4.18: *Pitch, loudness, and duration parameters computed automatically for the Spanish sentence "**Mi casa tiene tres cuartos**" (My house has three rooms). The non-shaded regions are voiceless speech sounds.*

Timing

Grabe and Low (2002) and Ramus et al. (1999) have proposed metrics that are *related* to speech rhythm[4], by considering timing information extracted from vowels and consonants. Three main descriptors are considered:

1. The raw and normalized Pairwise Variability Index (rPVI and nPVI, respectively) proposed by Grabe and Low (2002) to measure the duration

---

[4]Some authors question the validity of these metrics for speech rhythm analysis. See Arvaniti (2009); White and Malisz (2020)

variability of successive vowel and consonant intervals:

$$\text{rPVI} = \frac{1}{D-1} \sum_{i=1}^{D-1} |d_i - d_{i+1}| \tag{4.30}$$

$$\text{nPVI} = \frac{100}{D-1} \sum_{i=1}^{D-1} \left| \frac{d_i - d_{i+1}}{0.5(d_i + d_{i+1})} \right| \tag{4.31}$$

where D are the number of vowel (or consonants) in a speech signal and d_i is the duration of the i-th vowel (or consonant).

2. The Global Proportions of Intervals (GPI) proposed by Ramus et al. (1999) to measure the proportion of vowels (vowel produced per second/vowel rate)

$$\text{GPI} = \frac{\sum_{i=1}^{D} d_i}{L} \tag{4.32}$$

where L is the total duration of the signal

3. Ramus et al. (1999) also proposes to use the standard deviation of the vowel/consonant (dGPI) duration intervals to measure speech rhythm.

Note that computing these features requires phonetic segmentation. Thus, the same system used to computed the phoneme posterior probabilities (Section 4.2.3) is used to obtain the phoneme labels. Furthermore, the GPI is extended to compute the phoneme rate ($\text{GPI}-y[k]$) and variability ($\text{std} - y[k]$) for the groups described in Table 4.1.

Summary of features

Table 4.2: Summary of the features considered to model speech disorders.

Dimension	Task	Feature	Description
Phonation	Sustained vowel	meanF0	Average F0
	Sustained vowel	StdF0	Standard deviation of F0
	Sustained vowel	Jitter	F0 variation
	Sustained vowel	PPQ3	F0 variations in 3 pitch periods
	Sustained vowel	PPQ5	F0 variations in 5 pitch periods
	Sustained vowel	meanSPL	Average SPL
	Sustained vowel	StdSPL	Standard deviation of SPL
	Sustained vowel	Shimmer	SPL variation
	Sustained vowel	APQ3	SPL variation in 3 pitch periods
	Sustained vowel	APQ5	SPL variation in 5 pitch periods
Articulation	Vowels /a/, /i/, /u/	F1 and F2	Average formant frequency
	Vowels /a/, /i/, /u/	tVSA	Vowel space area
	Vowels /a/, /i/, /u/	LntVSA	Logarithm of the vowel space area
	Vowels /a/, /i/, /u/	FCR	Formant centralization ratio
	Reading text, /pa-ta-ka/	MaxPost	Maximum phoneme posteriors (Average) (x17)
	Reading text, /pa-ta-ka/	LLRPost	Average posterior log-likelihood ratio (x17)
	Reading text, /pa-ta-ka/	durPH	Average phoneme group duration (x17)
	Reading text, /pa-ta-ka/	CepsOn	MFCC/GFCC from onset transitions
	Reading text, /pa-ta-ka/	CepsOff	MFCC/GFCC from offset transitions
	/pa-ta-ka/	VOT	Voice Onset Time
Prosody	Reading text, monologue	meanF0	Average F0
	Reading text, monologue	stdF0	Standard deviation of F0
	Reading text, monologue	meanSPL	Average SPL
	Reading text, monologue	StdSPL	Standard deviation of SPL
	Reading text, monologue	rSpeech	Speech segments per second
	Reading text, monologue	dSpeech	Average duration of speech segments
	Reading text, monologue	rVoiced	Voiced segments per second
	Reading text, monologue	dVoiced	Average duration of voiced segments
	Reading text, monologue	rPause	Pauses per second
	Reading text, monologue	dPause	Average duration of pauses
	Reading text, monologue	$rPVI - Vow$	Vowel raw PVI
	Reading text, monologue	$rPVI - Con$	Consonant raw PVI
	Reading text, monologue	$nPVI - Vow$	Vowel normalized PVI
	Reading text, monologue	$nPVI - Con$	Consonant normalized PVI
	Reading text, monologue	$GPI - y[k]$	Phoneme rate (x17)
	Reading text, monologue	$GPI - Con$	Consonants rate
	Reading text, monologue	$std - y[k]$	Phoneme duration variability (x17)
	Reading text, monologue	$std - Con$	Consonant duration variability

4.3 Machine learning methods

In pathological speech signals, machine learning methods are used for the automatic detection of speech disorders (classify patient vs. healthy) or to predict a clinical score (e.g., the MDS-UPDRS/mFDA) based on a set of acoustic features extracted from speech recordings. This section describes the methods considered in this thesis for the automatic classification, regression, and modelling of pathological speech signals.

4.3.1 Support Vector Machine for classification

The general idea of the Support Vector Machine (SVM) algorithm (Vapnik, 1995) is to apply a nonlinear transformation $\phi(\boldsymbol{x})$ of the **input space** and map it into a higher dimensional **feature space** in which a linear decision boundary (centred on the training data) is used to divide the two classes. Such a transformation is performed in order to simplify the construction of the decision boundary. In the case of linearly separable classes, the SVM in commonly known as **hard-margin** SVM. When the two groups are overlapped, the decision boundary is constructed by allowing certain amount of errors and the SVM in called a **soft-margin** SVM.

Hard-margin SVM

For classification problems in which the two groups could be divided by a linear decision boundary, i.e., non-overlapping samples. In this case, two perfectly separable groups with N input vectors $\boldsymbol{x}_n = \{\boldsymbol{x}_1, \boldsymbol{x}_2, \ldots \boldsymbol{x}_N\}$ and targets $t_n \in \{-1, +1\}$, can be divided by an optimal hyperplane of the form

$$y(\boldsymbol{x}) = \mathbf{w}^T \phi(\boldsymbol{x}) + b \tag{4.33}$$

where $n = 1, 2, \ldots, N$ is the number of input/feature vectors that represent the samples in class 1 ($t_n = -1$) and class 2 ($t_n = +1$), $y(\boldsymbol{x})$ is the predicted class label, and $\phi(x)$ is the feature space; thus, there exists a vector $\mathbf{w}$ and scalar b

such that

$$\mathbf{w}^T \phi(\boldsymbol{x}_n) + b \geq 1 \quad \text{if } t_n = +1$$
$$\mathbf{w}^T \phi(\boldsymbol{x}_n) + b \leq -1 \quad \text{if } t_n = -1$$

which can be written in the canonical representation as

$$t_n(\mathbf{w}^T \phi(\boldsymbol{x}_n) + b) \geq 1 \tag{4.34}$$

and the optimal hyperplane is

$$\mathbf{w}^T \phi(\boldsymbol{x}_n) + b = 0 \tag{4.35}$$

In the SVM, the optimal decision boundary is found using the concept of *margin*, which is defined by the support vectors i.e., the points/vectors $\boldsymbol{x}_n$ for which $t_n(\mathbf{w}^T \phi(\boldsymbol{x}_n) + b) = 1$. Figure 4.19 shows an example of two perfect separable classes, the linear decision boundary (optimal hyperplane), the margin, and the support vectors. The distance of any input vector $\boldsymbol{x}_n$ to the

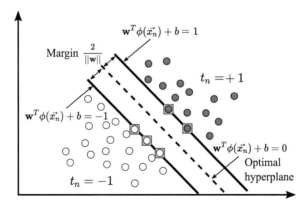

Figure 4.19: *Example of a hard-margin SVM. The support vectors (marked with squares) are the samples that define the margin. Based on Cortes and Vapnik (1995)*

separating hyperplane is given by

$$\frac{t_n(\mathbf{w}^T\phi(\boldsymbol{x}_n) + b)}{||\mathbf{w}||} \tag{4.36}$$

The distance $\mathbf{w}$ and scalar b are optimized to maximize the margin, which is given by the perpendicular distance to the support vectors: $\frac{|1-b|}{||\mathbf{w}||}$ for $t_n = +1$ and $\frac{|-1-b|}{||\mathbf{w}||}$ for $t_n = -1$. Thus, the maximum margin is found by solving for

$$\underset{\mathbf{w}}{\mathrm{argmax}} \, \frac{2}{||\mathbf{w}||} \tag{4.37}$$

This maximization problem is converted into a quadratic minimization problem as:

$$\begin{aligned} &\underset{\mathbf{w},b}{\mathrm{minimize}} \, \frac{1}{2}||\mathbf{w}||^2 \\ &\text{subject to } - t_n(\mathbf{w}^T\phi(\boldsymbol{x}_n) + b) + 1 \leq 0 \end{aligned} \tag{4.38}$$

In order to solve this, we must ensure that the gradients of the objective function and the constrain are pointing into the same direction by introducing Lagrange multipliers; thus, (4.38) becomes

$$L(\mathbf{w}, b, \boldsymbol{\alpha}) = \frac{1}{2}||\mathbf{w}||^2 - \sum_{n=1}^{N} \alpha_n[t_n(\mathbf{w}^T\phi(\boldsymbol{x}_n) + b) - 1] \tag{4.39}$$

where α_n are the Lagrange multipliers with $\alpha_n \geq 0$. The optimal solution is found by setting the gradients of $L(\mathbf{w}, b, \boldsymbol{\alpha})$ to zero:

$$\begin{aligned} \frac{\partial L}{\partial \mathbf{w}} &= \mathbf{w} - \sum_{n=1}^{N} \alpha_n t_n \phi(\boldsymbol{x}_n) = 0 \\ \Rightarrow \mathbf{w} &= \sum_{n=1}^{N} \alpha_n t_n \phi(\boldsymbol{x}_n) \end{aligned} \tag{4.40}$$

and

$$\frac{\partial L}{\partial b} = \sum_{n=1}^{N} \alpha_n t_n = 0 \qquad (4.41)$$

Note that in Equation 4.40 only the vectors $\phi(\boldsymbol{x}_n)$ where $\alpha_n > 0$ contribute to find the margin, i.e., the support vectors are the points in the feature space with $\alpha_n > 0$. Replacing (4.40) and (4.41) in (4.39) gives the dual representation of the Lagrangian

$$L_D(\boldsymbol{\alpha}) = \sum_{n=1}^{N} \alpha_n - \frac{1}{2} \sum_{n=1}^{N} \sum_{m=1}^{N} \alpha_n \alpha_m t_n t_m k(\boldsymbol{x}_n, \boldsymbol{x}_m) \qquad (4.42)$$

where $k(\boldsymbol{x}_n, \boldsymbol{x}_m) = \phi(\boldsymbol{x})^T \phi(\boldsymbol{x}')$ is known as the kernel function. The dual problem (**minimize** $L(\mathbf{w}, b, \boldsymbol{\alpha})$ for **w** and b and **maximize** L_D for $\boldsymbol{\alpha}$, can be solved by considering the Karush-Kuhn-Tucker (KKT) conditions, which provide the necessary and sufficient conditions for a point to be an optimum. The KKT conditions are:

- The primal constrains

$$t_n(\mathbf{w}^T \phi(\boldsymbol{x}_n) + b) - 1 \geq 0$$

- Complementary slackness

$$\alpha_n[\mathbf{w}^T \phi(\boldsymbol{x}_n) + b) - 1] = 0, \quad n = 1, 2, \ldots, N$$

- The dual constrains

$$\alpha_n \geq 0, \quad n = 1, 2, \ldots, N$$

Considering the above conditions and keeping in mind that the support vectors are the data points that define the margin, then they satisfy

$$t_n \left(\sum_{m \in \mathcal{S}} \alpha_m t_m k(\boldsymbol{x}_n, \boldsymbol{x}_m) + b \right) = 1 \tag{4.43}$$

where $\mathcal{S}$ denotes the set of indices of the support vectors. Now, b can be computed as

$$b = \frac{1}{N_{\mathcal{S}}} \sum_{n \in \mathcal{S}} \left(t_n - \sum_{m \in \mathcal{S}} \alpha_m t_m k(\boldsymbol{x}_n, \boldsymbol{x}_m) \right) \tag{4.44}$$

Soft-margin SVM

In speech processing applications is rarely the case that the data can be linearly discriminated without making errors, i.e., the classes are overlapped. In order to deal with this issue, Cortes and Vapnik (1995) proposed an extension of the hard-margin SVM in which certain amount of classification errors are allowed and penalized by introducing the slack variables ξ_n; thus, the decision function has the form

$$t_k(\mathbf{w}^T \phi(\boldsymbol{x}_n) + b) \geq 1 - \xi_n \tag{4.45}$$

Figure 4.20 illustrates the slack variables in a 2-dimensional feature space. Considering the class $t_n = +1$ as the reference, the slack variables take values of $\xi_n = 0$ for each data point that lies on the margin or in the correct side of the margin. For the data points inside the margin and in the correct side of the decision boundary, the slack variables take values in the range of $0 < \xi_n \leq 1$. For those data points on the wrong side of the margin, the values of the slack variables are $\xi_n > 1$. Now the goal is to maximize the margin while penalizing the data points for which $\xi_n > 1$. Therefore, we wish to minimize

$$\text{minimize} \quad C \sum_{n=1}^{N} \xi_n + \frac{1}{2} ||\mathbf{w}||^2 \tag{4.46}$$

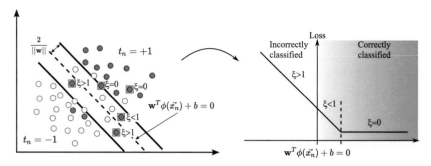

Figure 4.20: *Example of a soft-margin SVM and its respective loss function. Based on a figure found in Bishop (2006)*

and

where the parameter C controls the trade-off between ξ_n and the margin. This is a convex optimization problem where the goal is to minimize Equation 4.46 subject to the constrains introduced in Equation 4.45. Similar to the hard-margin SVM, Lagrange multipliers are introduced to solve the optimization problem

$$L = \frac{1}{2}||\mathbf{w}||^2 + C\sum_{n=1}^{N}\xi_n - \sum_{n=1}^{N}\alpha_n\{t_n(\mathbf{w}^T\phi(\boldsymbol{x}_n)+b)-1+\xi_n\} - \sum_{n=1}^{N}\mu_n\xi_n \quad (4.47)$$

where $\alpha_n \geq 0$ and $\mu_n \geq 0$ are Lagrange multipliers. For the soft-margin SVM, the set of KKT conditions are expressed as:

1. Primal constrains

$$\alpha_n \geq 0 \quad (4.48)$$

$$t_n(\mathbf{w}^T\phi(\boldsymbol{x}_n) + b) - 1 + \xi_n \geq 0 \quad (4.49)$$

2. Complementary slackness

$$\alpha_n(t_n(\mathbf{w}^T\phi(\boldsymbol{x}_n) + b) - 1 + \xi_n) = 0 \quad (4.50)$$

$$\mu_n\xi_n = 0 \quad (4.51)$$

3. Dual constrains

$$\alpha_n \geq 0 \qquad (4.52)$$

$$\mu_n \geq 0 \qquad (4.53)$$

The partial derivatives of L are

$$\frac{\partial L}{\partial b} = \sum_{n=1}^{N} \alpha_n t_n = 0$$

$$\frac{\partial L}{\partial \mathbf{w}} = \mathbf{w} - \sum_{n=1}^{N} \alpha_n t_n \phi(\boldsymbol{x}_n) = 0 \qquad (4.54)$$

$$\frac{\partial L}{\partial \xi_n} = C - \alpha_n - \mu_n = 0$$

Now the dual Lagrangian formulation is expressed as

$$L_D = \sum_{n=1}^{N} \alpha_n - \frac{1}{2} \sum_{n=1}^{N} \sum_{m=1}^{N} \alpha_n \alpha_m t_n t_m k(\boldsymbol{x}_n, \boldsymbol{x}_m) \qquad (4.55)$$

Subject to

$$0 \leq \alpha_n \leq C \qquad (4.56)$$

$$\sum_{n=1}^{N} \alpha_n t_n = 0 \qquad (4.57)$$

The support vectors for which $\alpha_n > 0$ should satisfy

$$t_n(\mathbf{w}^T \phi(\boldsymbol{x}_n) + b) = 1 - \xi_n \qquad (4.58)$$

From (4.54) it can be observed that if $\alpha_n < C$ then $\mu_n > 0$. It follows from Equation 4.51 that $\xi_n = 0$, which indicates that such data points lie on the margin. The data points where $\alpha_n = C$ can lie inside the margin and in this case the slack variables can be either $\xi_n \leq 1$ or $\xi_n > 1$. The support vectors for which $0 < \alpha_n < C$ have $\xi_n = 0$. Substituting in Equation 4.58, it follows that those support vectors will satisfy

$$t_n \left(\sum_{m \in \mathcal{S}} \alpha_m t_m k(\boldsymbol{x}_n, \boldsymbol{x}_m) + b \right) = 1 \tag{4.59}$$

To compute b, a numerically stable solution is obtained by averaging.

$$b = \frac{1}{N_{\mathcal{M}}} \sum_{n \in \mathcal{M}} \left(t_n - \sum_{m \in \mathcal{S}} \alpha_m t_m k(\boldsymbol{x}_n, \boldsymbol{x}_m) \right) \tag{4.60}$$

where $\mathcal{M}$ and $\mathcal{S}$ represent the set of data points such that $0 < \alpha_n < C$ and the set of total support vectors, respectively. The SM-SVM described before corresponds to the case of overlapped data with a linear decision boundary. However, in many applications a linear decision function may not exist or is not optimal to discriminate overlapped data. In those cases, kernel functions are considered to build a nonlinear decision boundary. One of the most common kernel used in Pattern Recognition is the Gaussian kernel, which is expressed as

$$k(\boldsymbol{x}_n, \boldsymbol{x}_m) = \mathrm{e}^{-\frac{2}{\gamma^2}|\boldsymbol{x}_n - \boldsymbol{x}_m|^2} \tag{4.61}$$

where γ is the bandwidth of the Gaussian kernel. The parameters C and γ are optimized using a grid-search scheme.

4.3.2 Support Vector Machine for regression

The goal of the Support Vector Regression (SVR) is to find a function $y(\boldsymbol{x})$ that has at most ϵ deviation from the targets $t_n \in R$. The main idea is to minimize the prediction error $|t_n - y(\boldsymbol{x}_n)|$ which can be above or below the target value and the margin is described by $y(\boldsymbol{x}_n) - t_n > \epsilon$ and $t_n - y(\boldsymbol{x}_n) > \epsilon$. In other words, the prediction error is tolerated if it's less than ϵ. In the case of linear regression, the optimization problem can be formulated as

$$\text{minimize} \quad \frac{1}{2}||\mathbf{w}||^2 + C \sum_{n=1}^{N} |t_n - y(\boldsymbol{x}_n)|_\epsilon \tag{4.62}$$

where C is a penalty parameter which determines the amount of trade-off between the flatness of $y(\boldsymbol{x})$ (Equation 4.33) and the amount of error larger than ϵ which is tolerated. To formulated Equation 4.62 as a constrained optimization problem, the slacks variables ξ and ξ^* are introduced. Assigning ξ to $y(\boldsymbol{x}_n) - t_n > \epsilon$ and ξ^* to $t_n - y(\boldsymbol{x}_n) > \epsilon$.

The primal objective function can be expressed as

$$
\begin{aligned}
\text{minimize} \quad & \frac{1}{2}||\mathbf{w}||^2 + C\sum_{n=1}^{N}(\xi_n + \xi_n^*) \\
\text{subject to} \quad & t_n - y(\boldsymbol{x}_n) \leq \epsilon + \xi_i \\
& y(\boldsymbol{x}_n) - t_n \leq \epsilon + \xi_n^* \\
& \xi_n, \xi_n^* \geq 0
\end{aligned}
\tag{4.63}
$$

Figure 4.21 illustrates the situation. Only the points outside the shaded region (ϵ-insensitive tube) contribute to the cost insofar, as the prediction errors are penalized in a linear fashion. Similar to the classification approach, the

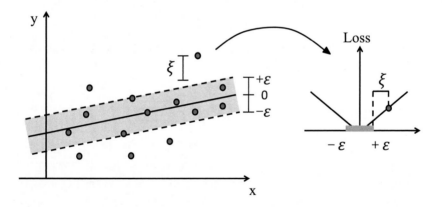

Figure 4.21: *Example of a Linear Support Vector Regressor and its corresponding loss function. Based on a figure found in Smola and Schölkopf (2004)*

optimization problem is solved by introducing Langrange multipliers:

$$
L = \frac{1}{2}||\mathbf{w}||^2 + C\sum_{n=1}^{N}(\xi_n + \xi_n^*) - \sum_{n=1}^{N}(\eta_n\xi_n + \eta_i^*\xi_n^*)
$$

$$
- \sum_{n=1}^{N}\alpha_n(\epsilon + \xi_n - t_n + y(\boldsymbol{x}_n)) - \sum_{n=1}^{N}\alpha_n^*(\epsilon + \xi_n^* + t_n - y(\boldsymbol{x}_n))
$$

(4.64)

where $\{\alpha_n, \alpha_n^*, \eta_n,$ and $\eta_n^*\} \geq 0$. Setting the gradients of L to zero:

$$
\nabla_b L = \sum_{n=1}^{N}(\alpha_n^* - \alpha_n) = 0
$$

$$
\nabla_{\mathbf{w}} L = \mathbf{w} - \sum_{n=1}^{N}(\alpha_n - \alpha_n^*)\boldsymbol{x}_n = 0 \qquad (4.65)
$$

$$
\nabla_{\xi_n} L = C - \alpha_n - \eta_n = 0
$$

$$
\nabla_{\xi_n^*} L = C - \alpha_n^* - \eta_n^* = 0
$$

Substituting the previous results in 4.64, the dual optimization problem is expressed as

$$
\text{maximize} \quad -\frac{1}{2}\sum_{n,m=1}^{N}(\alpha_n - \alpha_n^*)(\alpha_m - \alpha_m^*)\phi(\boldsymbol{x}_n, \boldsymbol{x}_m) - \epsilon\sum_{n=1}^{N}(\alpha_n + \alpha_n^*) + \sum_{n=1}^{N}t_n(\alpha_n -
$$

$$
\text{subject to} \quad \sum_{n=1}^{N}(\alpha_n - \alpha_n^*) = 0 \text{ and } \alpha_n, \alpha_m^* \in [0, C]
$$

(4.66)

From the partial derivatives we have that $\mathbf{w} = \sum_{n=1}^{N}(\alpha_n - \alpha_n^*)\boldsymbol{x}_n$. The regression function can be rewritten as

$$
y(\boldsymbol{x}) = \sum_{n=1}^{N}(\alpha_n - \alpha_n^*)\phi(\boldsymbol{x}_n, \boldsymbol{x}) + b \qquad (4.67)
$$

Now the weights $\mathbf{w}$ can be described as a linear combination of the training patterns $\boldsymbol{x}_n$. The KKT conditions state that at the point of the solution the product between dual variables and constrains has to vanish

$$\alpha_n(\epsilon + \xi_n - t_n + \mathbf{w}^T \phi(\boldsymbol{x}_n) + b) = 0$$
$$\alpha_n^*(\epsilon + \xi_n^* + t_n - \mathbf{w}^T \phi(\boldsymbol{x}_n) - b) = 0$$
(4.68)

and

$$(C - \alpha_n)\xi_n = 0$$
$$(C - \alpha_n^*)\xi_n^* = 0$$
(4.69)

From the previous result it can be concluded that only samples $(\boldsymbol{x}_n, t_n)$ with corresponding $\alpha_n = C$ and $\alpha_n^* = C$ lie outside the ϵ-insensitive tube. Additionally, there is never a set of dual variables α_n, α_n^* which are both simultaneously nonzero ($\alpha_n \alpha_n^* = 0$). From this we obtain that

$$b = t_n - \mathbf{w}^T \phi(\boldsymbol{x}_n) - \epsilon \quad \text{for } 0 < \alpha_n < C$$
(4.70)

and

$$b = t_n - \mathbf{w}^T \phi(\boldsymbol{x}_n) + \epsilon \quad \text{for } 0 < \alpha_n^* < C$$
(4.71)

Finally, from 4.68 it follows that for all samples inside the ϵ-insensitive tube the Lagrange multipliers α_n, α_n^* vanish for $|y(\boldsymbol{x}_n) - t_n| < \epsilon$.

4.3.3 Neural Networks

Neural Networks (NN) were developed in an attempt to find mathematical representations of the way the biological neurons process information (McCulloch and Pitts, 1943; Rosenblatt, 1958). One of the most successful NN model is the Multi-Layer Perceptron (MLP) (also known as feedforward network), in which a nonlinear transformation $\phi(\boldsymbol{x})$ is adapted to the data points during training, i.e., $\phi(\boldsymbol{x})$ is learned. This is in contrast to the SVM, where the nonlinear transformation (e.g. a Gaussian kernel) is known and training is performed in order to center the decision boundary on the data.

In general, a MLP consists of input, hidden(s), and output layers, however, only the last two layers processes the input data and determine the properties of the network. In the basic model of a neural network, the output is represented as a linear combination of nonlinear functions $\phi(\boldsymbol{x})$ of the form

$$y_k(\boldsymbol{x}, \mathbf{w}) = f\left(\sum_{j=1}^{M} \mathbf{w}_j \phi_j(\boldsymbol{x})\right) \tag{4.72}$$

where $y_k(\boldsymbol{x}, \mathbf{w})$ are the predicted targets, $f(.)$ is a nonlinear **activation function** and $\mathbf{w}$ are the learnable weights. The aim of the NN is to learn the functions $\phi_j(\boldsymbol{x})$ by adjusting its parameters along with the weights (Bishop, 2006). For this, M linear combinations of the input vectors $\boldsymbol{x}_d = \{\boldsymbol{x}_1, \boldsymbol{x}_2, \ldots \boldsymbol{x}_D\}$ are constructed in the first **hidden layer** using

$$a_j = \sum_{i=1}^{D} \mathbf{w}_{ji}^{(1)} \boldsymbol{x}_i + w_{j0}^{(1)} \tag{4.73}$$

where D is the number of features, the superscript (1) indicates the corresponding layer index, $j = 1, 2, \ldots M$ are the number of **neurons** in the hidden layer (1), and w_{j0} is the bias parameter. For simplicity, let's assume a two-layer network with a single hidden layer, where the superscript (1) corresponds to the hidden layer and (2) indicates operations in the output layer. The **activations** a_j are transformed using a nonlinear **activation function** $\phi(.)$, which is generally chosen to be the sigmoid function or the "tanh" function. The resulting quantities are known as the **hidden units** and have the form

$$z_j = \phi(a_j) \tag{4.74}$$

Using z_j, the **output units** are computed in the second layer as

$$a_k = \sum_{j=1}^{M} \mathbf{w}_{kj}^{(2)} z_j + w_{k0}^{(2)} \tag{4.75}$$

where $k = 1, 2, \ldots, K$ are the number of outputs (targets) and w_{k0} is the bias parameter. The predicted target labels $y_k(\boldsymbol{x})$ are computed by transforming the output units using an activation function

$$y_k(\boldsymbol{x}, \mathbf{w}) = f(a_k) \tag{4.76}$$

The choice of the **output unit activation function** ($f(.)$) depends on the problem to be addressed

- Bi-class/Multi-class: A softmax activation function is preferred because it converts each a_k into a probability ($\sum_{k=1}^{K} f(a_k) = 1$); thus, a sample is assigned to the class with the highest probability. The prediction of a class label using a softmax activation function has the form

$$y_k(\boldsymbol{x}, \mathbf{w}) = \text{Softmax}(a_k) = \frac{e^{a_k}}{\sum_{k=1}^{K} e^{a_k}} \tag{4.77}$$

- Multi-label: A sigmoid activation function is used because it produces independent probabilities for each a_k, which is suitable when a sample may belong to more than one class.

$$y_k(\boldsymbol{x}, \mathbf{w}) = \sigma(a_k) = \frac{1}{1 + e^{-a_k}} \tag{4.78}$$

- Regression: In this case, the nonlinear transformation is the identity, i.e., the predicted values are computed simply as

$$y_k(\boldsymbol{x}, \mathbf{w}) = a_k \tag{4.79}$$

Figure 4.22 shows an example of a feedforward network with a single hidden layer which is M linear combinations of the input vector $\boldsymbol{x}_d$. Note that if there are several samples N, the input layer is formed by a "matrix" with dimensions $N \times D$, where N is the total number of input vectors and D the number of features; thus, the operation on the hidden and output layers are performed for every $\boldsymbol{x}_d^n$, with $n = 1, 2, \ldots, N$ and $d = 1, 2, \ldots, D$.

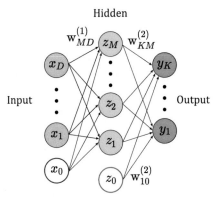

Figure 4.22: *Schematic view of a single-hidden layer feedforward network. The blue circles represent the input vectors with D features, the green circles represent the hidden layer with M neurons (hidden units), and the red circles represent the outputs with K target labels. The variables x_0 and Z_0 represent the bias parameters of each layer, and W are the learnable weights. Based on a figure found in Bishop (2006)*

Training of the network

The previous equations described how the information flows from the input to the output layer (forward propagation) in order to predict the class-label/real-value of an input vector. Now, it is described how to compute the optimal value of the weight parameters. The aim is to determine the weight matrix $\mathbf{W}$ that minimizes a **loss function** $L(\mathbf{W})$ given a set of N input vectors and target labels $(\boldsymbol{x}_n, t_n) = \{(\boldsymbol{x}_1, t_1), (\boldsymbol{x}_2, t_2), \ldots, (\boldsymbol{x}_N, t_N)\}$ with $n = 1, 2, \ldots, N$. Note that each $\boldsymbol{x}_n$ is a D-dimensional feature vector and each t_n is the target label of $\boldsymbol{x}_n$. The training process is based on minimizing the empirical risk:

$$E_{\boldsymbol{x}, t \sim \hat{p}_{\text{data}}(\boldsymbol{x}, t)} \left[L(\mathbf{W}, \boldsymbol{x}, t) \right] = \frac{1}{N} \sum_{n=1}^{N} L(\mathbf{W}, \boldsymbol{x}_n, t_n) \qquad (4.80)$$

where N is the number of training samples, $\hat{p}_{\text{data}}$ is the empirical distribution, and $L(\mathbf{W}, \boldsymbol{x}_n, t_n)$ is the loss function. Finding the optimal values of $\mathbf{W}$ means finding the minimum error between the predicted labels $y_k(\boldsymbol{x}_n)$ (Equation 4.72) and the target labels y_n for each x_n. If $L(\mathbf{W})$ is a **continuous function**, then the smallest value of the lost function occurs at the point in the *weight space* were the gradient vanishes, i.e., $\nabla L(\mathbf{W}) = 0$. The simplest approach to minimize the lost is by means of the **backpropagation**, which is an iterative algorithm that uses the gradient information to update the weights as

$$\mathbf{W}^{(\tau+1)} = \mathbf{W}^{(\tau)} - \eta \nabla L(\mathbf{W}^{(\tau)}), \tag{4.81}$$

where τ indicates the iteration step and η is the learning rate. After updating $\mathbf{W}$, the gradient is computed again for the new weight, and the process is repeated. The general method is called backpropagation because the error is computed on the output layer, and the weights are updated for the successive layers. This particular optimization method is known as **Stochastic Gradient Descent** (SGD) because after each step the weight matrix is "moved" towards the highest decreasing rate of the error function, i.e., the weight moves towards the direction of the negative gradient. In many applications, it is necessary to adapt the learning rate η during training. This can be achieved using the optimization Adaptive Moment Estimation (Adam), which allows computing individual adaptive learning rates for the weight parameters from estimates of first and second moments of the gradients (Kingma and Ba, 2014). Adam computes the parameters v^τ and r^τ, which are moving averages included in Equation 4.81 as follows

$$\mathbf{W}^{(\tau+1)} = \mathbf{W}^{(\tau)} - \eta \frac{v^\tau + \epsilon}{\sqrt{r^\tau} + \epsilon} \odot \nabla L(\mathbf{W}^{(\tau)}) \tag{4.82}$$

$$v^\tau = \beta_1 v^{\tau-1} + (1 - \beta_1)\nabla L(\mathbf{W}^{(\tau)}) \tag{4.83}$$

$$r^\tau = \beta_2 v^{\tau-1} + (1 - \beta_2)\nabla L(\mathbf{W}^{(\tau)}) \odot \nabla L(\mathbf{W}^{(\tau)}) \tag{4.84}$$

where β_1 and β_2 (typically $\beta_1 = 0.9$; $\beta_2 = 0.999$) are parameters used to control the decay rates of v^τ and r^τ, ϵ is a floating number used to prevent divisions by zero, and $\odot$ is the Hadamard product.

Similar to the output activation function, the choice of the **loss function**

$L(\mathbf{W})$ depends on the problem to be addressed:

- Bi-class/Multi-class: Cross entropy loss combined with softmax (Equation 4.77)

$$L(\mathbf{W}) = -\log(t_n \log(\text{Softmax}(a_n))) \tag{4.85}$$

- Multi-label: The Binary Cross-Entropy (BCE) with logistic loss uses the sigmoid function to compute the loss

$$L(\mathbf{W}) = -t_n \log \sigma(a_n) + (1 - t_n) \log(1 - \sigma(a_n)) \tag{4.86}$$

- Regression: The L2-norm (Mean Square Error) is the most common lost function used for regression

$$L(\mathbf{W}) = ||t_n - y_k(\boldsymbol{x}_n)||_2^2 \tag{4.87}$$

In summary, the parameters of the NN are computed by first forward propagating the feature vectors $\boldsymbol{x}_n$ from the input to the output layer. Then, the error between the predicted and target values (i.e., $\delta_k = y_k(\boldsymbol{x}_n, \mathbf{w}) - t_n$) is calculated for all the output units and back propagated in the network. Afterwards the weights $\mathbf{W}$ of each input neuron are updated and the process is repeated until finding the minimum value of the error function.

4.3.4 Convolutional Neural Networks

Convolutional Neural Networks (CNN) can capture the spatial and temporal dependencies of a grid-like input (e.g., spectrograms) through the application of relevant filters (LeCun et al., 1999). CNN has specialized layers (convolutional layers) that take advantage of the regularity in the input data to extract the most relevant features. Rather than convolutions, the operation performed in a CNN are cross-correlations where the input and a *kernel* (learnable weights) are combined to produce an output tensor or **feature map**. A convolutional layer is defined as

$$\mathbf{H}(i,j,h) = \sum_{k=1}^{C} \sum_{j=1}^{M} \sum_{i=1}^{N} \boldsymbol{X}(k,i+M,j+N)\mathbf{W}_h(k,M,N) \qquad (4.88)$$

where $\mathbf{W}_h$ is the *kernel* matrix, $\boldsymbol{X}$ is the input tensor with dimensions $M \times N$, which in speech processing applications can be a STFT, a Mel Spectrum or a Cochleagram (Section 4.1.2). C is the number of input channels. Figure 4.23 shows an example of a convolution operation performed in a 2-channel spectrogram. The first channel is the Mel spectrum, and the second one is a Cochleagram. In the example, four kernel matrices of size 3×3 are applied to each channel of the input tensor $\boldsymbol{X}$. The resulting feature maps are used processed by the hidden layers of a NN for classification or regression. The

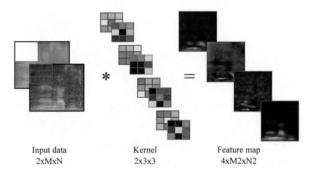

Input data   Kernel   Feature map
2xMxN   2x3x3   4xM2xN2

Figure 4.23: *Convolutional layer with four kernel matrices of size 3×3 applied to a 2D-spectrogram formed with a Mel spectrum and a Cochleagram. The resulting feature maps highlight different patterns from the input.*

kernel matrix can be applied using different methods. Commonly, **stride convolutions** are applied to the input data in order to skip some elements of $\boldsymbol{X}$, instead of multiplying the kernel at each position of the input data. The output of a convolution layer with stride is defined as

$$[(V + 2p - M + 1)/(s + 1)] \times [(D + 2p - N + 1)/(s + 1)] \times H \quad (4.89)$$

where s is an integer value that defines the size of the stride, and p is the amount of padding that can be applied to the input tensor. Typically, a CNN also includes a **pooling layer** which fuses information of the input across spatial locations, decreases the number of parameters, and reduces the computational costs and overfitting. The most common pooling operation is the *max pooling*, which propagates the maximum value in a *neighborhood* to the next layer. Furthermore, a stride, which is equal to the size of the pooling, is applied. Typical choices of pooling are 2×2 or 3×3 neighborhoods. During training, only one value contributes to the error, which is propagated along the path of the maximum value. In the forward propagation from the input to the output layer, it is common to keep track of the index of the max activation.

Figure 4.24 illustrates the max-pooling operation performed in a matrix of dimensions 4×4. The size of the pooling layer is a "filter" of size 2×2 with a stride of 2. The resulting output is a reduced version of the input data where only the highest value contained in the pooling "filter" are included.

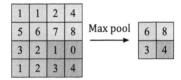

Figure 4.24: *Max pooling operation with a 2×2 filter and stride of 2.*

4.3.5 Recurrent Neural Networks

Recurrent Neural Networks (RNN) are specialized feedforward networks that process sequential data by 'giving" memory to the network. During the 70s, different NN architectures were proposed to analyze time series. However, the recurrent networks used today are based on the idea proposed by Elman (1990).

In order to understand how to give memory to a network, let us consider the case of a speech signal converted into a sequence of feature vectors $x_t = \{x_1, x_2, \ldots, x_T\}$ and used in the input layer of a NN with a single hidden

95

layer. The aim is to analyze the sequence at each time step t; thus, at a time step t, the output of the hidden layer is computed and forward propagated to activate the output layer. The outputs from the hidden layer are *fed back* into the network and used as inputs to activate the hidden layer at the time step $t + 1$. The variables that store the information of a sequence up to $t - 1$ are called **hidden states** (or hidden variables) and are represented by H_t. An RNN is simply a feedforward network with hidden states, where the calculation of the hidden state of the current time step t is determined by the input of the current time step together with the hidden state of the previous time step $t - 1$. Then, considering Equation 4.74 and changing z_j by H_t, the output of the hidden layer in an RNN is computed as

$$H_t = \phi(X_t W_{xh} + H_{t-1} W_{hh} + b_h) \tag{4.90}$$

where $X_t \in \mathbb{R}^{N \times D}$ is a *minibatch* (subset of training points) with N sequences and D inputs/features at time step t, $W_{xh} \in \mathbb{R}^{D \times h}$ is the weight parameter with h hidden *units* (neurons), $H_{t-1} \in \mathbb{R}^{h \times h}$ is the hidden state of the previous time step, $W_{hh} \in \mathbb{R}^{h \times h}$ is the weight parameter associated to the hidden state H_{t-1}, b_h are the bias parameters, and ϕ is the activation function of the hidden layer (commonly a tanh function). The output layer of an RNN is computed as

$$Y_t = f(H_t W_{hk} + b_k) \tag{4.91}$$

where $Y \in \mathbb{R}^{N \times K}$ is the output with K predictions, N sequences, and $f(.)$ is the output activation function that can take the form of Equations 4.77, 4.78, 4.79 or other. Figure 4.25 shows an schematic view of an "unfolded" RNN. Each unit passes the hidden state as additional input to the successor, thus, previous input can influence current output and the parameters W are shared across different parts of the model, which helps to compute the gradients (Graves, 2012).

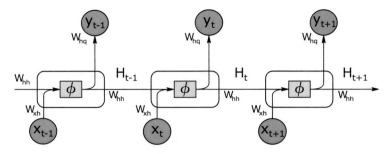

Figure 4.25: *Schematic view of an "unfolded" RNN. The blue circles represent the input layer, the green boxes are the hidden layers, and the red circles are the elements of the output layer. Based on a figure found in Zhang et al. (2021)*

Forward propagation in an RNN

Given a sequence of feature vectors $x_t = \{x_1, x_2, \ldots, x_T\}$, the input is propagated in an RNN cell with hidden layer activation $\phi(.) = \tanh(.)$ and output layer activation $f(.) = \sigma(.)$ as shown in Figure 4.26. Note that the activation function in the output layer can also be a Softmax function (for multiclass) of the identity (for regression). Furthermore, according to Equations 4.90 and 4.91, the loss is computed for every t in the sequence.

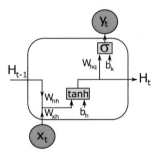

Figure 4.26: *Schematic view of the forward propagation procedure in an RNN cell. Based on a figure found in Olah (2021)*

Backpropagation in an RNN

The weight parameters are updated by computing the gradients from the time step $t = T$ through the full sequence down to $t = 0$ (back in time). Considering a tanh as activation function in the hidden layer, the gradients of the weights are computed as

$$\nabla W_{hh,t} = \nabla H_t \cdot \tanh'(X_t W_{xh} + H_{t-1} W_{hh} + b_h) \cdot H_{t-1}^\mathsf{T}$$
$$\nabla W_{xh,t} = \nabla H_t \cdot \tanh'(X_t W_{xh} + H_{t-1} W_{hh} + b_h) \cdot x_t^\mathsf{T}$$
$$\nabla b_{h,t} = \nabla H_t \cdot \tanh'(X_t W_{xh} + H_{t-1} W_{hh} + b_h)$$

Since the RNN shares the weights, each gradient can be computed as the sum over all time steps, for instance

$$\nabla W_{hh,t} = \sum_{t=1}^{T} \nabla H_t \cdot \tanh'(X_t W_{xh} + H_{t-1} W_{hh} + b_h) \cdot H_{t-1}^\mathsf{T} \qquad (4.92)$$

Note that one update of parameters requires backpropagation through a complete sequence, resulting in a high amount of computation time. One solution is to perform a *truncated* backpropagation through time, which consists of adapting the parameters every δ time steps.

Long-Short Term Memory units

Although the hidden states of an RNN can capture historical information of the sequence up to the current time step, for a relatively long sequence, the network has problems connecting relevant past and present inputs. The reason is that the hidden state is overwritten at each time step, leading to vanishing gradient problems, i.e., the network stops updating the parameters, even if the optimal solution is not reached (Bengio et al., 1994). The Long-Short Term Memory (LSTM) units were designed to solve vanishing gradient problems in a standard RNN cell and to help the NN to learn long-term dependencies for larger sequences (Hochreiter and Schmidhuber, 1997). The main idea of the

RNN with LSTM units (or cells) is to introduce **gates** that control writing and accessing "memory" in an additional **cell state**.

Figure 4.27 shows a schematic view of an LSTM unit. The elements of such a cell include the input x_t, the hidden state H_t/H_{t-1}, the cell state C_t/C_{t-1}, and the output y_t. The internal gates of the LSTM are updated in different

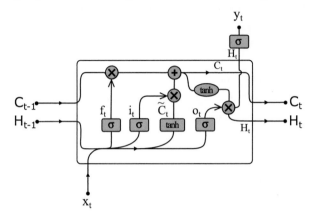

Figure 4.27: *Schematic view of a LSTM cell. The green boxes represent hidden layers and the orange circles represent point-wise operations. Based on a figure found in Olah (2021)*

steps:

- **Cell state** (C_t): Undergoes only linear changes, i.e. no activation function is used, thus, the cell state can be constant for multiple time steps.

- **Forget gate** (f_t): Controls how much of the previous cell state is "forgotten". Note that C_{t-1} is multiplied by f_t, which can only take values between 0 and 1 (the output is a sigmoid function), thus, C_{t-1} is 0 if f_t is 0.

$$f_t = \sigma \left(W_f \cdot [H_{t-1}, x_t] + b_f \right)$$

- **Input gate** (i_t): Combines the input and hidden state on two paths.

$$i_t = \sigma \left(W_i \cdot [H_{t-1}, x_t] + b_i \right)$$
$$\tilde{C}_t = \tanh \left(W_C \cdot [H_{t-1}, x_t] + b_C \right)$$

where $\tilde{C}_t$ is the "candidate memory". In the input gate $\tilde{C}_t$ is multiplied by i_t which can only take values between 0 and 1. Thus, the amount of information that is added to the cell state will depend on i_t.

- **Updating the cell state**: The new cell state is the sum of the "remaining information" from C_{t-1} and new information from input and hidden state ($\odot$: element-wise multiplication)

$$C_t = f_t \odot C_{t-1} + i_t \odot \tilde{C}_t$$

- **Output gate** (o_t): The output y_t directly depends on the hidden state H_t:

$$o_t = \sigma \left(W_o [H_{t-1}, x_t] + b_o \right)$$
$$H_t = o_t \odot \tanh \left(C_t \right)$$
$$y_t = \sigma \left(H_t \right)$$

Note also that the cell and hidden states are updated **separately**. Note that the operation $\tanh (C_t)$ does not corresponds to an activation layer.

Gated Recurrent Units

Another alternative to learn long term dependencies and reduce vanishing gradient problems in the standard RNN, is to use Gated Recurrent Units (GRUs), a variant of the LSTM. Cho et al. (2014) proposed the GRU as a recurrent cell that controls the flow of "memory" only with the hidden states; thus, removing the cell state, which simplifies the network by reducing the number of trainable parameters. Figure 4.28 shows an schematic view of a GRU. The parameters

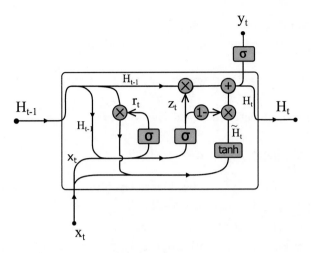

Figure 4.28: *Schematic view of a GRU cell. The green boxes represent hidden layers and the orange circles represent point-wise operations. Based on a figure found in Olah (2021)*

of the GRU are updated in different steps:

- **Reset gate** (r_t): Determines the influence of the previous hidden state (similar to the "forget gate" in the LSTM).

$$r_t = \sigma \left(\boldsymbol{W}_r \cdot [\boldsymbol{H}_{t-1}, \boldsymbol{x}_t] + \boldsymbol{b}_r \right)$$

- **Update gate** (z_t): Determines the influence of an "update proposal" on the new hidden state:

$$z_t = \sigma \left(\boldsymbol{W}_z \cdot [\boldsymbol{H}_{t-1}, \boldsymbol{x}_t] + \boldsymbol{b}_z \right)$$

- **Candidate update**: Combination of input and "reset" hidden state (similar to the candidate memory $\tilde{\boldsymbol{C}}_t$ in the LSTM).

$$\tilde{\boldsymbol{H}}_t = \tanh \left(\boldsymbol{W}_h \cdot [\boldsymbol{r}_t \odot \boldsymbol{H}_{t-1}, \boldsymbol{x}_t] + \boldsymbol{b}_h \right)$$

- **Computing the updated hidden state**: The update gate controls the way that the old state and the proposed update are combined:

$$H_t = (1 - z_t) \odot H_{t-1} + z_t \odot \tilde{H}_t$$

The node output is computed as $\hat{y}_t = \sigma(H_t)$

Bidirectional RNNs (BRNN)

This variant of RNN connects two hidden layers of opposite directions to the same output Schuster and Paliwal (1997). The idea of a BRNN is to split the hidden states into **forward** and **backward** states. In the forward state, the hidden states are computed starting from $t = 0$ up to $t = T$ (like in the standard RNN). In the backward state, the hidden states are computed starting from $t = T$ up to $t = 0$. Figure 4.29 shows a schematic view of a BRNN. Note that the outputs of the forward and backward states are concatenated in order to compute the output. Other operations include a sum or multiplication of the forward-backward states in order to compute the output. Additionally, note that the RNN cells can also be LSTM or GRUs. The sequence of feature vectors X is fed to the recurrent net with RNN cells, which computes the forward ($\overrightarrow{H}$) and backward ($\overleftarrow{H}$) hidden sequences. The sequence $\overrightarrow{H}$ is computed by iterating Equation 4.93 from $t = 1$ to $t = T$. In the case of $\overleftarrow{H}$, the hidden states are computed by iterating Equation 4.94 from $t = T$ to $t = 1$:

$$\overrightarrow{H}_t = \phi(X_t W_{x\overrightarrow{h}} + H_{t-1} W_{\overrightarrow{h}\overrightarrow{h}} + b_h) \qquad (4.93)$$

$$\overleftarrow{H}_t = \phi(X_t W_{x\overleftarrow{h}} + H_{t-1} W_{\overleftarrow{h}\overleftarrow{h}} + b_h) \qquad (4.94)$$

The output of the recurrent network is the sequence r_T formed with the concatenation of $\overrightarrow{H}$ and $\overleftarrow{H}$. For each time frame, the output is defined as

$$r_t = (W_{\overrightarrow{h}r}\overrightarrow{H}_t \oplus W_{\overleftarrow{h}r}\overleftarrow{H}_t) + b_r \qquad (4.95)$$

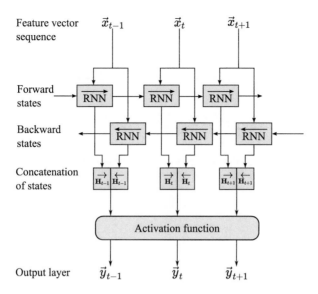

Feature vector sequence $\vec{x}_{t-1}$ $\vec{x}_t$ $\vec{x}_{t+1}$

Forward states

Backward states

Concatenation of states

Activation function

Output layer $\vec{y}_{t-1}$ $\vec{y}_t$ $\vec{y}_{t+1}$

Figure 4.29: *Schematic view of a BRNN cell. The green boxes represent the forward states and the orange boxes represent the backward states. In order to compute the output, the forward-backward states are concatenated. Based on a figure found in Schuster and Paliwal (1997)*

Besides concatenation, other operations such as the sum can be used to combine the forward and backward states.

4.4 Speaker models

4.4.1 Gaussian Mixture Models

The Gaussian Mixture Model (GMM)-based systems are capable of representing arbitrary probabilistic densities. GMMs are parametric probabilistic models represented as a weighted sum of M Gaussian densities (Figure 4.30). For a D-dimensional feature vector x a GMM is defined as:

$$p(\boldsymbol{x}|\lambda) = \sum_{i=1}^{M} \omega_i p_i(\boldsymbol{x}) \tag{4.96}$$

103

The Gaussian densities $p_i(x)$ are parameterized by the mixture weights ω_i, a D $\times 1$ mean vector μ_i, and a D$\times$D covariance matrix Σ_i (Reynolds et al., 2000). The parameters of the density models can be denoted as $\lambda = (\omega_i, \mu_i, \Sigma_i)$ and the Gaussian densities as

$$p_i(x) = \frac{1}{(2\pi)^{D/2}|\Sigma_i|^{1/2}} \exp\{-\frac{1}{2}(x - \mu_i)^T \Sigma_i^{-1}(x - \mu_i)\} \qquad (4.97)$$

In speech processing GMMs are used to represent the distribution of feature

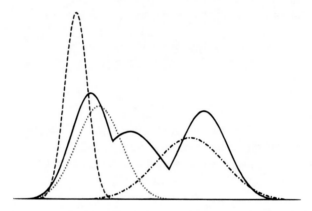

Figure 4.30: *Graphical representation of a one-dimensional GMM. The solid black curve is the weighted sum of the Gaussian distributions represented by the gray dashed curves.*

vectors extracted from a single speaker or a group of speakers. If the GMM is trained using features extracted from a large sample of speakers, the resulting model is called Universal Background Model (UBM). Therefore, the UBM is trained to represent the entire space of possible speakers. For a given set of speakers, the conditional probability $p(X_{UBM}|\lambda)$ is known as the maximum likelihood function that better represents the population of speakers, where X_{UBM} are the set of feature vectors extracted from the group of speakers. The parameters λ of the maximum likelihood function can be estimated using the Expectation Maximization (EM) algorithm. The EM approach is used to increase the likelihood of the UBM, i.e., for iterations k and $k + 1$,

$p(\boldsymbol{X}|\lambda^{(k+1)}) > p(\boldsymbol{X}|\lambda^{(k)})$. The steps of the EM algorithm are as follows:

- Initialize $\omega_k, \boldsymbol{\mu}_k, \boldsymbol{\Sigma}_k$. This is commonly achieved with a clustering algorithm such as K-means.

- Compute the new weights ω_{ik} with $1 \leq i \leq N$ and $1 \leq k \leq M$.

$$\omega_{ik} = \frac{p_k(\boldsymbol{x}_i|\lambda_k)\omega_k}{\sum_{m=1}^{M} p_m(\boldsymbol{x}_i|\lambda_m)\omega_m} \tag{4.98}$$

Where N is the number of feature vectors extracted from the speakers, M is the number of Gaussian components in the GMM, $\omega_k = N_k/N$. N_k is the number of feature vectors contained in each Gaussian component.

- Compute the new mean vector $\boldsymbol{\mu}_k$

$$\boldsymbol{\mu}_k = \frac{1}{N_k} \sum_{i=1}^{N} \omega_{ik}\boldsymbol{x}_i \tag{4.99}$$

- Compute the new covariance matrix $\boldsymbol{\Sigma}_k$

$$\boldsymbol{\Sigma}_k = \frac{1}{N_k} \sum_{i=1}^{N} \omega_{ik}(\boldsymbol{x}_i - \boldsymbol{\mu}_k)(\boldsymbol{x}_i - \boldsymbol{\mu}_k)^T \tag{4.100}$$

Then ω_{ik} is computed again and the procedure is repeated until the convergence. In a GMM-UBM system the single speaker model is derived from the population of speakers by adapting the parameters of the UBM using the training data from the speaker to be modeled. There are different approaches used to obtain the speaker model. One method is the Maximum A Posteriori (MAP) adaptation which consist of a two step estimation process. In the first step the training vectors from the speaker to be modeled are aligned into the UBM mixture components. That is, given a UBM and the training vectors from the speaker $X = \{x_1, x_2, ..., x_T\}$, for mixture i in the UBM, we compute

$$Pr(i|x_t) = \frac{\omega_i p_i(x_t)}{\sum_{j=1}^{M} \omega_j p_j(x_t)} \qquad (4.101)$$

Then $Pr(i|x_t)$ and x_t are used to compute the sufficient statistics of the weight, mean, and variance

$$n_i = \sum_{t=1}^{T} Pr(i|x_t) \qquad (4.102)$$

$$E_i(x) = \frac{1}{n_i} \sum_{t=1}^{T} Pr(i|x_t)x_t \qquad (4.103)$$

$$E_i(x^2) = \frac{1}{n_i} \sum_{t=1}^{T} Pr(i|x_t)x_t^2 \qquad (4.104)$$

The second step of the adaptation process consists of using these sufficient statistics to update the parameters of the UBM for the mixture i using the following equations

$$\hat{\omega}_i = [\alpha_i^\omega n_i/T + (1 - \alpha_i^\omega)\omega_i]\gamma \qquad (4.105)$$

$$\hat{\mu}_i = \alpha_i^m E_i(x) + (1 - \alpha_i^\omega)\mu_i \qquad (4.106)$$

$$\hat{\sigma}_i^2 = \alpha_i^v E_i(x^2) + (1 - \alpha_i^v)(\sigma_i^2 + \mu_i^2) - \hat{\mu}_i^2 \qquad (4.107)$$

Where $\{\alpha_i^\omega, \alpha_i^m, \alpha_i^v\}$ are the adaptation coefficients used to control the balance between the old and new estimates for the weights, means, and variances, respectively. The scale factor, γ, is computed to ensure that the weights sum to unity. T is the number of feature vectors extracted from the speaker. The resulting adapted model can be used to assess the progression of the disease from the patients, considering the changes with respect to the UBM.

4.4.2 i–vectors

Speaker models obtained with the GMM-UBM may adapt not only to the the speaker-specific features, but also to the channel conditions of the recordings. The i–vector approach is an alternative way to obtain speaker models and at the same time other acoustic factors embedded in the recordings. This approach is based on Joint Factor Analysis (JFA), which assumes that a speaker model can be decomposed into a speaker independent, speaker dependent, channel dependent, and residual components. Thus, in JFA a speaker model has the form

$$s = m + Vy + Ux + Dz \qquad (4.108)$$

where s is the speaker **supervector**, m is the speaker independent component (e.g. mean vector from a UBM), Vy is the speaker dependent component, Ux is the channel dependent component, and Dz are the residual components. The factors $x, y,$ and z are obtained by first computing the matrices $V, U,$ and D in the following way (Kenny et al., 2008):

- V is computed assuming that U and D are zero.

- U is computed given V and assuming that D is zero.

- D is computed given V and U, from the previous steps.

Dehak et al. (2011) proposed the i–vector approach after showing that channel factors in the JFA model also contained information about the speakers and proposed combining the channel and speaker spaces into a total variability space. In this approach the speaker supervector s is given by:

$$s = m + T\,\omega \qquad (4.109)$$

where m is the channel- and speaker-independent supervector (from UBM), T is the total variability matrix which is trained in the same way as the matrix V, and the components of ω are the total factors, and ω itself is known as the identity vector or i–vector. According to Dehak et al. (2011), ω is defined by its posterior distribution conditioned to the Baum-Welch statistics. Given a sequence of L frames $\{y_1, y_2, \ldots, y_L\}$ and a UBM Ω composed of C mixture components, the Baum-Welch statistics N_c and F_c of utterance u are given by:

$$N_c = \sum_{t=1}^{L} P(c|y_t, \Omega) \tag{4.110}$$

$$F_c = \sum_{t=1}^{L} P(c|y_t, \Omega)y_t \tag{4.111}$$

where $c = 1, \ldots, C$ is the Gaussian index and $P(c|\boldsymbol{y_t}, \Omega)$ is the posterior probability of mixture component c generating the vector $\boldsymbol{y_t}$. The first-order Baum-Welch statistic centralized around the mean of the UBM mixture component c (i.e., m_c) is given by:

$$\tilde{F}_c = \sum_{t=1}^{L} P(c|y_t, \Omega)(y_t - m_c) \tag{4.112}$$

Then, the identity vector $\boldsymbol{\omega}$ for a given utterance u can be found as follows:

$$\boldsymbol{\omega} = (I + T^t \Sigma^{-1} N(u)T)^{-1} T^t \Sigma^{-1} \tilde{F}(u) \tag{4.113}$$

where $N(u)$ is a diagonal matrix whose diagonal blocks are $N_c I$, $\hat{F}(u)$ is a supervector that concatenates all of the first-order Baum-Welch statistics $\tilde{F}_c$ for a given utterance u, and Σ models the residual variability not captured by the total variability matrix $\boldsymbol{T}$.

4.4.3 x–vectors

The GMM-UBM and i–vector approaches estimates the probability distribution of the speakers in order to model their speech. An alternative approach proposed by Snyder et al. (2018) consists of transforming the speech data by means of several hidden layers and using the output of one of these layers as a speaker embedding or x–vector. Table 4.3 shows the configuration of the DNN used

108

to compute the speaker embeddings. The method considers a Deep Neural

Table 4.3: DNN architecture for x–vectors. **Layer:** name of the hidden, pooling, or activation layer. **Layer context:** Frames considered for analysis on each layer.

Layer	Layer context	Total context
frame 1	[t-2,t+2]	5
frame 2	{t-2, t, t+2}	9
frame 3	{t-3, t, t+3}	15
frame 4	{t}	15
frame 5	{t}	15
stats pooling	[0, T)	T
segment 6	{0}	T
segment 7	{0}	T
Softmax	{0}	T

Network (DNN) to process a sequence of feature vectors $x_t = \{x_1, x_2, \ldots x_T\}$ where $t = \{1, 2, \ldots, T\}$ and T is the total number of frames. The first five layers **frame** i ($i = \{1, 2, 3, 4, 5\}$) process the speech signal at frame level (time steps), with a temporal context (**Layer context**) centered at the current time step t. For example, the layer **frame 1** has a temporal context of 5 speech frames ($t - 2, t - 1, t, t + 1, t + 2$) for processing. The total temporal context of the second layer **frame 2** builds on the temporal context of the earlier layers: the input to **frame 2** is the output of **frame 1** (which has a temporal context of 5 frames) and the layer context of **frame 2** is $\{t - 2, t, t + 2\}$. The statistics pooling layer computes the mean and standard deviation of all T frame-level outputs from layer **frame 5**. These statistics are concatenated together and propagated through the rest of the network. After training, the x-vectors are extracted from layer **segment 6**. The layers **segment 7** and **Softmax** are not considered as speaker embeddings because these are only used as the classification layer during the training stage.

Summary

Speech production involves the fast interaction of regions in the brain, the vocal tract, and the respiratory system. Thus, when one of these areas is considerably affected by a clinical condition, abnormal variations in speech can be detected and measured automatically for further analysis. On the one hand, classification methods are suitable for the detection of speech disorders from recordings. On the other hand, regression analysis allows predicting the progression of the speech symptoms based on a clinical evaluation. Furthermore, speaker models include relevant information about a person's speech which can be helpful to detect changes through time. The following chapter describes the datasets considered in this thesis to implement automatic methods for acoustic analysis of speech signals of PD patients and CI users.

Chapter 5

Data collection

5.1 Parkinson's disease

5.1.1 PCGITA (Spanish)

This dataset was collected by Orozco-Arroyave et al. (2014). It consists of speech recordings of 50 PD patients and 50 age/gender balanced healthy speakers. The speech tasks performed by the participants are reported in Appendix A.1. The recordings were captured in a sound-proof booth. The speech signals were captured at 44.1 kHz with 16-bit resolution. For this thesis, the signals are down sampled to 16 kHz in order to match the sampling frequency of the trained models. All of the PD patients were diagnosed by a neurologist expert and were labeled according to the motor sub-scale MDS-UPDRS-III. None of the speakers in the healthy groups had symptoms associated with PD or any other neurological disease. Additionally, the dysarthria level of the patients and the healthy speakers was evaluated by speech therapists according to the m-FDA (Table 1.3). Table 5.1 summarizes the information about the PD patients and HC speakers.

Table 5.1: Information about the PCGITA dataset

| | PD patients | | Healthy speakers | |
	Male	Female	Male	Female
Number of speakers	25	25	25	25
Age [years]	60.5±11.6	61.4±7.0	61.6±11.6	60.8±7.6
Range of age [years]	33-81	49-75	31-86	49-76
MDS-UPDRS-III	9-92	19-71	-	-
mFDA	17-41	13-51	0-29	0-25

5.1.2 PD At-home (Spanish)

This dataset was captured during the Third Frederick Jelinek Memorial Summer Workshop at Johns Hopkins University[1]. Seven PD patients were recorded four times per day (every two hours), once per month during four months. Thus, there is a total of 16 recording sessions per patient. As it was not possible to have a neurologist expert during all day long with each patient, the at-home test set does not have MDS-UPDRS-III scores. The speech recordings of this set were evaluated according to the m-FDA scale. Table 5.2 summarizes the information of the m-FDA scale of the patients in the at-home test set.

Table 5.2: Dysarthria scores of the at-home test set.

| ID | Age | Gender | m-FDA (At-home) | | | | | | | | | | | | | | |
			H1	H2	H3	H4	H5	H6	H7	H8	H9	H10	H11	H12	H13	H14	H15	H16
P1	68	Male	20	23	21	12	21	18	17	16	17	20	25	20	27	23	22	20
P2	59	Female	35	35	35	35	33	35	34	34	36	37	39	39	42	42	42	42
P3	55	Female	19	15	20	19	14	19	18	16	20	20	17	17	24	23	23	23
P4	63	Male	20	25	24	23	28	26	25	25	29	29	29	27	28	28	28	28
P5	70	Male	25	24	26	25	24	30	27	28	28	25	28	28	25	24	24	25
P6	59	Female	26	32	31	30	32	30	31	31	33	33	30	34	37	38	37	34
P7	69	Male	40	35	38	36	37	34	35	34	33	28	37	37	36	36	37	38

5.1.3 PD Longitudinal (Spanish)

Speech recordings of the same 7 PD patients from the At-Home dataset were recorded in at least four sessions from 2012 to 2017: In 2012 (June), 2014 (June), 2015 (February), 2015 (August), 2016 (February), and 2017 (February).

[1]https://bit.ly/3pYrGGY

112

The speech recordings of this set were evaluated according to the m-FDA scale. Table 5.3 summarizes the information from the patients.

Table 5.3: Dysarthria scores of the longitudinal test set.

ID	Age	Gender	m-FDA 2012	2014	2015-1	2015-2	2016	2017
P1	62	Male	31	15	21	19	-	18
P2	55	Female	29	29	27	26	34	27
P3	51	Female	15	37	10	14	20	23
P4	59	Male	22	22	19	19	22	26
P5	66	Male	13	28	23	24	28	27
P6	55	Female	24	42	21	23	21	31
P7	67	Male	-	40	31	38	-	33

5.1.4 Apkinson (Spanish)

This dataset was collected with the Android application Apkinson [2], which was designed for motor evaluation and monitoring of PD patients (Orozco-Arroyave et al., 2020). The speech protocol includes the sentences and DDK exercises described in Appendix A.1. Additionally, the protocol includes the sustained phonation of vowels /a/, /i/, and /u/, the rapid and sequential repetition of /si-fa-schu/, and the description of a picture. The dataset considered in this thesis consists of speech recordings of 37 PD patients (17 females) and 37 healthy speakers (17 females) captured with a sampling frequency of 16 kHz in different acoustic environments and with different smartphones. The age (average±standard deviation) of the patients and healthy speakers are 68±11 and 65±7, respectively. None of the speakers in this dataset has mFDA nor MDS-UPDRS-III scores.

[2] https://bit.ly/3iM03lu

5.2 Cochlear implants

5.2.1 LMU TAPAS (German)

This dataset was collected during the development of this thesis, as part of the TAPAS project[3]. It consists of speech recordings of 72 CI users and 72 NH German native speakers. The speech protocol followed by the speakers is reported in Appendix A.2. The recordings were captured in a quiet room at the Clinic of the Ludwig-Maximillians University in Munich (LMU) and in a retirement home (Augustinum Seniorenresidenz München-Neufriedenheim[4]) with a sampling frequency of 16 kHz and a 16 bit resolution. Table 5.4 summarizes the information of the German speakers considered in this experiments. Only postlingually deafened CI users were considered in this dataset.

Table 5.4: CI: postlingually deafened CI users. NH: normal hearing speakers.

	CI		NH	
	Male	Female	Male	Female
Number of speakers	36	36	36	36
Range of age [years]	51-83	50-80	50-75	50-78
Age [years]	66±9	66±9	61±8	60±9

5.2.2 LMU Onset (German)

This is a subset of the datasets collected by Ruff et al. (2017). It consists of speech recordings of 60 CI users and 20 NH German native speakers. The CI users are divided into three groups of speakers: 20 prelingual (PRE), 20 postlinguals with long duration of time between onset of deafness and implantation (LONG), and 20 postlinguals with short duration of time between onset of deafness and implantation (SHORT). Note that the prelinguals are younger than the other two groups of postlingually deafened CI users. That is because cochlear implantation has been performed since the late 80's of the last

---

[3]https://www.tapas-etn-eu.org/
[4]https://augustinum.de/muenchen-neufriedenheim/

century, and congenital deaf children who were implanted are much younger than postlinguals.

The speech signals were captured in noise-controlled conditions at the Clinic of the LMU, with a sampling frequency of 44.1 kHz and a 16 bit resolution. The speech signals were re-sampled to 16 kHz. All of the patients were asked to read 97 words (Fox-Boyer, 2002), which contain every phoneme of the German language in different positions within the words (See Appendix A.2.3). Additionally, all of the participants were asked to read 5 sentences extracted from the *Heidelberger Rhinophoniebogens* (See Appendix A.2.2). Table 5.5 summarizes the information of the German speakers considered in these experiments.

Table 5.5: PRE: prelingual CI users. LONG: Postlingual CI users with long duration of deafness before cochlear implantation (> 2 years). SHORT: Postlingual CI users with short duration of deafness before cochlear implantation (< 2 years). NH: normal hearing speakers.

	PRE	LONG	SHORT	NH
Number of male/female	4/16	6/14	4/16	11/9
Range of age [Years]	12 - 71	51 - 82	51 - 79	31 - 62
Age [years] ($\mu \pm \sigma$)	32 ± 18	67 ± 9	64 ± 8	44 ± 9

5.3 Supporting datasets

5.3.1 Young healthy controls (Spanish)

This dataset contains recordings of 25 male and 25 female Spanish native speakers from Colombia. The age of the yHC group ranges from 17 to 38 (mean 22±4). The recordings were captured in a sound-proof booth using a professional audio-card and a dynamic omni-directional microphone. The speech signals were captured at 44.1 kHz with 16-bit resolution. The speech signals were re-sampled to 16 kHz. None of the speakers had symptoms associated with any neurological disease or other clinical conditions that may result in speech disorders.

5.3.2 PhonDat 1 Corpus (German)

This dataset was extracted from the Bavarian Archive For Speech Signals (BAS), which is freely available for European academic users[5]. The complete corpus contains speech recordings of 201 (100 male/101 female) German speakers captured at four different sites in Germany (University of Kiel, University of Bonn, University of Bochum, University of Munich). All speakers were older than 20 years at the moment of the recordings. No information about the age is available, however, there was a rough classification into "old" (78) and "young" (123) speakers. The recordings were performed in controlled conditions at a sampling rate of 48 kHz at 16 Bit resolution. The speech signals were filtered with a low-pass filter with 8 kHz cutoff frequency and downsampled to 16 kHz.

5.3.3 Verbmobil subset (German)

This dataset is a subset of the speech recordings collected by Wahlster (2013). The Verbmobil subset considered in this thesis consists of speech recordings from 586 German native speakers (308 male, 278 female). The database contains about 29 hours of dialogues with their corresponding phonetic transcriptions. The data was captured in controlled acoustic conditions with a close-talk microphone at a sampling frequency of 16 kHz and a resolution of 16-bit. The age of the speakers ranges from 20 up to 40 years.

5.3.4 TEDx Spanish Corpus - TSC (Spanish)

This dataset consists of a program of self-organized events that bring people together to share experiences. The TSC contains 24 hours and 29 minutes of speech recordings manually segmented and transcribed, however, phonetic transcriptions were not available for this dataset. It consists of spontaneous speech of 142 Mexican-Spanish native speakers (102 male, 40 female) which were recorded during different TEDx events[6]. The audio files were captured

---

[5]http://hdl.handle.net/11858/00-1779-0000-000C-DAAF-B
[6]https://www.ted.com/watch/tedx-talks

at a sampling frequency of 16 kHz and a resolution of 16-bit. This dataset is freely available under a Creative Commons Attribution-Non-Commercial-No-Derivatives 4.0 International license and can be found at `http://www.ciempiess.org/downloads`.

Chapter 6

Experiments and results

6.1   Models for speech analysis

This section presents the methods, experiments, and performance results of the machine learning models that are used later for analysis of pathological speech signals (Sections 6.2 and 6.3) and the influence of aging in speech (Section 6.4). Particularly, two systems are presented here: automatic phoneme recognition (used for phonemic analysis) and automatic detection of VOT.

6.1.1   Phoneme posterior probabilities

Aim: To train a RNN-based model for the automatic classification of phonemes grouped according to voicing, manner, and place of articulation.

Hypothesis:

- Automatic detection of phoneme is possible without the use of a language model.

Two automatic phoneme recognition systems were trained in German and Spanish to measure the phoneme articulation precision (Section 4.2.3). Only two languages were considered because of the data available for PD patients

(Colombian Spanish) and CI users (German). For Spanish data, recordings of Mexican speakers were used because, to the best of my knowledge, there is not a database of recordings from Colombian speakers big enough to train a system like the one proposed here.

Data

German data: The Verbmobil dataset described in Section 5.3.3 is considered to train the RNN model for the automatic recognition of phonemes classes in the German language. The data is divided into train, validation, and test sets. The train set is used to update the model's weights, the validation set is used to compute the loss, and the test set is used to evaluate the performance. The number of hours on each set is 26 for train, 1.5 for validation, and 1.5 for test.

Spanish data: The TEDx Spanish Corpus (Section 5.3.4) is considered for evaluation. This dataset does not include phonetic transcriptions. Thus, all of the phonemes in the TEDx corpus were labeled automatically using the BAS CLARIN web service[1], which allows performing forced alignment using an ASR system. The web platform returns the transcriptions in the TextGrid format, including the time stamps for the words and phonemes represented in the SAMPA format. The number of hours on the train, validation and test sets are 21, 1.5, and 1.5, respectively.

Methods

Regardless of the language, the following network architecture is considered to train the German and Spanish models (Figure 6.1). The speech recordings are divided into 500 ms sequences, which are extracted every 250 ms. Then, Mel-spectrograms are computed for each sequence considering a 64 triangular filterbank. The filterbank energies are extracted from Hanning windows of 25 ms, taken every 10 ms. Thus, the size of each input tensor to the network is

---

[1] https://clarin.phonetik.uni-muenchen.de/BASWebServices/interface

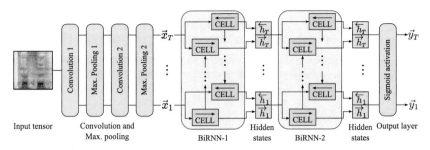

Figure 6.1: *General architecture of the automatic phoneme recognizer. The green boxes represent the forward states and the orange boxes represent the backward states. The "CELL" boxes can be either standard RNN, GRU, or LSTM cells.*

50×64 (50 speech frames and 64 Mel-filters).

Each sequence is time-aligned with its corresponding phonetic transcription. Thus, each speech frame is labeled according to the 18 phoneme classes (including silence) described in Table 4.1 (Section 4.2.3). Since each phoneme can belong to more than one class (e.g. the phoneme /p/ belongs to the classes Stop, Labial, and Voiceless), a multilabel RNN with sigmoid activation function and BCE logistic loss was considered for training. Two convolution layers process the input tensors with ReLU activation functions, two max-pooling layers, and dropout. The output of the first and second convolution layers are 8 and 16, respectively. The convolution operation is performed in both frequency and time axis with a kernel size of 3×3. In order to keep a one-to-one relation between the length of the input (speech sequences) and the output (phoneme prediction), padding of 1 is included in the time-axis. The max-pooling operation is performed with a kernel size of 1×2 (only in the frequency axis).

After convolution, the resulting feature maps are concatenated to form the sequence of feature vectors processed by two stacked bidirectional recurrent layers. The Adam optimization algorithm with a learning rate of $\eta = 10^{-4}$ is considered for training (Section 4.3.3). Class weights are also computed and used in the loss function to account for class unbalance. Such weights are computed as the total number of samples (for each phoneme class) in the training set. The batch size is set to 100 and an *early stopping* strategy is used to end the training of the network when the training loss does not decrease for 7 consecutive epochs. The performance of the multilabel RNN is measured at frame level in the test set using the precision, recall, and unweighted F1-score.

Results: German model

Table 6.1 shows the results obtained for the German model. The recurrent networks were trained with 512 hidden units and three variations of recurrent cells: standard RNN, GRU, and LSTM. In general, the best performance was obtained with the LSTM cells. Although the performance of the GRU and LSTM were very similar, in this thesis, the RNN with LSTM cells is preferred to extract phoneme-based features. Figure 6.2 shows the results of predicting the sequence of phonemes with the German model for the sentence "Peter spielt auf der Strasse" (Peter plays on the street). The results are presented for the manner of articulation, the place of articulation, and voicing. The silence/pause segments are also displayed. Phoneme prediction errors are inevitable when using fully automatic methods. However, it is still possible to use such systems to find patterns in pathological speech signals compared to a proper baseline e.g., healthy speakers in the same age group, language, and others. On the one hand, the prediction labels (shaded regions) can be used for automatic segmentation of phonemes, which allows evaluating duration, rate, and timing parameters (Section 4.2.4). On the other hand, the sequence of probabilities (colored lines) generated by the network can evaluate phoneme precision.

Table 6.1: Performance of the RNN models trained for automatic recognition of phoneme classes from the German language. The values highlighted in bold indicates the highest recognition performance.

Dimension	Class	RNN			GRU			LSTM		
		Prec	Rec	F1	Prec	Rec	F1	Prec	Rec	F1
	Silence	0.90	0.86	0.88	0.89	0.86	0.88	0.90	0.87	0.88
Manner	Stop	0.85	0.81	0.83	0.85	0.80	0.82	0.86	0.81	0.83
	Nasal	0.84	0.84	0.84	0.83	0.84	0.83	0.84	0.83	0.84
	Trill	0.86	0.64	0.73	0.83	0.68	0.75	0.85	0.70	**0.76**
	Fricative	0.89	0.87	0.88	0.88	0.87	0.88	0.89	0.88	0.88
	Approximant	0.88	0.74	0.80	0.86	0.77	0.81	0.84	0.81	**0.83**
	Lateral	0.82	0.61	0.70	0.78	0.65	0.71	0.79	0.68	**0.73**
	Vowel	0.87	0.89	0.88	0.87	0.88	0.88	0.88	0.89	0.88
Place	Labial	0.86	0.80	0.83	0.85	0.82	0.83	0.85	0.83	**0.84**
	Alveolar	0.87	0.86	0.87	0.87	0.86	0.86	0.88	0.86	0.87
	Velar	0.86	0.76	0.81	0.86	0.78	0.82	0.86	0.80	**0.83**
	Palatal	0.87	0.81	0.84	0.88	0.81	0.84	0.88	0.83	**0.85**
	Postalveolar	0.87	0.84	0.85	0.86	0.86	0.86	0.86	0.87	**0.87**
	Central	0.82	0.82	0.82	0.83	0.81	0.82	0.84	0.82	**0.83**
	Front	0.85	0.77	0.81	0.82	0.79	0.81	0.83	0.81	**0.82**
	Back	0.84	0.81	0.83	0.83	0.82	0.82	0.83	0.84	**0.84**
Voicing	Voiceless	0.89	0.90	0.89	0.90	0.88	0.89	0.91	0.88	**0.90**
	Voiced	0.95	0.94	0.95	0.94	0.95	0.95	0.94	0.96	0.95
	AVG	0.87	0.81	0.83	0.86	0.82	0.84	0.86	**0.83**	**0.85**

AVG: Average performance. **Prec**: Precision. **Rec**: Recall. **F1**: F1-score. **RNN**: Recurrent Neural Network. **GRU**: Gated Recurrent Units. **LSTM**: Long-Short Term Memory

Results: Spanish model

As described before, phonemic transcriptions were not available for the Spanish data. Thus, phoneme alignment was performed using an ASR system. This automatic alignment is prone to labeling errors, especially at the transitions from one phoneme to the other; thus, it is expected to have relatively lower performance for the Spanish model compared to the system trained in German. Since manual correction was not an option (the dataset is too large and it would take too much time), a transfer learning approach was implemented: the parameters learned by the German model were used as starting point for the Spanish model. Furthermore, it was observed that the best way to perform training is by stopping the network in the epoch where the F1-score drops. Two different training strategies were used for the Spanish models: 1) the

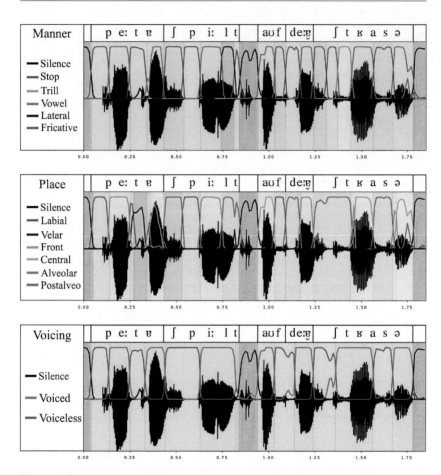

Figure 6.2: *Sequence of phoneme posterior probabilities (colored lines) and predictions (shaded regions) for the German sentence "Peter spielt auf der Strasse" (Peter plays on the street).*

Spanish model is trained **without** considering the pre-trained German model as initialization and 2) the German model is used for initialization, but the training is performed until the F1-score does not improve anymore. Table 6.2 shows the results for the Spanish model trained with the proposed training strategies. On average, the performance of the Spanish model improved from 0.75 up to 0.77 (F1-score) using the German model as weight initialization.

Table 6.2: Performance of the LSTM models trained for automatic recognition of phoneme classes from the Spanish language. The values highlighted in bold indicates the highest recognition performance.

Dimension	Class	Spanish-Spanish			German-Spanish		
		Prec	Rec	F1	Prec	Rec	F1
	Silence	0.87	0.91	0.89	0.90	0.89	**0.90**
Manner	Stop	0.77	0.68	0.72	0.82	0.68	**0.74**
	Nasal	0.79	0.72	0.75	0.83	0.71	**0.77**
	Trill	0.63	0.54	0.58	0.73	0.51	**0.60**
	Fricative	0.82	0.78	0.80	0.85	0.76	0.80
	Approximant	0.70	0.50	**0.58**	0.68	0.50	0.57
	Lateral	0.71	0.58	0.63	0.76	0.59	**0.67**
	Vowel	0.85	0.85	0.85	0.87	0.87	**0.87**
Place	Labial	0.73	0.68	0.71	0.80	0.69	**0.74**
	Alveolar	0.79	0.74	0.76	0.83	0.73	**0.78**
	Velar	0.74	0.64	0.69	0.82	0.63	**0.71**
	Palatal	0.74	0.59	0.66	0.73	0.61	**0.67**
	Postalveolar	0.86	0.68	0.76	0.88	0.71	**0.79**
	Central	0.81	0.80	0.80	0.83	0.81	**0.82**
	Front	0.82	0.76	0.79	0.84	0.78	**0.81**
	Back	0.79	0.75	0.77	0.85	0.75	**0.80**
Voicing	Voiceless	0.82	0.76	0.79	0.85	0.75	**0.80**
	Voiced	0.95	0.95	0.95	0.94	0.96	0.95
	AVG	0.79	0.72	0.75	**0.82**	0.72	**0.77**

AVG: Average. **Prec**: Precision. **Rec**: Recall. **F1**: F1-score.

Figure 6.3 shows an example of the sequence of phoneme predictions and posterior probabilities computed by the network for the sentence "Laura sube al tren que pasa" (Laura gets on the passing train) uttered by a Spanish speaker. One of the prediction errors made by the network occurs in the Stop-Vowel syllable "que" (IPA: kɛ), which is detected as a vowel by the Spanish model. However, in this particular case, the Spanish speaker does not produce any pause during the utterance, which is more likely to result in the voicing of the closure stage (obstruction of airflow resulting in a silence region) or "consonant weakening" during the release stage (absence of the burst after the closure stage) of the stop sound.

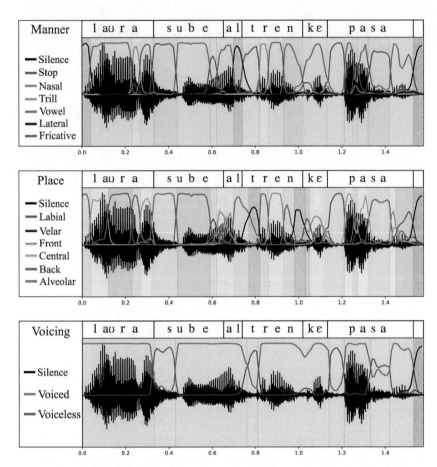

Figure 6.3: *Phoneme posterior probabilities (colored lines) and predictions (shaded regions) for the Spanish sentence "Laura sube al tren que pasa" (Laura gets on the passing train).*

Conclusions

The output of a recurrent network can be used to evaluate segmental aspects such as phoneme duration (using the predicted labels) and phoneme precision (using the posterior probabilities). One limitation is that fully automatic methods are prone to labeling errors. Thus, it is recommended to include healthy

126

speakers when analyzing pathological speech signals to have a proper baseline for comparison.

The main limitation of the Spanish model is the low performance achieved compared to the German model. Using the latter as an initialization improved the accuracy of recognizing phoneme groups in the Spanish language. It was also shown that the best way to use the pre-trained German model for parameter initialization is to train the Spanish model until the F1-score drops and not until the early stopping criterion is met. The reason is that the latter causes the network to modify the network entirely, thus, losing the advantage of having a relatively well-trained model as the starting point.

Another strategy would be to merge both German and Spanish data to have a language-independent model and thus have a better performance. The reason to keep two separated models for German and Spanish is that merging the data may cause biased results for the analysis of speech production, i.e., instead of speech deviations produced by a clinical condition, there will be variations due to the language. There are other approaches such as the connectionist temporal classification loss (Graves et al., 2006) which allows performing phoneme alignment by considering the transcriptions of the audio signals without further annotation.

6.1.2 Automatic detection of voice onset time

Aim: To train a RNN-based model for the automatic detection of VOT in voiceless stop sounds produced during the rapid repetition of the syllables /pa-ta-ka/.

Hypotheses:

- It is possible to perform automatic recognition of VOT using recurrent networks.

- VOT that can be automatically detected in speech signals of people with PD.

In this section PD patients are included to observed the influence of dysarthric speech in the automatic detection of VOT. Further analysis on speech problems related to PD will be addressed in Section 6.2. Speech recordings of CI users are not included here because there are not annotations of VOT available to compare with recordings of normal hearing speakers.

Data

The 50 PD patients and 50 healthy speakers (HC) described in the PC-GITA database (Section 5.1.1) are considered for the experiments. In the case of the healthy controls, only the dysarthria score is available. The speech task considered for the analysis is the alternating and sequential repetition of /pa-ta-ka/ (DDK). The labeling procedure of the VOT was performed by an expert in linguistics. Manual labels are placed at the initial burst of the consonants and vowel onsets using the software Praat.

Methods

A similar architecture to the one presented in Section 6.1.1 was used for detection of the VOT. The speech recordings are divided into sequences of 500 ms,which are extracted every 250 ms. Then, Mel-spectrograms are computed for each sequence considering a 64 triangular filterbank. The filterbank energies are extracted from Hanning windows of 25 ms, taken every 1 ms. Thus, the size of each input tensor to the network is 500×64 (500 speech frames and 64 Mel-filters).

Each sequence is time-aligned with their corresponding phonetic transcription, thus, each speech frame is labeled according to 5 classes: VOT, /p/, /t/, /k/, and non-VOT. The non-VOT class consists of speech frames that are either vowels, silence, or stop sounds without VOT (stop sounds characterized by the absence of the burst).

A multi-label LSTM with sigmoid activation function, 512 hidden units, and BCE logistic loss was considered for training. The input tensors are processed by two convolution layers (with 8 and 16 output channels) with ReLU activation functions, two max-pooling layers,and dropout. The convolution operation is performed in both frequency and time axis with a kernel size of 3×3. In order to keep a one-to-one relation between the length of the input (speech sequences) and the output (VOT prediction), a padding of 1 is added to the time-axis. The max-pooling operation is performed with a kernel size of 1×2 (only in the frequency axis). After convolution, the resulting feature maps are concatenated to form the sequence of feature vectors processed by two stacked bidirectional recurrent layers. The Adam optimization algorithm with a learning rate of $\eta = 10^{-4}$ is considered for training. Additionally, class weights are computed and used in the loss function in order to account for class unbalance. Such weights are computed as the total number of samples (for each phoneme class) in the training set. The batch size is set to 100 and a *early stopping* strategy is used to end the training of the network when the training loss does not decrease for 7 consecutive epochs.

Note that the number of recordings available to train the model is very limited; thus, the following data augmentation techniques were performed:

- The pitch was shifted up and down by 200 cents.

- Noisy speech signals (Gaussian noise) with signal-to-noise ratios (SNR) of 10 dB, 20 dB, and 30 dB were included.

- Reverberation of 30% was applied to the speech signals.

The data is divided into 80 speakers for the train set (40 HC and 40 PD), 10 for validation (5 HC and 5 PD) and 10 for the test (5 HC and 5 PD). A median filter mask of 3 ms is applied to the sequence of predicted VOTs in order to interpolate the missing values. The performance of the multi-label LSTM is measured at frame level using the precision, recall, and unweighted F1-score.

Results: Prediction of VOT

Table 6.3 shows the classification results for the automatic detection of VOT. The model's performance to detect VOT speech frames is higher for healthy speakers (F1=0.78) than for PD patients (F1= 0.73). This result is expected considering the reduced range of articulatory movements associated with PD (Section 2.2.2). Regarding the detection of stop consonants, the lowest performance was obtained for /p/, followed by /t/, and then /k/. These results can be explained considering the consonant weakening phenomena described in Section 4.2.3. Consonant weakening occurs when there is an absence of burst during the release stage when producing stop sounds. It can be produced by both healthy and PD patients in intermediate positions during the DDK tasks, e.g., in the transition between /ka/ and /pa/. Figure 6.4 shows the bar plots with the number of VOT and Non-VOT stop consonants produced by patients and healthy speakers. These measurements correspond to the manual annotations made by the human expert. The patients produce the highest number of Non-VOT segments (due to consonant weakening). Additionally, consonant weakening segments are higher when speakers produce the stop sound /p/, followed by /t/, and then /k/. Thus, the information given in Figure 6.4 can clearly explain the results reported in Table 6.3. The time errors between the manual annotations and predicted VOT of the initial burst (E_{Burst}) and the vowel onset (E_{Vowel}) were: (1) $E_{Burst} = 4.3 \pm 1.9$ ms and $E_{Vow} = 3.4 \pm 1.4$ ms for the healthy controls and (2) $E_{Burst} = 5.0 \pm 1.5$ ms and $E_{Vow} = 5.1 \pm 1.7$ ms for the PD patients. These

130

Table 6.3: Performance of the LSTM models trained for automatic detection of VOT.

Class	HC			PD		
	Prec	**Rec**	**F1**	**Prec**	**Rec**	**F1**
VOT	0.73	0.84	0.78	0.73	0.74	0.73
Non-VOT	0.97	0.97	0.97	0.94	0.97	0.96
/p/	0.72	0.60	0.65	0.58	0.36	0.44
/t/	0.71	0.73	0.72	0.71	0.52	0.60
/k/	0.83	0.84	0.84	0.74	0.55	0.63
AVG	0.79	0.80	0.79	0.74	0.63	0.67

AVG: Average. **Prec**: Precision. **Rec**: Recall.
F1: F1-score.

deviations are acceptable considering that another human annotator might have consider different time stamps for the VOTs.

Figure 6.5 shows an example of the predicted VOT and non-VOT segments from the recording of a PD patient. The shaded regions represent the VOT segment manually annotated by the expert, the dashed black lines are the predictions of the system (after post-processing with a median filter), and the colored straight lines are posterior probabilities of the /p/, /t/, and /k/. Note that

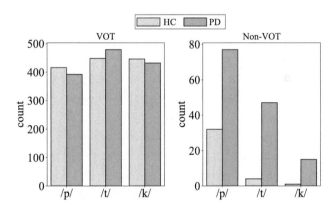

Figure 6.4: *Number of VOT (left) and Non-VOT (right) measurements (labeled by a human expert) in the HC and PD groups. In some cases the VOT can not be measured due to the absence of burst in the release stage when producing stop consonants.*

for the last syllable (a transition from /ta/ to /ka/), the posterior probability of the stop sound /k/ is greater than zero, but neither the human expert nor the system predicted such a segment as a VOT. In this case the /k/ is weakened and perceived as a /g/ due to the absence of burst. Thus, the posterior probability can also be use as an indication of consonant mis-articulation.

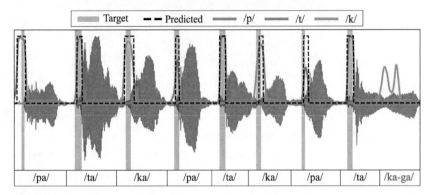

Figure 6.5: *The shaded regions represent the VOT segment manually annotated by the expert, the dashed black lines are the predictions of the system (after post-processing with a median filter), and the colored straight lines are posterior probabilities of the /p/ (red), /t/ (green), and /k/ (blue).*

Results: Prediction of VOT with noisy speech

Figure 6.6 shows the classification results for the automatic detection of VOT with noisy speech signals. The model's performance increased when noisy recordings were used for testing, indicating that the model was over-fitted. For healthy speakers, the F1-score increased when noisy and reverberated speech were considered for the test. For patients, the model's performance was lower for signals with an SNR of 10 dB than for the original signals; however, there are slight improvements for recordings with SNRs of 20 dB, 30 dB, and reverberation. Besides overfitting, another reason for the mixed results between HC and PD is that the noise component appears to remove part of the acoustic property that characterizes the stop consonants resulting in two

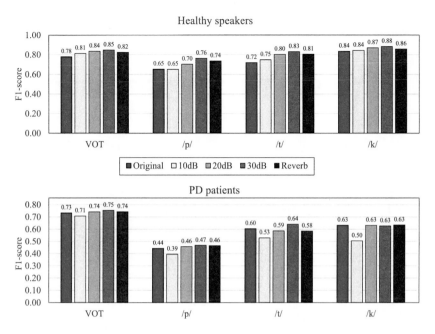

Figure 6.6: *F1-scores for the automatic detection of VOT speech frames and the consonants /p/, /t/, and /k/. The model is tested using clean signals (original), noisy signals with SNRs of 10 dB, 20 dB, and 30 dB and reverberation of 30%.*

different situations: On the one hand, the reduced phoneme precision of the patients combined with the Gaussian noise affects the model's performance to predict the correct sequence of consonants. On the other hand, the noise component improves the detection of vowels' onset, leading to higher F1-scores for the HC because they do not produce as many misarticulations as the patients, e.g., weakened consonants. Figure 6.7 shows the VOT prediction of two recordings from the same PD patient: the original version and a noisy version with an SNR of 20dB. In the clean version, the model can predict the correct phoneme sequence. Additionally, the burst of energy that characterizes the stop consonants can it is visible in the spectrum. In the case of the noisy signal, the energy burst is weaker (and in some cases disappears), leading to more mistakes from the system to detect the correct sequence of phonemes.

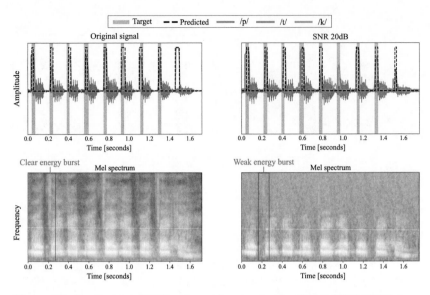

Figure 6.7: *Prediction of VOT using a clean and noisy signal (SNR 20dB) from a PD patient. The corresponding Mel-spectrograms are shown in the bottom.*

Finally, Table 6.4 shows the time error to predict the initial burst (E_{Burst}) and the vowel onset (E_{Vowel}). Since the prediction of the onsets is more accurate with noise (especially for the vowel), the number of speech frames that were correctly classified increased the performance of the model to predict the VOT.

Table 6.4: Time error to predict the initial burst (E_{Burst}) and the vowel onset (E_{Vowel}). The time errors are reported in milliseconds.

Group	Error	Original	SNR 10dB	SNR 20dB	SNR 30dB	Reverb
HC	E_{Burst}	4.3 ± 1.9	4.1 ± 1.3	3.3 ± 0.8	3.0 ± 0.6	3.4 ± 0.9
	E_{Vowel}	3.4 ± 1.4	2.2 ± 0.7	2.3 ± 0.6	2.3 ± 0.5	2.9 ± 1.0
PD	E_{Burst}	5.8 ± 2.4	5.7 ± 1.8	5.3 ± 2.2	4.3 ± 1.4	3.9 ± 1.2
	E_{Vowel}	5.4 ± 2.1	3.0 ± 1.1	3.2 ± 1.2	3.6 ± 1.5	4.6 ± 1.9

Conclusions

Automatic detection for VOT speech frames was possible with F1-scores of up to 0.78 for healthy speakers and 0.73 for PD patients. The VOT segments were predicted with average time errors of 3.8 ms for healthy speakers and 5.6 ms for PD patients. Regarding the detection of stop consonants, the lowest performance was obtained for /p/, followed by /t/, and then /k/. This decrease in performance was mainly caused by the consonant weakening which occurs more frequently when the stop sound /p/ is produced in intermediate positions. This phenomenon can be explained considering the speakers perform rapid movements of the articulators during the DDK task, which results from difficulties in controlling the vocal folds' movement when alternating from vowels to voiceless stop sounds Louzada et al. (2011). PD patients produced more weakened consonants than the healthy speakers, resulting in a lower performance to detect VOT segments. It was also shown that the posterior probability calculated by the automatic model can provide information about weakened consonants.

One limitation of this approach is that it might not be suitable for continuous speech tasks, e.g., monologues, picture descriptions, conversations. However, as is going to be demonstrated in Section 6.2, the DDK task might provide sufficient information for automatic detection and prediction of the state of PD. Another limitation is the relatively low number of recordings considered for training. One solution was to use data augmentation to increase the sample size. However, the performance of the model was better using noisy versions of the original signals. This result showed that the noise component improved the detection of vowel onsets and the prediction of VOT speech frames for healthy speakers. On the contrary, the Gaussian noise combined with phoneme imprecision resulted in the lower prediction of phoneme sequences produced by PD patients.

6.2 Parkinson's disease patients

6.2.1 Automatic methods for the assessment of PD from speech

Aim: To evaluate the suitability of different features and speech tasks for the assessment of PD from speech signals.

Hypotheses:

- Combining the information of different features sets and speech tasks improves the performance of automatic methods to detect disordered speech in PD patients.

- The neurological state and the dysarthria level can be estimated using automatic methods.

Data

The 50 PD patients and 50 healthy speakers described in the PC-GITA database (Section 5.1.1) are considered for the experiments. All of the PD patients were evaluated according to neurological (MDS-UPDRS-III) and dysarthria (mFDA) scales. In the case of the healthy controls, only the dysarthria score is available. The speech tasks considered for the analysis are the sustained phonation of the Spanish vowels /a/, /e/, /i/, /o/, and /u/, reading of a text, a monologue, and the alternating and sequential repetition of /pa-ta-ka/ (DDK).

Methods

Phonation features include pitch, loudness, and perturbation measures extracted from the sustained phonation of the vowels /a/, /e/, /i/, /o/, and /u/. Furthermore, the vowels /a/, /i/, and /u/ are considered to extract the first and second formant frequencies, the tVSA (and the logarithm) and the FCR. The formants are extracted by removing 100 ms at the beginning and the end of each recording.

This procedure is performed in order to avoid the miscalculations of F1 and F2 at the vowel onset and offset. Acoustic articulation is evaluated by extracting filterbank features (13 MFCC and 13 GFCC) from the onset/offset transitions extracted from the reading, monologue, and DDK tasks. In the case of prosody analysis, the set of parameters considered are pitch, loudness, duration, rate, and timing based features. Phonemic analysis is performed with the LSTM model trained for the Spanish language (Section 6.1.1). Phonemic analysis is divided into voicing, manner, and place of articulation (Table 4.1). For each dimension, the set of phonemic parameters includes $\mathrm{MaxPost}$ and $\mathrm{LLRPost}$ (which are related to phoneme articulation) and the durPH and $\mathrm{GPI} - y[k]$ (which are related to speech prosody) (Table 4.2). Phonemic features are extracted from the reading, monologue, and DDK speech tasks. In the case of the DDK task, however, only the stop (/p/, /t/, and /k/), vowels (/a/), labial (/p/), alveolar (/t/), and velar (/k/) phoneme groups were considered in the feature sets.

Automatic classification with a radial basis function SVM is considered for further analysis. The margin C and kernel γ parameters are optimized through a grid search with $10^{-4} < C < 10^4$ and $10^{-4} < \gamma < 10^4$. The parameters are optimized as follows:

1. 10-fold cross validation strategy is considered to train and test the model.

2. An internal 9-fold cross validation strategy is used to select the best set of parameters for testing.

3. After evaluating every fold, the medians of the resulting C and γ parameters are computed and the 10-fold cross validation strategy was performed again with fixed parameters.

4. The performance of the bi-class SVM is evaluated by means of the accuracy, sensitivity, specificity, and AUC.

Regression analysis is performed by means of a linear SVR in order to evaluate the suitability of the selected features and speech tasks to estimate the dysarthria level and the neurological state of the patients according to the mFDA and MDS-UPDRS-III, respectively. The parameters are optimized with a similar approach than the classifier, however, the performance is measured by means of the of the Pearson's (r) and Spearman's (ρ) correlation coefficients. Additionally, 5-fold cross validation is performed when predicting the MDS-UPDRS-III because only the PD patients are evaluated. Figure 6.8 shows an schematic view of the methodology implemented in this section.

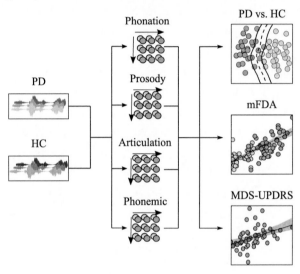

Figure 6.8: *Schematic view of the methodology implemented in this section.*

Results: Automatic classification of PD

Table 6.5 shows the classification results obtained for PD patients vs. HC speakers. Overall, phonemic features contributed more to the automatic classification of PD patients. The highest performance was obtained when combining phonation, articulation, and phonemic features from the sustained vowels, DDK, and monologue tasks. The most relevant features to detect PD appear to be the offset transitions (filterbank energies) and phonemic features. Transitions work better in the monologue due to the amount of information obtained during

Table 6.5: Results for automatic classification of PD patients and HC speakers. C and γ are the final parameters selected to evaluate the performance of the SVM. The values highlighted in bold indicate the highest results obtained per speech task.

Task	Feat ID	Features	Acc	Sen	Spe	AUC	C	γ
Vowel	V1	Phonation	70	60	80	0.75	1	0.01
	V2	Articulation Vowel	67	54	80	0.71	10	0.01
	V3	**V1+V2**	**75**	**66**	**84**	**0.79**	**1**	**0.01**
Read text	R1	Articulation On	69	84	54	0.75	5.5	0.01
	R2	Articulation Off	66	60	72	0.75	10	0.0001
	R3	R1+R2	70	66	74	0.77	10	0.001
	R4	Prosody	63	54	72	0.69	1	0.055
	R5	Phonemic Manner	72	58	86	0.73	1	0.001
	R6	**Phonemic Place**	**81**	**82**	**80**	**0.82**	**1**	**0.01**
	R7	Phonemic Voicing	73	72	74	0.76	10	0.0055
	R8	R5+R6+R7	78	76	80	0.82	1	0.01
Monologue	M1	Articulation On	69	74	64	0.77	1	0.01
	M2	**Articulation Off**	**75**	**74**	**76**	**0.81**	**100**	**0.00055**
	M3	M1+M2	72	74	70	0.81	100	0.00055
	M4	Prosody	61	50	72	0.64	100	0.001
	M5	Phonemic Manner	65	50	80	0.75	1	0.001
	M6	Phonemic Place	73	74	72	0.77	1	0.01
	M7	Phonemic Voicing	63	66	60	0.64	550	0.001
	M8	M5+M6+M7	66	58	74	0.75	0.001	0.001
DDK	D1	Articulation On	65	62	68	0.69	1	0.01
	D2	Articulation Off	62	58	66	0.68	10	0.01
	D3	**Phonemic Manner**	**82**	**76**	**88**	**0.81**	**1**	**0.01**
	D4	Phonemic Place	75	74	76	0.81	0.001	0.1
	D5	Phonemic Voicing	75	66	84	0.80	100	0.0055
	D6	D3+D4+D5	73	62	84	0.83	0.5005	0.01
Fusion	**F1**	**V3+D3+D4+M2+M6**	**84**	**82**	**86**	**0.89**	**10**	**0.00055**
	F2	**F1+R6+R7**	**84**	**86**	**82**	**0.87**	**10**	**0.0001**
	F3	D3+D4+M2+M6	83	82	84	0.84	10	0.001
	F4	F3+R6+R7	81	80	82	0.85	10	0.0001
	F5	V3+R6+R7	81	78	84	0.86	1	0.0055

Fusion: Early fusion of features (top five highest performances). **Acc**: Accuracy[%].
Sen: Sensitivity[%]. **Spe**: Specificity[%]. **AUC**: Area under the ROC curve.

this task. On average, the speakers produced 83 onset/offset transitions in the monologue, 29 in the reading task, and 20 in the DDK. Thus, the amount of variation in the transitions is likely to be the most relevant factor to affect the classification. It is not clear, however, why offset transitions work better than onset in the monologue. One possible reason is a process called "resyllabification", which in the Spanish language occurs when word-initial vowels are merged with the end of the previous word (Colina, 2009) e.g., in the reading task, the sentence "...ya sabemos que es..." (we already know what it is) it's syllabified as "pu.es.ya.sa.be.mos.**ques**". This process produces misalignments between word boundaries and syllable structures in both healthy and PD patients. However, it might be the case that the "resyllabification" process affects more the patients. Further analysis is necessary to validate this hypothesis.

The results reported in this section also show the advantage of considering different tasks to evaluate speech disorders. Combining similar features sets and tasks (e.g. phonemic place of articulation from monologue and DDK) improves the automatic classification of PD patients and HC speakers. In the case of the DDK, the kinematic vocal movements performed by the speakers highlight specific articulation deficits related to the production of stop consonants by generating constrictions in the lips (/p/), alveolar ridge (/t/), and the velum (/k/). For the monologue and read text, problems related to the place of articulation are more likely due to the imprecision of the patients to produce a wider variety of sounds. The main limitation of the monologue task is that there is no control of what the speakers say. However, using non-planned speech tasks might evidence problems due to the relatively higher cognitive load (compared to reading) required (García et al., 2021, 2016).

Figure 6.9 shows the maximum posterior probability (MaxPost) for the place of articulation produced in the reading, monologue, and DDK tasks. As

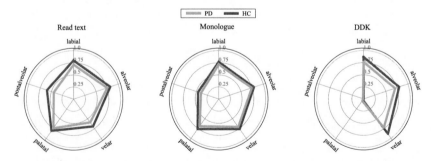

Figure 6.9: *Radar plot of the phoneme place of articulation precision* (MaxPost)

described in previous chapters, the MaxPost allows measuring the phoneme precision of the speakers. These parameters can only take values between 0 and 1, where 1 represents the "perfect" production of speech sounds. In this case, PD patients produced lower probabilities than the healthy speakers in all three tasks. In the case of the DDK, only the three phoneme groups (labial, alveolar, and velar) stand out, as expected. Note that postalveolar sounds appear to have a relatively low articulation precision, even for the healthy controls. In Section 6.4 will be shown that imprecision of articulation may be related to physiological and anatomical changes due to aging.

Results: Regression analysis

The results obtained in the estimation of the dysarthria level and neurological state of the patients are reported in Tables 6.6 and 6.7, respectively. Similar to the classification task, phonemic features showed to be more relevant to assess the severity of the disease. All of the features resulted in considerable high correlations between predicted values and mFDA scores (p-value<0.001). The highest correlation was obtained with the combination of features from reading (phonemic), DDK (phonemic), and sustained phonation of vowels. In the case of the neurological state, the combination of articulation and phonemic features resulted in a better prediction of the MDS-UPDRS-III. However, this estimation is relatively lower than the prediction of the mFDA, which is not surprising considering that the MDS-UPDRS-III consists of the evaluation of other motor aspects such as postural instability, gait, writing, and others. Nevertheless, two main patterns consistently repeat for the prediction of mFDA and MDS-UPDRS-III: the DDK task and the phonemic features strongly highlight motor speech problems in PD patients, not only in the regression analysis but also in the classification task.

141

Table 6.6: Estimation of the dysarthria level according to the mFDA. C and ϵ are the final parameters selected to test the performance of the SVR. The values highlighted in bold indicate the highest results obtained per speech task.

Task	Feat ID	Features	r	p-value	ρ	p-value	C	ϵ
Vowel	V1	Phonation	0.49	<0.001	0.48	<0.001	0.1	10
	V2	Articulation Vowel	0.40	<0.001	0.42	<0.001	1	0.55
	V3	**V1+V2**	**0.64**	**<0.001**	**0.64**	**<0.001**	**1**	**1**
Read text	R1	Articulation On	0.49	<0.001	0.47	<0.001	0.1	10
	R2	Articulation Off	0.46	<0.001	0.45	<0.001	0.1	10
	R3	R1+R2	0.53	<0.001	0.52	<0.001	0.1	10
	R4	Prosody	0.37	<0.001	0.35	<0.001	1	10
	R5	Phonemic Manner	0.59	<0.001	0.56	<0.001	1	10
	R6	**Phonemic Place**	**0.70**	**<0.001**	**0.67**	**<0.001**	**0.1**	**1**
	R7	Phonemic Voicing	0.60	<0.001	0.56	<0.001	1	10
	R8	R5+R6+R7	0.69	<0.001	0.66	<0.001	0.1	1
Monologue	M1	Articulation On	0.24	<0.05	0.25	<0.05	0.1	10
	M2	Articulation Off	0.44	<0.001	0.43	<0.001	0.1	10
	M3	M1+M2	0.34	<0.01	0.32	<0.01	0.1	10
	M4	Prosody	0.43	<0.001	0.43	<0.001	1	0.55
	M5	**Phonemic Manner**	**0.60**	**<0.001**	**0.59**	**<0.001**	**0.1**	**1**
	M6	**Phonemic Place**	**0.62**	**<0.001**	**0.58**	**<0.001**	**0.1**	**0.001**
	M7	Phonemic Voicing	0.49	<0.001	0.50	<0.001	100	10
	M8	M5+M6+M7	0.59	<0.001	0.55	<0.001	0.1	0.1
DDK	D1	Articulation On	0.41	<0.001	0.37	<0.001	0.1	10
	D2	Articulation Off	0.42	<0.001	0.40	<0.001	0.55	10
	D3	Phonemic Manner	0.67	<0.001	0.64	<0.001	10	5.5
	D4	**Phonemic Place**	**0.71**	**<0.001**	**0.67**	**<0.001**	**1**	**0.1**
	D5	Phonemic Voicing	0.60	<0.001	0.61	<0.001	1000	10
	D6	D3+D4+D5	0.66	<0.001	0.66	<0.001	0.1	5.5
Fusion	**F1**	**V3+R6+D4+D3**	**0.80**	**<0.001**	**0.78**	**<0.001**	**0.1**	**1**
	F2	V3+R6+D4	0.79	<0.001	0.78	<0.001	0.1	1
	F3	V3+R6	0.79	<0.001	0.77	<0.001	0.1	0.55
	F4	V3+D4	0.75	<0.001	0.74	<0.001	1	1
	F5	R6+D4+D3	0.74	<0.001	0.72	<0.001	0.1	0.0055

Fusion: Early fusion of features and tasks (top five highest performances).
r: Pearson's correlation coefficient. ρ: Spearman's correlation coefficient.

Table 6.7: Estimation of the neurological state according to the MDS-UPDRS-III. C and ϵ are the final parameters selected to test the performance of the SVR. The values highlighted in bold indicates the highest results obtained per speech task.

Task	Feat ID	Features	r	p-value	ρ	p-value	C	ϵ
Vowel	V1	Phonation	-0.25	0.084	-0.30	0.033	0.001	10
	V2	Articulation Vowel	-0.15	0.300	-0.13	0.370	0.1	10
	V3	V1+V2	-0.25	0.085	-0.24	0.094	0.001	10
Read text	R1	Articulation On	0.29	<0.05	0.37	<0.01	0.1	10
	R2	**Articulation Off**	**0.33**	**<0.05**	**0.43**	**<0.01**	**0.1**	**10**
	R3	**Articulation All**	**0.36**	**<0.05**	**0.43**	**<0.01**	**0.1**	**10**
	R4	Prosody	0.10	0.494	0.14	0.334	1	10
	R5	Phonemic Manner	-0.18	0.212	-0.13	0.354	0.01	10
	R6	Phonemic Place	0.17	0.242	0.07	0.639	0.1	10
	R7	Phonemic Voicing	-0.24	0.092	-0.22	0.124	0.001	10
	R8	Phonemic All	-0.01	0.943	-0.07	0.634	0.01	10
Monologue	**M1**	**Articulation On**	**0.38**	**<0.01**	**0.45**	**<0.01**	**0.1**	**10**
	M2	Articulation Off	0.38	<0.01	0.40	<0.01	1	10
	M3	**Articulation All**	**0.38**	**<0.01**	**0.46**	**<0.01**	**0.1**	**10**
	M4	Prosody	-0.24	0.087	-0.24	0.098	0.001	10
	M5	Phonemic Manner	0.20	0.169	0.12	0.418	0.1	10
	M6	Phonemic Place	0.21	0.143	0.15	0.291	0.1	10
	M7	Phonemic Voicing	0.00	0.999	-0.06	0.661	0.1	10
	M8	Phonemic All	0.18	0.211	0.17	0.235	0.1	10
DDK	D1	Articulation On	0.18	0.223	0.21	0.146	0.1	10
	D2	Articulation Off	0.09	0.520	0.09	0.552	0.1	10
	D3	**Phonemic Manner**	**0.40**	**<0.01**	**0.39**	**<0.01**	**1**	**1**
	D4	Phonemic Place	0.14	0.340	0.10	0.490	0.1	10
	D5	Phonemic Voicing	0.08	0.580	0.04	0.806	0.1	10
	D6	Phonemic All	0.31	0.027	0.31	0.030	0.1	10
Fusion	**F1**	**R2+M1+D3**	**0.40**	**<0.01**	**0.53**	**<0.01**	**1**	**10**
	F2	**R2+D3**	**0.41**	**<0.001**	**0.52**	**<0.001**	**0.1**	**10**
	F3	R3+D3	0.41	<0.01	0.47	<0.01	0.1	10
	F4	**M3+D3**	**0.40**	**<0.01**	**0.45**	**<0.01**	**1**	**10**
	F5	R3+M3	0.38	<0.01	0.48	<0.001	0.1	1

Fusion: Early fusion of features and tasks (top five highest performances).
r: Pearson's correlation coefficient. ρ: Spearman's correlation coefficient.

Figure 6.10 shows the regression plots of the best performances obtained for the estimation of the dysarthria level (mFDA: $r = 0.80$; $\rho = 0.78$) and the neurological state (MDS-UPDRS-III: $r = 0.40$; $\rho = 0.53$). The differences in the performances can be explained considering that the mFDA is a scale completely focused on evaluating speech impairments. On the contrary, the MDS-UPDRS-III only includes speech in 1 item from 33. Nevertheless, automatic speech analysis shows a close relationship to the general clinical score.

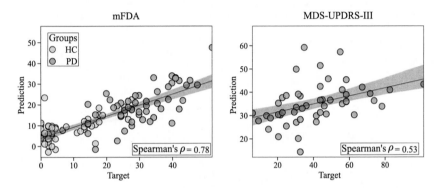

Figure 6.10: *Regression plots of the best performances obtained for the estimation of the mFDA and the MDS-UPDRS-III*

Conclusions

The results obtained in both classification and regression tasks validated the first hypothesis. The prediction of mFDA and MDS–UPDRS-III was better using phonemic features extracted from the DDK task. However, combining different speech tasks improves the performance of the automatic methods. For instance, the combination of articulation and phonemic features resulted in the highest classification performance and estimation of the neurological state. Additionally, phonemic features combined with phonation and articulation features from the vowels improved the prediction of the mFDA.

The estimation of the dysarthria level (regression analysis) was considerably higher than the prediction of the general neurological state. There are several reasons for these results. First, the neurological scales consider other motor skills than speech to estimate the severity of the disease. It is highly optimistic to expect that only speech signals will capture all other motor disorders. Thus, future work should consider the multimodal analysis of PD patients using other bio-signals such as writing, movement of the limbs, gait, among others. Another reason for the low performance might be the relatively low variability in the clinical score due to the number of speakers available to perform regression analysis. For the mFDA evaluations, speakers without any speech disorders and with different levels of impairments were available. Thus, the SVR can model better the dysarthria level because of the variability in the training set. For the neurological scale, only patients (with relatively low scores) have an MDS–UPDRS-III with low variability in the clinical score.

6.2.2 Speaker embeddings to monitor Parkinson's disease

Aim: To evaluate the suitability of speaker embeddings to capture the progression of speech symptoms over the time.

Hypotheses:

- It is possible to monitor the progression of speech symptoms considering recordings captured in different sessions.

- The progression of the symptoms can be improved considerably when speaker embeddings are combined with acoustic features.

Data

Three datasets were considered to validate the hypotheses of this section: one is used as the baseline and the other two are considered to test the short- and long-term progression of PD. The speech tasks considered for the analysis are the reading of a text, a monologue, and the alternating and sequential repetition of /pa-ta-ka/. The sustained phonation task is not considered here because only the vowel /a/ was recorded for the short-term dataset, thus, it is not possible to compute all of the vowel articulation features. Additionally, only speech recordings that were evaluated according to the mFDA were considered for the experiments. The reason is that not all of the recordings were evaluated according to the MDS-UPDRS.

Short-term: This dataset include speech signals of 7 patients recorded in their house (Section 5.1.2). The patients were recorded four times per day (every two hours), once per month during four months; thus, there is a total of 16 recording sessions per patient. Each recording session was assessed according to the mFDA.

Long-term: Speech recordings of the same 7 patients were collected in 6 recording sessions from 2012 to 2017 (Section 5.1.3). However, one patient

146

was recorded in 5 sessions and another in 4 sessions. All of the patients were evaluated according to the mFDA.

Baseline: Speech recordings of 50 PD patients and 50 healthy speakers are considered for the experiments (Section 5.1.1). Note that 6 of the patients in PC-GITA are also included in the longitudinal datasets. Thus, the speech recordings of these patients were replaced with PD patients from another dataset.

Methods

The recording protocol and the acoustic conditions of the recordings vary from session to session. For the short-term recordings, every patient was recorded with the same device in his/her house during all sessions. For the long-term recordings, the recording sessions were performed in a soundproof booth (2012) or the Parkinson's foundation (2014-2017). However, the recording devices varied for all sessions. Considering the previous information, the denoising system presented in (Schröter et al., 2020) was used on all of the recordings to reduce the variability in the acoustic conditions. The system uses a linear combination of complex-valued coefficients applied in the frequency domain considering the current and previous time frames.

Speaker embeddings are extracted from the monologue task using pre-trained i-vector and x-vector models (Section 4.4). Such models were pre-trained using the Vox-Celeb dataset [2]. Furthermore, the x-vector system was trained on augmented data i.e, speech recordings with different noise and acoustic conditions. The i-vector embedding consists of a 400-dimensional feature vector which is assumed to contain the necessary information to identify a speaker. The x-vector embedding is a 512-dimensional vector formed with the output from a fully connected layer.

The dysarthria level of the patients is evaluated using a linear SVR. The parameters C and ϵ are optimized through a grid search with $10^{-4} < C < 10^3$ and $10^{-4} < \epsilon < 10^3$. The parameters are optimized as follows:

---

[2]https://kaldi-asr.org/models/m7

1. A Leave-one-speaker-out strategy is considered to train and test the model. All of the recordings from one patient (from the short/long term datasets) are considered for testing and the remaining speakers (including the ones in the baseline dataset) are considered for training.

2. An internal 20-fold cross validation strategy is used to select the best set of parameters.

3. After evaluating every speaker from the longitudinal datasets, the medians of the resulting C and ϵ parameters are computed and leave-one-speaker-out is performed again with fixed parameters.

4. The performance is measured by means of the Pearson's (r) and Spearman's (ρ) correlation coefficients.

Figure 6.11 shows a schematic diagram of the methodology implemented in this section. The predicted mFDA scores are evaluated for each patient individually and the progression curves are assessed using the Spearman's (ρ) and the Mean Absolute Error (MAE).

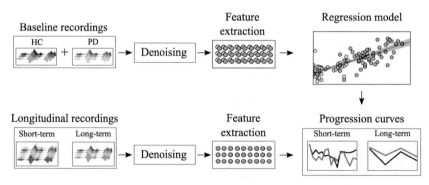

Figure 6.11: *Schematic view of the methodology implemented in this section.*

Results

Table 6.8 shows the performance of the SVR to predict the mFDA score of the 7 patients recorded in longitudinal datasets. The x-vector approach outperformed the i-vectors in the estimation of the dysarthria level. This might be since the x-vector system was pre-trained with augmented data. Other studies have shown that x-vectors exploit speaker's information from a large amount of data better than the i-vectors (Kelly et al., 2019; Snyder et al., 2018). Regarding the acoustic analysis, phonemic features are the most suitable to predict the dysarthria level of the patients in the short- and long-term datasets. Furthermore, the prediction of the mFDA scores improved when phonemic features (from the DDK task) were combined with the x-vector embeddings.

The same experiments were performed for the original recordings i.e., without speech enhancement. These results are reported in Table 6.9. From the table, it can observed that the performance of the x-vector was not affected by the acoustic conditions: x-vectors without denoising: $r = 0.67$, $\rho = 0.65$; with denoising: $r = 0.66$; $\rho = 0.65$. Additionally, in the same table, the performance of the SVR trained with the acoustic features was considerably affected by the variability of the acoustic conditions. For instance, **without** denoising the performance of the SVR trained with phonemic manner of articulation features was $r = 0.19$; $\rho = 0.14$ (read text), whereas the performance with denoised recordings was $r = 0.50$; $\rho = 0.48$. Figure 6.12 shows the dysarthria progression curves obtained from the prediction of the mFDA score (x-vector+phonemic DDK features with speech enhancement) for each patient in short- and long-term speech recording sessions. For the short-term sessions (At-home dataset), most of the estimated scores are in the same range as the target values. There is a mismatch between the target and predicted values. However, the progression curves follow a similar trend. For instance, the scores predicted for PD6 (short-term progression) are lower than the real mFDA. However, the estimation of the clinical scores follows a similar trend to the targets. Thus, the system can capture the variations in the speech signal similar to the speech therapist. In the case of the long-term progression curves, the SVR has

149

Table 6.8: Estimation of the dysarthria level according to the mFDA in the short- and long-term datasets (with speech enhancement). C and ϵ are the final parameters obtained to test the performance of the SVR. The values highlighted in bold indicate the highest results obtained per speech task.

Task	Feat ID	Features	r	p-value	ρ	p-value	C	ϵ
Speaker	S1	i-vector	0.13	0.125	0.13	0.113	0.01	0.0001
embeddings	**S2**	**x-vector**	**0.66**	**<0.001**	**0.65**	**<0.001**	**0.1**	**0.1**
	S3	S1+S2	0.51	<0.001	0.51	<0.001	0.01	0.1
Read text	R1	Articulation On	-0.29	<0.001	-0.26	<0.01	0.1	10
	R2	Articulation Off	0.04	0.653	0.06	0.493	0.1	10
	R3	R1+R2	-0.01	0.894	-0.04	0.641	0.1	1
	R4	Prosody	0.08	0.322	0.04	0.641	1	10
	R5	**Phonemic Manner**	**0.50**	**<0.001**	**0.48**	**<0.001**	**1**	**10**
	R6	Phonemic Place	0.27	<0.01	0.27	<0.01	0.1	1
	R7	Phonemic Voicing	0.08	0.310	0.04	0.651	1	1
	R8	R5+R6+R7	0.40	<0.001	0.37	<0.001	0.1	10
Monologue	M1	Articulation On	-0.05	0.583	-0.02	0.772	0.1	1
	M2	Articulation Off	0.27	<0.01	0.27	<0.01	0.1	1
	M3	M1+M2	-0.01	0.914	0.02	0.836	0.1	0.1
	M4	Prosody	0.20	<0.05	0.16	<0.05	0.1	0.1
	M5	**Phonemic Manner**	**0.56**	**<0.001**	**0.52**	**<0.001**	**0.1**	**1**
	M6	Phonemic Place	0.46	<0.001	0.43	<0.001	0.1	0.1
	M7	Phonemic Voicing	0.37	<0.001	0.33	<0.001	10	10
	M8	**M5+M6+M7**	**0.56**	**<0.001**	**0.54**	**<0.001**	**0.1**	**0.0001**
DDK	D1	Articulation On	-0.22	<0.01	-0.28	<0.01	0.1	10
	D2	Articulation Off	0.01	0.909	0.05	0.514	0.1	10
	D3	**Phonemic Manner**	**0.49**	**<0.001**	**0.44**	**<0.001**	**1**	**10**
	D4	Phonemic Place	0.43	<0.001	0.42	<0.001	1	10
	D5	Phonemic Voicing	0.37	<0.001	0.39	<0.001	10	10
	D6	D3+D4+D5	0.42	<0.001	0.42	<0.001	0.1	10
Fusion	**F1**	**S2+D6**	**0.75**	**<0.001**	**0.73**	**<0.001**	**0.1**	**0.1**
	F2	**S2+D3+D5**	**0.74**	**<0.001**	**0.73**	**<0.001**	**0.1**	**0.1**
	F3	S2+D3	0.74	<0.001	0.72	<0.001	0.1	0.1
	F4	S2+D5	0.72	<0.001	0.70	<0.001	0.1	0.1
	F5	S2+M6	0.71	<0.001	0.70	<0.001	0.1	1

Fusion: Early fusion of features and speech tasks (top five highest performances).
r: Pearson's correlation coefficient. ρ: Spearman's correlation coefficient.

more difficulties to capture high variations between sessions (e.g. PD1, PD3, PD6). However, the trend of the progression is similar to the target values. Overall, combining speaker embeddings with acoustic features improved the performance of the SVR to estimate the dysarthria level of the patients. Although it might be possible to improve the performance, even more, we must

Table 6.9: Estimation of the dysarthria level according to the mFDA in the short- and long-term datasets (without speech enhancement). C and ϵ are the final parameters selected to test the performance of the SVR. The values highlighted in bold indicate the highest results obtained per speech task.

Task	Feat ID	Features	r	p-value	ρ	p-value	C	ϵ
Monologue	S1	i-vector	0.36	<0.001	0.36	<0.001	0.1	0.001
	S2	**x-vector**	**0.67**	**<0.001**	**0.65**	**<0.001**	**0.1**	**1**
	S3	S1+S2	0.48	<0.001	0.48	<0.001	0.01	1
Read text	R1	Articulation On	0.03	0.680	-0.02	0.801	0.1	1
	R2	Articulation Off	0.07	0.370	0.07	0.427	0.1	1
	R3	R4+R5	0.08	0.305	0.05	0.521	0.1	1
	R4	Prosody	-0.13	0.116	-0.14	0.097	0.1	1
	R5	Phonemic Manner	0.19	<0.05	0.14	0.085	0.1	1
	R6	**Phonemic Place**	**0.27**	**<0.01**	**0.26**	**<0.01**	**0.1**	**1**
	R7	Phonemic Voicing	0.10	0.224	0.02	0.838	1	0.1
	R8	R5+R6+R7	0.25	<0.01	0.24	<0.01	0.1	1
Monologue	M1	Articulation On	0.08	0.346	0.09	0.289	0.1	0.001
	M2	Articulation Off	0.10	0.222	0.13	0.120	0.1	1
	M3	M4+M5	0.02	0.803	0.05	0.552	0.1	1
	M4	Prosody	0.19	0.022	0.15	0.060	0.1	1
	M5	**Phonemic Manner**	**0.51**	**<0.001**	**0.48**	**<0.001**	**0.1**	**0.1**
	M6	Phonemic Place	0.40	<0.001	0.38	<0.001	0.1	1
	M7	Phonemic Voicing	0.33	<0.001	0.28	<0.001	1	1
	M8	M5+M6+M7	0.46	<0.001	0.44	<0.001	0.1	1
DDK	D1	Articulation On	-0.12	0.155	-0.16	0.045	0.1	10
	D2	Articulation Off	-0.03	0.676	-0.04	0.659	0.1	10
	D3	Phonemic Manner	0.31	<0.001	0.30	<0.001	1	10
	D4	**Phonemic Place**	**0.32**	**<0.001**	**0.34**	**<0.001**	**1**	**10**
	D5	Phonemic Voicing	0.14	0.084	0.17	<0.05	10	10
	D6	D3+D4+D5	0.18	<0.05	0.17	<0.05	0.1	10

r: Pearson's correlation coefficient. ρ: Spearman's correlation coefficient.

keep in mind that the clinical evaluation is based on a perceptual score which might change depending on the experience of the speech therapist, the number of patients (or recordings) rated during the day, among others. Thus, rather than predicting the same values as the human expert, automatic methods should focus on capturing the changes in speech with sufficiently good accuracy to provide an objective second opinion to the medical expert.

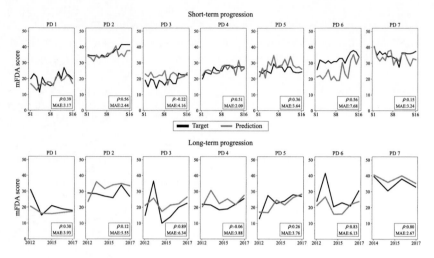

Figure 6.12: *Prediction of the dysarthria level in the short- and long-term recording sessions.*

Conclusions

Overall, it is possible to capture the progression of the speech symptoms over time. Speaker embeddings provide the most relevant information to identify a person. However, it seems that it is not sufficient to capture the level of speech impairments. Thus, combining both speaker embeddings with acoustic information results in a more accurate model to predict the progression of the speech symptoms. The x-vector embeddings (from the monologue) combined with phonemic DDK features improved the performance of the SVR considerably. Future work should consider language, motor skills, depression, response to the medicament, among others.

Regarding the acoustic conditions of the recordings, speech enhancement considerably improved the performance of the SVR for the acoustic features. In the case of the speaker embeddings, the x-vector system was not affected by the variability in the acoustic conditions, and the main reason is that the model used in this thesis was pre-trained on augmented data. Thus, the recommendation is to include a pre-processing stage when using automatic methods to reduce the

152

influence of noise.

The influence of the interviewer in the speech protocol should also included (Pérez-Toro et al., 2021). For instance, five different interviewers supervised the recordings of the At-home dataset (short-term progression). However, it might be the case that the attitude of one of the patients towards an interviewer resulted in a more familiar conversation during the monologue task. In the controlled tasks (such as the DDK), the interviewer with more experience knows when the exercise was successful.

The experience of the neurologist/speech therapist and the number of patients/recordings assessed during the day play a key role in clinical evaluation (mFDA/MDS–UPDRS–III). Thus, automatic methods should aim to capture the variations in speech over time to provide a second opinion to the expert.

6.3 Cochlear Implant users

6.3.1 Quantification of phoneme precision to evaluate onset and duration of deafness

Aim: To evaluate the phoneme precision of CI users considering a RNN approach.

Hypotheses:

- Phoneme errors are more common in CI users compared with healthy speakers and such errors can be quantified using a RNN.

- The duration and onset of deafness influence the phoneme precision of CI users.

Data

The speech recordings considered are from the 60 CI users and 20 NH German native speakers described in Section 5.2.2. The CI users include 20 prelingually deafened CI users (PRE), 20 postlinguals with a long duration of time between the onset of deafness and implantation (LONG), and 20 postlinguals with a short duration of time between the onset of deafness and implantation (SHORT). The speech tasks considered are the 97 words from the PLAKSS test (See Appendix A.2.3) and the 5 sentences extracted from the *Heidelberger Rhinophoniebogens* (See Appendix A.2.2).

Methods

Phoneme precision is measured by computing phoneme posterior probabilities using the LSTM model trained for the German language (Section 6.1.1). The $MaxPh$ is computed for the classes reported in Table 4.1 in order to validate the hypotheses. Automatic classification with a radial basis function SVM is considered for further analysis. The margin C and kernel γ parameters are

154

optimized through a grid search with $10^{-4} < C < 10^4$ and $10^{-4} < \gamma < 10^4$. Due to the relatively low amount of speakers on each class the parameters are optimized as follows:

1. Leave-one-speaker-out strategy is considered to train and test the model. The remaining speakers are used to optimize the parameters of the classifier with an internal 19-fold cross validation strategy so at least 1 speaker from each class is used during training-development stage.

2. After evaluating every fold, the medians of the resulting C and γ parameters are computed and Leave-one-speaker-out is performed again with fixed parameters.

An omnibus test of normality based on the Shapiro-Wilk test is performed on the computed acoustic parameters. If all of the parameters showed a normal distribution, then an ANOVA statistical test is performed. However, if not all features have a normal distribution, then the non-parametric Mann–Whitney U-test is considered to compare the groups. Furthermore, the Null-hypothesis is accepted or rejected considering the p-values **and** the effect size, which in this thesis is measured using Cohen's d coefficient. According to (Cohen, 1988), the effect size can be interpreted as small ($d= 0.20$), medium ($d=0.50$), or high ($d=0.80$). These values should be taken with care; however, they are used here as a general guideline to understand the results better. The performance of the multi-class SVM is evaluated using precision, recall, and F1-score.

Figure 6.13 shows the general methodology implemented in this section.

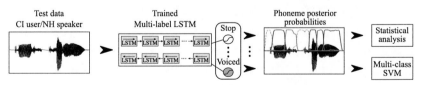

Figure 6.13: *Schematic view of the methodology implemented in this section. The LSTM trained for phoneme recognition is used as feature extraction to analyze phoneme precision.*

155

Results: Phoneme precision

Table 6.10 shows the mean and standard deviation (Avg ± Std) values for the maximum posterior probabilities (MaxPh) computed from the reading of the PLAKSS words, and Figure 6.14 shows the radar plots for such values to compare the speakers from the NH, SHORT, LONG, and PRE groups.

Table 6.10: Mean and standard deviation (Avg ± Std) values for the maximum posterior probabilities (MaxPh)

Dimension	Feature	NH	SHORT	LONG	PRE
Manner	Stop	0.86 ± 0.03	0.82 ± 0.03	0.80 ± 0.03	0.81 ± 0.05
	Nasal	0.73 ± 0.04	0.75 ± 0.04	0.74 ± 0.03	0.75 ± 0.04
	Trill	0.81 ± 0.07	0.70 ± 0.12	0.69 ± 0.10	0.71 ± 0.15
	Fricative	0.84 ± 0.04	0.80 ± 0.05	0.78 ± 0.05	0.79 ± 0.05
	Approximant	0.75 ± 0.13	0.68 ± 0.11	0.67 ± 0.11	0.67 ± 0.10
	Lateral	0.83 ± 0.05	0.77 ± 0.06	0.75 ± 0.07	0.77 ± 0.05
	Vowel	0.86 ± 0.03	0.86 ± 0.03	0.84 ± 0.03	0.86 ± 0.03
Place	Labial	0.77 ± 0.04	0.75 ± 0.04	0.74 ± 0.05	0.76 ± 0.04
	Alveolar	0.78 ± 0.04	0.78 ± 0.03	0.77 ± 0.03	0.77 ± 0.04
	Velar	0.82 ± 0.04	0.76 ± 0.05	0.73 ± 0.06	0.76 ± 0.05
	Palatal	0.72 ± 0.10	0.68 ± 0.07	0.66 ± 0.06	0.68 ± 0.06
	Postalveolar	0.94 ± 0.06	0.88 ± 0.09	0.83 ± 0.11	0.77 ± 0.22
	Central	0.84 ± 0.04	0.81 ± 0.04	0.79 ± 0.05	0.81 ± 0.04
	Front	0.78 ± 0.04	0.77 ± 0.04	0.76 ± 0.04	0.77 ± 0.03
	Back	0.80 ± 0.05	0.77 ± 0.08	0.74 ± 0.08	0.76 ± 0.08
Voicing	Voiceless	0.90 ± 0.03	0.88 ± 0.04	0.85 ± 0.03	0.87 ± 0.04
	Voiced	0.85 ± 0.01	0.86 ± 0.02	0.86 ± 0.02	0.86 ± 0.02

In most cases, NH speakers produced higher phoneme precision than CI users, particularly for manner and place of articulation. Regarding the manner of articulation, the MaxPh features indicate that the CI users have more difficulties to produce stops (like /p/ or /g/), trills (/r/), fricatives (/f/, /ʃ/), approximants (/j/), and lateral (/l/) sounds. However, when comparing the three groups of CI users (PRE, LONG, SHORT), there are no noticeable differences regarding the manner of articulation. In place of articulation, CI users produced similar values to NH speakers for labial and alveolar phonemes.

As discussed in Chapter 1 (Section 1.2.2), one reason may be that hearing-impaired people produce *visible* phonemes (sounds produced with the lips

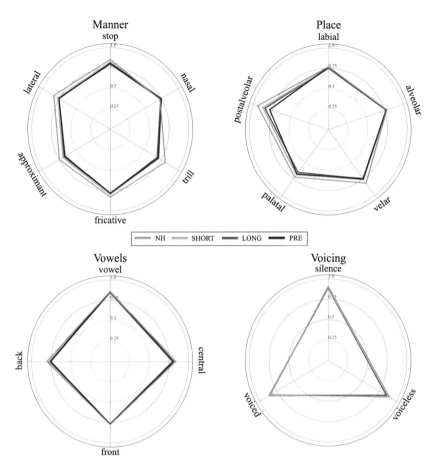

Figure 6.14: *Radar plots of the phoneme precision* (MaxPh) *in the word list read by normal hearing speakers, prelingual CI users, postlingual with long and short duration of deafness.*

or/and teeth) with greater precision than non-visible sounds produced, for instance, with the back of the tongue and the velum. Compared to the NH speakers, CI users produced velar (like /k/), palatal (/j/), and postalveolar (/ʃ/) sounds with lower precision. Furthermore, there is a visible difference in the production of postalveolar sounds; particularly, postlingually deafened CI users with long and short duration of deafness produce higher posterior probabilities than the prelingually deafened CI users. This result is consistent with findings from Neumeyer et al. (2015), which hypothesized that these changes are produced due to a limited spectral resolution of the implant. Thus, CI users shift the production of the sibilant sounds (postalveolar-fricative) into the frequency range perceived by them. This frequency shift may also explain why the difference is more considerable between postlingually and prelingually deafened CI users, since the latter lost their hearing before speech acquisition and thus have always heard a "shifted" version of these sounds. On the contrary, postlingual CI users had heard the standard way to produce the sound before losing their hearing. However, perception (and production) may have changed over time due to hearing loss and the device.

Results: NH vs. CI users

An omnibus test of normality based on the Shapiro-Wilk test was performed on the computed acoustic parameters. The normality test results showed that not all of the features have a normal distribution; thus, the non-parametric Mann–Whitney U-test is considered to evaluate differences between CI and NH speakers. Table 6.11 shows the obtained results of the statistical analysis. The silence class is not considered for the analysis. Differences regarding phoneme precision are more evident in stop, trill, fricative, lateral, velar, postalveolar, central vowels, and voiced sounds. For pre- and post-lingually CI users (LONG), differences to NH speakers are also found on voiceless consonants. Additionally, differences were found for palatal sounds between postlingually deafened adults with a long duration of deafness and NH speakers.

Results: Onset and duration of deafness

Table 6.12 shows the results of the statistical analysis for the comparison of CI users regarding onset (PRE vs. POST) and duration (LONG vs. SHORT) of deafness. For these experiments, differences were only found for the production of voiceless sounds, which is surprising considering that Figure 6.14 shows that, on average, CI users from the PRE class produces more phoneme errors

Table 6.11: Mann–Whitney U-test to compare NH vs. CI users according to phoneme posteriors (MaxPh) produced in the PLAKSS test. The values highlighted in bold indicate strong differences.

Feature	NH vs. SHORT			NH vs. LONG			NH vs. PRE		
	U-test	p-value	E. size	U-test	p-value	E. size	U-test	p-value	E. size
Stop	311	<0.01	1.071	358	<0.001	1.796	324	<0.01	1.121
Nasal	147	0.156	0.489	155	0.229	0.336	151	0.190	0.434
Trill	315	<0.01	1.068	330	<0.001	1.312	280	<0.05	0.805
Fricative	282	<0.05	0.747	318	<0.01	1.204	311	<0.01	1.000
Approximant	249	0.190	0.520	264	0.086	0.600	261	0.102	0.598
Lateral	302	<0.01	0.986	329	<0.01	1.245	323	<0.01	1.226
Vowel	200	0.989	0.005	261	0.102	0.479	213	0.735	0.113
Labial	247	0.208	0.420	261	0.102	0.566	206	0.882	0.119
Alveolar	201	0.989	0.014	241	0.273	0.241	244	0.239	0.245
Velar	340	<0.001	1.341	357	<0.001	1.614	333	<0.001	1.314
Palatal	256	0.133	0.537	290	<0.05	0.784	257	0.126	0.535
Postalveolar	290	<0.05	0.762	319	<0.01	1.139	337	<0.001	1.011
Central	279	<0.05	0.731	313	<0.01	1.073	274	<0.05	0.645
Front	219	0.617	0.188	228	0.457	0.274	225	0.508	0.203
Back	257	0.126	0.467	293	<0.05	0.919	258	0.120	0.580
Voiceless	262	0.096	0.671	360	<0.001	1.706	286	<0.05	0.698
Voiced	107	<0.05	0.907	119	<0.05	0.675	123	<0.05	0.864

U-test: Mann-Whitney U statistic. E. size: Effect size.

for postalveolar sounds compared to postlingually deafened CI users (LONG and SHORT). These results can be explained considering that the speech of prelingually CI users shows a high variability with relatively high standard deviation values for the speakers in the PRE group (Postalveolar MaxPh [Avg ± Std]: NH 0.94 ± 0.06; SHORT: 0.88 ± 0.09; LONG: 0.83 ± 0.11; PRE: 0.77 ± 0.22; from Appendix 6.10).

Results: Phoneme precision in connected speech

Multi-classification using an SVM is performed considering the PLAKSS words and the 5 Rhino sentences individually. The aims of this experiment are: (1) to observe how many speakers are correctly classified when the SVM is trained with the MaxPh posteriors and (2) to identify which of the Rhino sentences is/are the most suitable to evaluate phoneme precision with the MaxPh features. Rhino sentences are also included to evaluate whether phoneme pre-

Table 6.12: Mann–Whitney U-test to compare onset (pre vs. post) and duration (long vs. short) of deafness according to phoneme posteriors (MaxPh) produced in the PLAKSS test. The values highlighted in bold indicate strong differences.

Feature	PRE vs. SHORT			PRE vs. LONG			SHORT vs. LONG		
	U-test	p-value	E. size	U-test	p-value	E. size	U	p-value	E. size
Stop	212	0.756	0.265	149	0.172	0.274	131	0.064	0.668
Nasal	202	0.968	0.016	187	0.735	0.150	182	0.636	0.183
Trill	168	0.394	0.088	148	0.164	0.189	179	0.579	0.111
Fricative	226	0.490	0.242	173	0.473	0.170	145	0.140	0.417
Approximant	227	0.473	0.069	191	0.818	0.009	180	0.598	0.077
Lateral	228	0.457	0.053	157	0.250	0.277	142	0.120	0.290
Vowel	208	0.839	0.115	156	0.239	0.379	146	0.148	0.473
Labial	149	0.172	0.311	143	0.126	0.471	179	0.579	0.190
Alveolar	242	0.262	0.275	204	0.925	0.029	158	0.262	0.276
Velar	203	0.935	0.001	164	0.337	0.390	152	0.199	0.395
Palatal	190	0.797	0.047	179	0.579	0.352	164	0.337	0.267
Postalveolar	264	0.086	0.608	221	0.579	0.330	150	0.181	0.427
Central	175	0.508	0.035	143	0.126	0.454	157	0.250	0.452
Front	204	0.925	0.006	201	0.989	0.099	192	0.839	0.082
Back	199	0.989	0.131	168	0.394	0.259	158	0.262	0.410
Voiceless	209	0.818	0.101	107	**<0.05**	**0.590**	112	**<0.05**	**0.793**
Voiced	201	0.989	0.014	178	0.561	0.211	180	0.598	0.207

U-test: Mann-Whitney U statistic. **E. size**: Effect size.

cision is worse on connected speech. As discussed before, not all CI users produce phoneme errors; thus, misclassifications are expected. Table 6.13 shows the performance for each class and per speech task. The speech task with the highest performance is the sentence Peter strasse (*"Peter spielt auf der Strasse"*), followed by the PLAKSS words. Figure 6.15 shows the confusion matrices obtained for the two speech tasks with the highest performance. Compared to the PLAKSS task, the sentence is less accurate to differentiate between NH speakers and CI users. However, identifying prelingually deafened CI users is better on single words than on connected speech. Particularly for this sentence, phoneme precision might be worse due to the combinations of stop (/p/, /t/), fricative-alveolar (/s/), and fricative-postalveolar (/ʃ/) phonemes.

Table 6.13: Average precision, recall, and F1-score obtained from the multi-class SVM trained with MaxPh features extracted from the PLAKSS and Rhino speech tasks. The sentences are labeled according to the first word of each task in Appendix A.2.2.

Speech task	Performance			SVM parameters	
	Prec	Rec	F1	C	γ
PLAKSS words	0.41	0.44	0.42	100	0.001
Nenne	0.12	0.08	0.09	1	0.01
Peter strasse	**0.46**	**0.46**	**0.46**	1	0.1
Pferd	0.12	0.08	0.09	0.001	0.0001
Schokolade	0.32	0.34	0.33	1	0.1
Vater	0.00	0.00	0.00	1	1

Prec: Precision. **Rec**: Recall. **F1**: F1-score.

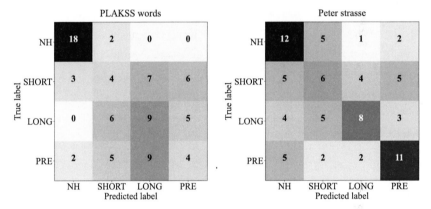

Figure 6.15: *Confusion matrices obtained for the PLAKSS words (Left) and sentence "Peter spielt auf der Strasse" (Right).*

Conclusions

The two hypotheses formulated in this section were partially confirmed. Posterior probabilities are suitable to evaluate phoneme precision in CI users and speakers without hearing loss. The results showed that CI users have lower phoneme precision than NH speakers. A statistical analysis comparing NH speakers and CI users revealed that the differences were significant for stop, trill, fricative, and lateral phonemes regarding the manner of articulation. Regarding

161

the place of articulation, the trend is that "non-visible" phonemes are the most affected (postalveolar, velar, palatal). The main interest in performing this kind of analysis is the suitability to identify which sounds are the most difficult for the CI users to produce. Thus, speech therapy can be more personalized by targeting these particular phonemes.

Regarding the onset and duration of deafness, the phoneme precision for postalveolar sounds was higher for NH speakers, followed by postlingual CI users with short and long duration of deafness and prelingual CI users. This result reflects the role of auditory feedback in speech production. However, to validate this hypothesis, hearing status and data from the implant should be considered together with the speech analysis. There are no significant differences in the results to support this claim entirely. However, this outcome should not be considered to reject the hypothesis previously stated. It has to be considered that even though in **average** the phoneme precision difference is visible, some CI users may still produce the sounds without difficulties, which in turn affect the statistical outcome considering the relatively low amount of speakers in each class. This claim is supported by the experiments performed with the sentences that showed that difficulties in producing phonemes could be more evident on connected speech tasks.

6.3.2 Segmental and suprasegmental speech analysis of postlingually deafened CI users

Aim: To perform automatic evaluation of speech prosody and acoustic articulation of postlingually CI users during the reading of a standard text.

Hypothesis:

- Even after implantation, the speech of the postlingually deafened CI users is affected in different dimensions namely prosody, acoustic articulation, and phonemic production.

Data

Speech recordings of 72 CI users (36 male, 36 female) and 56 NH German native speakers (26 male, 30 female) from Section 5.2.1 are considered for the experiments. In order to balance the two groups, the remaining 16 NH elder speakers (10 male, 6 female) are extracted from the PhonDat 1 dataset (Section 5.3.2). All participants read the "Der Nordwind und die Sonne" (The North Wind and the Sun; Appendix A.2.1).

Methods

The analysis of speech prosody is divided into 5 main parameters: pitch (meanF0, stdF0), loudness (meanSPL, stdSPL), duration (dVoiced, dUnvoiced, dPause, dSpeech), ratio (rVoiced, rUnvoiced, rPause, rSpeech), and timing (nPVI − Consonants, nPVI − Vowels). The timing features are extracted from the consonants and vowels detected by means of the LSTM model trained for the German language (Section 6.1.1). Additionally, phoneme precision is evaluated by computing the average of the maximum posterior probabilities (MaxPh) for manner, place, and voicing phonemes. Acoustic articulation is evaluated by extracting filterbank features (13 MFCC and 13 GFCC) from the onset/offset transitions (Section 4.2.2).

The non-parametric Mann–Whitney U-test is considered for statistical analysis. Furthermore, the Null-hypothesis is accepted or rejected considering the p-values **and** the effect size using Cohen's d coefficient.

Automatic classification with a radial basis function SVM is considered to analyze the filterbank features extracted from the onset/offset transitions. The reason is the limited interpretability of the cepstral coefficients (MFCC/GFCC) used for filterbank analysis. Thus, changes in articulation are analyzed by investigating the suitability of automatic methods to detect speech articulation problems in CI users. The margin C and kernel γ parameters are optimized through a grid search with $10^{-4} < C < 10^4$ and $10^{-4} < \gamma < 10^4$ as follows:

1. 10-fold cross validation strategy is considered to train and test the model.

2. An internal 9-fold cross validation strategy is used to select the best set of parameters for testing.

3. After evaluating every fold, the medians of the resulting C and γ parameters are computed, and the 10-fold cross-validation strategy is performed again with fixed parameters. The performance of the bi-class SVM is evaluated with the accuracy, sensitivity, specificity, and AUC.

Results: Speech prosody

Statistical analysis of speech prosody was performed for male and female speakers individually. The reason is that parameters such as pitch highly depend on the gender of the speaker: generally, male speakers produce speech sounds with lower F0 values than females. Table 6.14 shows the mean and standard deviation (Avg $\pm$ Std) values for the speech prosody features computed from the reading of the text "Der Nordwind und die Sonne". Figure 6.16 shows the boxplots with the prosody features computed for male and female speakers from the CI and NH groups. Table 6.15 shows the results of the non-parametric Mann–Whitney U-test. In general, differences between CI users and NH speakers were found for all of the **parameters** except for "Pitch". However,

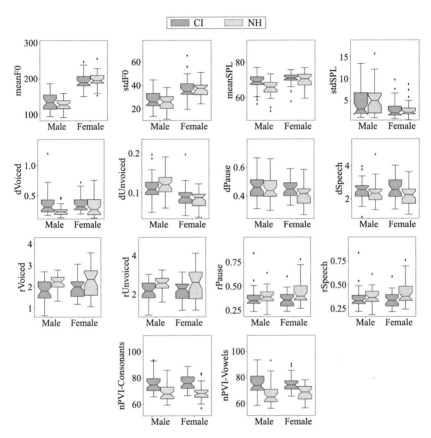

Figure 6.16: *Boxplots with the distribution of prosody-based features extracted from CI users (light blue) and NH speakers (light grey).*

Table 6.14: Mean and standard deviation (Avg $\pm$ Std) values for speech prosody features.

Parameter	Feature	Female		Male	
		CI	HC	CI	HC
Pitch	meanF0	192.7 ± 24.4	195.9 ± 20.7	135.2 ± 24.6	126.3 ± 16.5
	stdF0	37.1 ± 9.1	36.8 ± 6.9	27.8 ± 7.8	25.6 ± 6.5
Loudness	meanSPL	70.7 ± 3.0	69.5 ± 4.0	68.8 ± 4.7	65.6 ± 4.8
	stdSPL	2.9 ± 2.1	2.8 ± 1.7	4.4 ± 3.1	4.9 ± 3.4
Duration	dVoiced	0.36 ± 0.14	0.32 ± 0.17	0.37 ± 0.19	0.25 ± 0.08
	dUnvoiced	0.09 ± 0.03	0.08 ± 0.02	0.11 ± 0.03	0.12 ± 0.03
	dPause	0.45 ± 0.07	0.41 ± 0.08	0.46 ± 0.09	0.45 ± 0.09
	dSpeech	2.63 ± 0.65	2.16 ± 0.61	2.53 ± 0.62	2.36 ± 0.60
Ratio	rVoiced	1.92 ± 0.44	2.23 ± 0.66	1.83 ± 0.51	2.20 ± 0.35
	rUnvoiced	2.18 ± 0.50	2.51 ± 0.78	2.16 ± 0.54	2.54 ± 0.40
	rPause	0.36 ± 0.08	0.44 ± 0.12	0.37 ± 0.11	0.39 ± 0.08
	rSpeech	0.37 ± 0.04	0.42 ± 0.05	0.36 ± 0.11	0.37 ± 0.08
Timing	nPVI $-$ Con	76.1 ± 5.7	68.53 ± 5.4	75.7 ± 7.1	68.9 ± 6.4
	nPVI $-$ Vow	75.1 ± 5.9	68.28 ± 5.47	75.0 ± 7.6	66.8 ± 8.2

nPVI $-$ Con: Consonant timing. nPVI $-$ Vow: Vowel timing.

lower loudness values were found only for the male speakers (Figure 6.16), but not for female CI users, which produced loudness values in the same range as both male and female NH speakers. The speaking rate of hearing-impaired people has been reported to be slower compared to NH speakers due to a prolongation of speech segments and insertion of pauses (Osberger and McGarr, 1982). The results reported in Figure 6.16 and Table 6.15 are consistent with these findings; however, differences between CI users and NH speakers are more considerable for some features than others. Female CI users produced longer pauses and speech segments than female NH speakers and slower voice rate, pause rate, and speech ratios. In male speakers, CI users showed a prolongation of voiced segments and slower rates for voiced and unvoiced segments. In addition to the duration and rate features, timing features based on the variability of consecutive vowel and consonant duration (nPVI) were found to be higher for CI users compared to NH speakers. Timing changes may be related to difficulties in controlling and coordinating the larynx and oral gestures necessary to produce voicing contrast for an instant.

Table 6.15: Mann–Whitney U-test to compare postlingually deafened CI users vs.NH speakers considering speech prosody features extracted from the reading text. The values highlighted in bold indicate strong differences.

Parameter	Feature	Female			Male		
		U-test	p-value	E. size	U-test	p-value	E. size
Pitch	meanF0	573	0.401	0.136	774	0.158	0.415
	stdF0	609	0.665	0.031	740	0.303	0.297
Loudness	meanSPL	720	0.421	0.287	903	**<0.01**	**0.671**
	stdSPL	612	0.689	0.061	593	0.539	0.154
Duration	dVoiced	821	0.052	0.278	940	**<0.01**	**0.763**
	dUnvoiced	713	0.468	0.252	562	0.336	0.155
	dPause	837	**<0.05**	**0.592**	699	0.570	0.120
	dSpeech	883	**<0.01**	**0.73**	795	0.099	0.274
Ratio	rVoiced	457	**<0.05**	**0.532**	374	**<0.01**	**0.824**
	rUnvoiced	484	0.066	0.488	386	**<0.01**	**0.791**
	rPause	392	**<0.01**	**0.751**	493	0.082	0.210
	rSpeech	410	**<0.01**	**0.724**	514	0.133	0.175
Timing	nPVI – Con	1102	**<0.001**	**1.339**	996	**<0.001**	**0.989**
	nPVI – Vow	1024	**<0.001**	**1.172**	1024	**<0.001**	**1.014**

U-test: Mann-Whitney U statistic. **E. size**: Effect size. $nPVI - Con$: Consonant timing. $nPVI - Vow$: Vowel timing.

Results: Phoneme precision

Table 6.16 shows the mean and standard deviation (Avg $\pm$ Std) values for the maximum posterior probabilities (MaxPh) computed from the reading of "Der Nordwind und die Sonne" and the results of the Mann–Whitney U-test comparing CI users and NH speakers. Figure 6.17 shows radar plots with the MaxPh values computed for NH speakers and CI users. Statistical analysis shows that postlingually deafened CI users produced lower values for most phoneme classes except for "Approximants". Compared to the PLAKSS words (Table 6.11), precision is lower for the reading of a text (even for the "visible" phonemes). Thus, increasing the "complexity" of the task exposes other articulation issues that are not evident when a single word has to be uttered. Nevertheless, features extracted from the phoneme classes Nasal, Vowel, Alveolar, Central, Front, Voiceless, and Voiced have more than 0.80 (80%) precision for both CI and NH speakers. Thus, even if CI users (on

Table 6.16: Mann–Whitney U-test to compare postlingually deafened CI users vs.NH speakers considering phoneme precision-based features extracted from the reading text. The values highlighted in bold indicate significant differences.

Dimension	Features	CI	NH	U-test	p-value	E. size
Manner	Stop	0.74 ± 0.08	0.84 ± 0.08	947	**<0.001**	**1.246**
	Nasal	0.81 ± 0.06	0.88 ± 0.06	914	**<0.001**	**1.278**
	Trill	0.68 ± 0.13	0.78 ± 0.11	1391	**<0.001**	**0.857**
	Fricative	0.78 ± 0.07	0.87 ± 0.07	877	**<0.001**	**1.326**
	Approximant	0.60 ± 0.16	0.55 ± 0.26	2874	0.261	0.247
	Lateral	0.66 ± 0.08	0.75 ± 0.08	1161	**<0.001**	**1.100**
	Vowel	0.90 ± 0.03	0.93 ± 0.03	1028	**<0.001**	**1.188**
Place	Labial	0.76 ± 0.06	0.84 ± 0.07	1057	**<0.001**	**1.184**
	Alveolar	0.81 ± 0.05	0.88 ± 0.06	903	**<0.001**	**1.292**
	Velar	0.69 ± 0.08	0.79 ± 0.09	1062	**<0.001**	**1.113**
	Palatal	0.66 ± 0.09	0.73 ± 0.11	1663	**<0.001**	**0.721**
	Postalveolar	0.78 ± 0.21	0.88 ± 0.13	1741	**<0.01**	**0.590**
	Central	0.81 ± 0.04	0.84 ± 0.04	1365	**<0.001**	**0.916**
	Front	0.81 ± 0.04	0.86 ± 0.05	1124	**<0.001**	**1.104**
	Back	0.78 ± 0.07	0.83 ± 0.07	1512	**<0.001**	**0.749**
Voicing	Voiceless	0.81 ± 0.05	0.88 ± 0.06	972	**<0.001**	**1.220**
	Voiced	0.94 ± 0.02	0.96 ± 0.02	1188	**<0.001**	**0.967**

CI/NH: Mean and standard deviation (Avg $\pm$ Std) values for the maximum posterior probabilities (MaxPh). **U-test**: Mann-Whitney U statistic. **E. size**: Effect size.

average) produce such phonemes with lower precision, the overall intelligibility for these classes may still be good enough for oral communication.

Results: Onset/offset transitions

The automatic classification was performed to investigate the suitability of these features to detect abnormal energy changes in the transitions produced by CI users. Table 6.17 shows the classification results and Figure 6.18 shows the obtained confusion matrices. In general, the performance of the classifier is similar for both onset and offset transitions and the concatenation of both feature sets. In terms of sensitivity, the SVM can recognize better the CI users than the NH. This result can be explained considering that not all CI users might develop speech production problems. As discussed in Section 2.3.3, imprecise articulation may be caused due to changes in the internal model

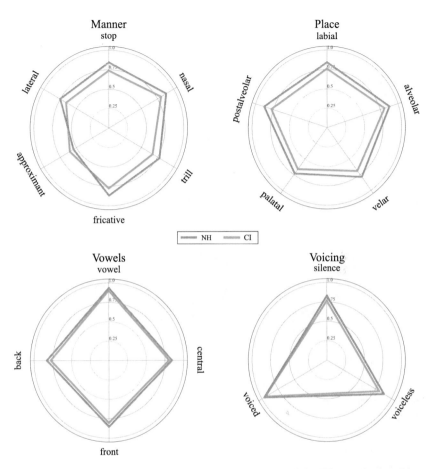

Figure 6.17: *Radar plots of the phoneme precision (*MaxPh*) in the reading task by the normal hearing speakers and postlingually deafened CI users.*

used by the brain to plan speech movements. Such a model is acquired and maintained with the use of auditory feedback. Thus, with ongoing hearing loss, the sensory-motor control decreases as one tend to use only as much force and effort for all movements as necessary. Onset/offset transitions combined with filterbank features appear to be suitable to capture such changes. However, it is necessary to include data from neural activity (for instance, functional

Magnetic Resonance Imaging- fMRI) during speech production and perception in order to have more conclusive results (Guenther and Hickok, 2016).

Table 6.17: Results for automatic classification of CI users and NH speakers. C and γ are the final parameters selected to evaluate the performance of the SVM.

Features	Acc	Sen	Spe	AUC	C	γ
Onset transitions	86	97	76	0.90	1	0.01
Offset transitions	84	93	75	0.87	1	0.01
Onset/offset transitions	86	97	75	0.88	1	0.001

Acc: Accuracy[%]. **Sen**: Sensitivity[%]. **Spe**: Specificity[%].
AUC: Area under the ROC curve.

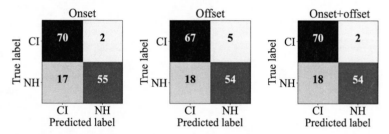

Figure 6.18: *Confusion matrices form the automatic classification of CI users and NH speakers considering offset (left), onset (middle) and onset/offset (right) transitions.*

Conclusions

Speech production of postlingual CI users differs from that of age-matched NH speakers at the supra-segmental (prosody) and segmental (phoneme precision, onset/offset transitions) levels. Thus, even after rehabilitation by cochlear implantation, the speech of CI users deviates from "normal" speech. For speech prosody, CI users produced higher variability in the duration of vowels/consonants and read the text with a slower voiced rate than the NH speakers. On the one hand, male CI users produced longer voiced segments resulting in a slower voiced rate. On the other hand, a slow voiced rate in females was due to a prolongation of pauses and speech segments within the text. Further research is necessary to determine whether these differences affect the oral communication of CI users positively or negatively. For instance, speech prosody deficits may negatively impact the expression of emotions and the intended linguistic information provided, such as word focus and sentence stress to distinguish between questions and statements and phrase boundary marking. On the contrary, a slow speaking rate may positively impact overall intelligibility. However, this may not be the case for the CI users considered in this study. The phonemic analysis shows that CI users produced lower phoneme precision even for "visible" phonemes when reading a text. Furthermore, automatic classification of CI users vs. healthy speakers using onset/offset transitions showed that there are difficulties of the patients to start/stop movements like the vibration of the vocal folds.

Some limitations include the lack of longitudinal data to monitor speech production over time. Additionally, specifics about the hearing state of the patients, ear side of implantation, insertion depth, active electrodes, manufacturer, filter settings of the input filters, and duration of CI usage should be taken into consideration, as well as possible influences on the acoustic parameters of speech production.

6.4 Aging and speech

Aim: To analyze the influence of aging in speech production in the context of PD.

Hypothesis

- Aging affects different aspects of speech production and such changes can be captured by most of the features considered to analyze pathological speech.

Only PD patients are considered because with this data it is possible to compare phonation, vowel articulation, prosody, and phoneme articulation precision of elderly and young speakers.

Data

Three groups of Spanish native speakers (from Colombia) are considered: 50 young, healthy speakers (YHC), 50 elderly healthy speakers (EHC), and 50 PD patients (PD). Each group contains speech signals from 25 males and 25 females. The recordings of the elderly speakers (EHC and PD) were extracted from the PCGITA dataset, and the recordings of the young speakers were presented in Section 5.3.1. All of the speakers were recorded in controlled noise conditions in a soundproof booth. The speech tasks considered for the analysis are the sustained phonation of the vowels /a/, /e/, /i/, /o/, and /u/, read text (Appendix A.1.3), and the repetition of /pa-ta-ka/.

Methods

Only standardized speech tasks are considered in this section for better group comparisons. Phonation analysis was performed by estimating pitch, loudness, and perturbation features from the sustained phonation of the Spanish vowels /a/, /e/. /i/, /o/ and /u/. Articulation analysis was performed by constructing the vowel space of /a/, /i/, and /u/. Filterbank analysis was not included in this section due to the limited interpretability of the cepstral coefficients (MFCC/GFCC). Prosody analysis was evaluated by considering pitch, loudness, duration, ratio, and timing parameters extracted from the reading task. Phonemic analysis was performed considering voicing, manner, and place of articulation features extracted from the text and the repetition of /pa-ta-ka/.

The non-parametric Mann–Whitney U-test was considered for analysis (a normality test was performed before). The Null-hypothesis is accepted or rejected considering the p-values **and** the effect size measured using Cohen's d coefficient.

Regression analysis was performed to estimate the age of a speaker using the selected feature sets. For this, a linear SVR is considered for further analysis. The parameters C and ϵ were optimized through a grid search with $10^{-4} < C < 10^3$ and $10^{-4} < \epsilon < 10^3$. The parameters are optimized as follows:

1. 10-fold cross-validation strategy is considered to train and test the model.

2. An internal 9-fold cross-validation strategy is used to select the best set of parameters for testing.

3. After evaluating every fold, the medians of the resulting C and γ parameters are computed, and the 10-fold cross-validation strategy is performed again with fixed parameters. The performance is measured using Pearson's (r) and Spearman's (ρ) correlation coefficients.

Results: Phonation analysis

Table 6.18 shows the mean and standard deviation (Avg $\pm$ Std) values for the phonation features. The corresponding boxplots are displayed in Figure 6.19. Male elderly speakers tend to produce higher F0 values than the young speakers, whereas the elderly female speakers produced lower F0 than the young speakers. Such deviations are even more significant in male and female PD patients. The increased mean F0 in elderly males and decreased mean F0 in elderly females have been reported to be related to changes in the larynx, mainly the length of the vocal folds (Titze et al., 2016). However, the exact reasons are still unclear. For instance, it has been hypothesized the menopause affects the larynx of the female, and these changes might account for deviations in the fundamental frequency (D'haeseleer et al., 2009). In the case of PD, alterations in F0 have been associated with increased rigidity of the laryngeal muscles (Chiaramonte and Bonfiglio, 2020; Miller, 2017; Ramig et al., 2001). Regarding the F0 variability (stdF0), elderly speakers (especially the PD patients) produced higher values than the young speakers.

In the case of loudness, elderly speakers (especially from the PD patients) tend to produce lower SPL levels (meanSPL) and higher variability (stdSPL) than the young speakers. Alteration in vocal loudness of elderly speakers has been reported to be related to changes in the laryngeal and respiratory mechanism (Baker et al., 2001; Linville, 1996). Particularly for PD, these changes are often associated with rigidity of respiratory and laryngeal muscles (Colton et al., 2011). Perturbation measurements do not appear to be related to aging. Only the female PD patients showed high instability of the vibration of the vocal folds during the sustained phonation.

Tables 6.19 and 6.20 show the results of the statistical analysis performed for females and males, respectively. Significant differences between groups were mainly found in the female speakers. In particular, phonation of the PD patients

Table 6.18: Mean and standard deviation (Avg $\pm$ Std) values for phonation features from PD patients, elderly healthy (EHC), and young healthy (YHC) speakers.

Parameter	Feature	Female			Male		
		PD	EHC	YHC	PD	EHC	YHC
Pitch	meanF0	192.8 ± 36.3	210.4 ± 31.2	224.2 ± 24.4	157.1 ± 39.8	134.9 ± 22.3	123.9 ± 12.9
	stdF0	22.1 ± 13.8	11.1 ± 8.1	7.7 ± 5.3	10.2 ± 7.1	5.9 ± 4.0	5.1 ± 5.9
Loudness	meanSPL	80.5 ± 1.9	82.3 ± 1.5	83.3 ± 0.9	81.31 ± 1.0	82.1 ± 1.6	82.6 ± 1.4
	stdSPL	3.8 ± 1.1	2.5 ± 0.8	2.5 ± 0.7	3.48 ± 1.12	2.84 ± 0.88	2.41 ± 0.86
Perturbation	Jitter	0.54 ± 0.47	0.19 ± 0.12	0.19 ± 0.09	0.33 ± 0.27	0.22 ± 0.12	0.26 ± 0.22
	PPQ3	0.49 ± 0.48	0.14 ± 0.14	0.15 ± 0.11	0.27 ± 0.30	0.16 ± 0.14	0.22 ± 0.27
	PPQ5	0.84 ± 0.82	0.25 ± 0.23	0.26 ± 0.19	0.46 ± 0.49	0.25 ± 0.17	0.37 ± 0.46
	Shimmer	0.30 ± 0.13	0.20 ± 0.07	0.18 ± 0.05	0.28 ± 0.10	0.24 ± 0.06	0.22 ± 0.07
	APQ3	0.18 ± 0.09	0.12 ± 0.05	0.12 ± 0.03	0.18 ± 0.05	0.18 ± 0.07	0.18 ± 0.08
	APQ5	0.33 ± 0.15	0.20 ± 0.07	0.20 ± 0.06	0.30 ± 0.09	0.25 ± 0.06	0.24 ± 0.07

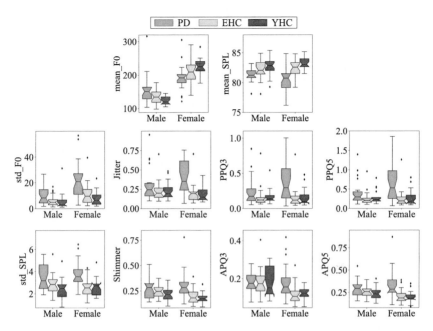

Figure 6.19: *Boxplots with the distribution of phonation-based features extracted from PD patients (light blue), elderly healthy speakers (light gray), and young healthy speakers (dark gray).*

appears to deviate more from the healthy speakers. In the case of male speakers, pitch and loudness produced by the patients seem to be considerably different from the healthy controls. Some of the perturbation features also appear to provide information about the presence of PD. However, the differences between patients and healthy speakers were inconsistent for elderly and young, e.g., the PPQ5 of the male PD patients is considerably higher than the elderly healthy speakers, but not higher than the young speakers. Phonation analysis appears to account more for the presence of PD rather than changes caused by aging (e.g., only the average SPL seems to be considerably lower in females from the EHC group compared with young speakers). Nevertheless, for acoustic features such as F0 and SPL, the voice of the patients, healthy elderly, and young speakers tend to be different.

Table 6.19: Mann–Whitney U-test to compare female PD patients, elderly healthy (EHC), and young healthy (YHC) speakers considering phonation features extracted from the sustained vowels. The values highlighted in bold indicate significant differences.

Parameter	Feature	PD vs. EHC			EHC vs. YHC			PD vs. YHC		
		U-test	p-value	E. size	U-test	p-value	E. size	U-test	p-value	E. size
Pitch	meanF0	211	0.050	0.501	220	0.074	0.474	**127**	**<0.001**	**0.977**
	stdF0	**474**	**<0.01**	**0.945**	394	0.116	0.479	**527**	**<0.001**	**1.337**
Loudness	meanSPL	**138**	**<0.01**	**1.007**	**201**	**<0.05**	**0.734**	**48**	**<0.001**	**1.783**
	stdSPL	**503**	**<0.001**	**1.209**	312	1.000	0.004	**520**	**<0.001**	**1.249**
Perturbation	Jitter	**515**	**<0.001**	**0.971**	308	0.938	0.035	**507**	**<0.001**	**0.995**
	PPQ3	**504**	**<0.001**	**0.960**	284	0.587	0.069	**484**	**<0.01**	**0.949**
	PPQ5	**502**	**<0.001**	**0.948**	286	0.614	0.076	**488**	**<0.01**	**0.933**
	Shimmer	**494**	**<0.001**	**0.973**	350	0.473	0.309	**538**	**<0.001**	**1.238**
	APQ3	**465**	**<0.01**	**0.844**	254	0.260	0.102	**447**	**<0.01**	**0.844**
	APQ5	**501**	**<0.001**	**0.995**	307	0.923	0.103	**513**	**<0.001**	**1.077**

U-test: Mann-Whitney U statistic. **E. size**: Effect size.

Table 6.20: Mann–Whitney U-test to compare male PD patients, elderly healthy (EHC), and young healthy (YHC) speakers considering phonation features extracted from the sustained vowels. The values highlighted in bold indicate significant differences.

Parameter	Feature	PD vs. EHC			EHC vs. YHC			PD vs. YHC		
		U-test	p-value	E. size	U-test	p-value	E. size	U-test	p-value	E. size
Pitch	meanF0	**429**	**<0.05**	**0.663**	393	0.121	0.581	**524**	**<0.001**	**1.081**
	stdF0	**429**	**<0.05**	**0.716**	381	0.187	0.144	**471**	**<0.01**	**0.746**
Loudness	meanSPL	**199**	**<0.05**	**0.609**	249	0.222	0.331	**131**	**<0.001**	**1.059**
	stdSPL	405	0.074	0.617	405	0.074	0.475	**472**	**<0.01**	**1.035**
Perturbation	Jitter	378	0.207	0.501	296	0.756	0.206	371	0.260	0.278
	PPQ3	391	0.130	0.473	244	0.187	0.261	330	0.742	0.192
	PPQ5	**425**	**<0.05**	**0.557**	236	0.140	0.331	359	0.372	0.185
	Shimmer	381	0.187	0.432	397	0.103	0.416	**428**	**<0.05**	**0.729**
	APQ3	345	0.535	0.052	337	0.641	0.059	352	0.449	0.113
	APQ5	402	0.084	0.531	368	0.286	0.248	**430**	**<0.05**	**0.693**

U-test: Mann-Whitney U statistic. **E. size**: Effect size.

Results: Articulation analysis

Table 6.21 shows the mean and standard deviation of the articulation features extracted from the sustained phonation of vowels. Figure 6.20 shows the vowel space formed with the first and second formant frequencies extracted from the vowels /a/, /i/, and /u/. Tables 6.22 and 6.23 shows the results of the statistical analysis performed with vowel articulation features. In the context of sex and

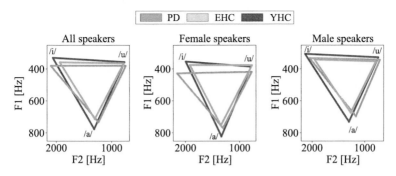

Figure 6.20: *Triangular vowel space area extracted from PD patients (light blue), elderly healthy speakers (light gray), and young healthy speakers (dark gray). The vowel space area was also extracted for all speakers (left), only females (center), and only males (right).*

aging, changes in formant frequencies have been linked to the size and shape of the vocal tract. In the case of PD, such changes have been related to the reduced amplitude of the speech articulators (Sapir et al., 2010; Skodda et al., 2011).

For the vowel space, the elderly speakers (PD and EHC) appear to have a smaller area than the young speakers, indicating a reduction in the articulatory movements. The statistical analysis revealed that such a reduction was significant only for male speakers. Furthermore, the FCR appears to increase when

Table 6.21: Mean and standard deviation (Avg $\pm$ Std) values for vowel articulation features from PD patients, elderly healthy (EHC), and young healthy (YHC) speakers.

Feature	Female			Male		
	PD	EHC	YHC	PD	EHC	YHC
$F1_{/a/}$	751 ± 102	768 ± 129	820 ± 83	672 ± 80	695 ± 84	729 ± 47
$F2_{/a/}$	1353 ± 129	1316 ± 103	1345 ± 168	1276 ± 106	1183 ± 105	1310 ± 129
$F1_{/i/}$	373 ± 65	425 ± 88	352 ± 61	339 ± 47	330 ± 58	304 ± 30.34
$F2_{/i/}$	1917 ± 446	2149 ± 276	1994 ± 454	1950 ± 211	2044 ± 163	2129 ± 178
$F1_{/u/}$	374 ± 58	416 ± 63	383 ± 48	351 ± 48	340 ± 36	325 ± 28
$F2_{/u/}$	789 ± 106	797 ± 110	809 ± 163	807 ± 150	732 ± 65	763 ± 48
tVSA [$\times 10^5$]	21.61 ± 12.05	23.99 ± 10.79	27.20 ± 8.92	18.62 ± 6.97	23.64 ± 7.09	28.32 ± 5.98
LntVSA	12.12 ± 0.59	12.23 ± 0.66	12.45 ± 0.37	12.05 ± 0.44	12.33 ± 0.30	12.53 ± 0.22
FCR	1.12 ± 0.21	1.03 ± 0.15	1.06 ± 0.27	1.07 ± 0.14	0.95 ± 0.09	0.95 ± 0.08

the vowel space decreases, which is more notable in male PD patients.

Table 6.22: Mann–Whitney U-test to compare female PD patients, elderly healthy (EHC), and young healthy (YHC) speakers considering articulation features extracted from the sustained vowels. The values highlighted in bold indicate significant differences.

| Feature | Female speakers | | | | | | | | |
| | PD vs. EHC | | | EHC vs. YHC | | | PD vs. YHC | | |
	U-test	p-value	E. size	U-test	p-value	E. size	U-test	p-value	E. size
$F1_{/a/}$	252	0.244	0.139	256	0.277	0.457	**195**	**<0.05**	**0.708**
$F2_{/a/}$	359	0.372	0.306	263	0.342	0.197	322	0.861	0.055
$F1_{/i/}$	**198**	**<0.05**	**0.643**	**480**	**<0.01**	**0.931**	376	0.222	0.332
$F2_{/i/}$	233	0.125	0.603	381	0.187	0.400	288	0.641	0.163
$F1_{/u/}$	**196**	**<0.05**	**0.659**	408	0.065	0.552	286	0.614	0.166
$F2_{/u/}$	279	0.522	0.068	356	0.404	0.083	320	0.892	0.137
tVSA	254	0.260	0.201	265	0.362	0.313	**202**	**<0.05**	**0.509**
log −tVSA	254	0.260	0.165	265	0.362	0.399	**202**	**<0.05**	**0.641**
FCR	394	0.116	0.483	294	0.727	0.158	380	0.194	0.222

U-test: Mann-Whitney U statistic. **E. size**: Effect size.

Table 6.23: Mann–Whitney U-test to compare male PD patients, elderly healthy (EHC), and young healthy (YHC) speakers considering articulation features extracted from the sustained vowels. The values highlighted in bold indicate significant differences.

| Feature | Male speakers | | | | | | | | |
| | PD vs. EHC | | | EHC vs. YHC | | | PD vs. YHC | | |
	U-test	p-value	E. size	U-test	p-value	E. size	U-test	p-value	E. size
$F1_{/a/}$	290	0.669	0.277	**177**	**<0.01**	**0.476**	**172**	**<0.01**	**0.839**
$F2_{/a/}$	**450**	**<0.01**	**0.855**	**141**	**<0.01**	**1.043**	267	0.383	0.277
$F1_{/i/}$	354	0.426	0.162	403	0.081	0.546	**454**	**<0.01**	**0.859**
$F2_{/i/}$	228	0.103	0.476	229	0.107	0.484	**157**	**<0.01**	**0.884**
$F1_{/u/}$	364	0.322	0.238	378	0.207	0.436	**433**	**<0.05**	**0.617**
$F2_{/u/}$	406	0.071	0.623	217	0.065	0.518	347	0.509	0.379
tVSA	**200**	**<0.05**	**0.689**	**182**	**<0.05**	**0.687**	**98**	**<0.001**	**1.439**
logtVSA	**200**	**<0.05**	**0.725**	**182**	**<0.05**	**0.743**	**98**	**<0.001**	**1.338**
FCR	**471**	**<0.01**	**0.962**	297	0.771	0.021	**467**	**<0.01**	**0.985**

U-test: Mann-Whitney U statistic. **E. size**: Effect size.

There is an interesting pattern when phonation and vowel articulation features are considered for the detection of PD. While phonation features appear to be more suitable for discriminating between female PD patients and healthy speakers, the vowel space area appears to be more suitable for highlighting deficits in male PD patients. However, there is no information about the anatomical changes of the vocal tract and by that acoustic properties to have definitive conclusions.

Results: Prosody analysis

Table 6.24 shows the mean and standard deviation (Avg $\pm$ Std) values for the speech prosody features computed from the reading of the standard text, and Figure 6.21 shows the corresponding boxplots. In general, young healthy speakers have higher ratio values than the elderly speakers (PD and EHC) which is associated with a faster reading. Furthermore, PD patients produced longer pause segments than the healthy controls (EHC/YHC), and there is a tendency from the patients to produce higher vowel duration variability (nPVI − Vow).

Similar to the phonation analysis, male elderly speakers produced higher F0 values than the YHC group; however, PD patients do not exhibit higher F0 values than the age-matched healthy speakers. Additionally, the pitch of the elderly male and healthy female speakers is higher during the reading task compared with the sustained phonation. The statistical analysis reveals that pitch values of male elderly speakers (PD and ECH) are considerably higher

Table 6.24: Mean and standard deviation (Avg $\pm$ Std) values for speech prosody features from PD patients and elderly/young healthy speakers.

Paramater	Feature	Female			Male		
		PD	EHC	YHC	PD	EHC	YHC
Pitch	meanF0	196.1 $\pm$ 36.3	220.1 $\pm$ 22.5	222.9 $\pm$ 19.3	150.0 $\pm$ 34.6	148.2 $\pm$ 25.3	128.3 $\pm$ 16.1
	stdF0	39.3 $\pm$ 16.3	40.7 $\pm$ 8.9	36.8 $\pm$ 7.3	25.4 $\pm$ 12.5	28.7 $\pm$ 8.6	18.6 $\pm$ 5.8
Loudness	meanSPL	66.7 $\pm$ 6.7	65.9 $\pm$ 4.9	66.1 $\pm$ 4.3	64.9 $\pm$ 6.9	65.3 $\pm$ 5.2	64.8 $\pm$ 3.4
	stdSPL	4.0 $\pm$ 3.1	4.3 $\pm$ 2.8	3.8 $\pm$ 2.3	5.4 $\pm$ 4.0	5.3 $\pm$ 3.6	5.3 $\pm$ 2.8
Duration	dVoiced	0.35 $\pm$ 0.11	0.35 $\pm$ 0.09	0.26 $\pm$ 0.05	0.50 $\pm$ 0.20	0.34 $\pm$ 0.07	0.27 $\pm$ 0.04
	dUnvoiced	0.12 $\pm$ 0.06	0.11 $\pm$ 0.03	0.1 $\pm$ 0.02	0.15 $\pm$ 0.07	0.13 $\pm$ 0.04	0.12 $\pm$ 0.03
	dPause	0.37 $\pm$ 0.10	0.34 $\pm$ 0.07	0.29 $\pm$ 0.05	0.38 $\pm$ 0.13	0.35 $\pm$ 0.07	0.30 $\pm$ 0.06
	dSpeech	1.44 $\pm$ 0.30	1.48 $\pm$ 0.32	1.21 $\pm$ 0.18	1.45 $\pm$ 0.33	1.45 $\pm$ 0.37	1.22 $\pm$ 0.2
Ratio	rVoiced	1.67 $\pm$ 0.53	1.69 $\pm$ 0.35	2.07 $\pm$ 0.24	1.23 $\pm$ 0.48	1.59 $\pm$ 0.36	1.87 $\pm$ 0.28
	rUnvoiced	2.27 $\pm$ 0.53	2.24 $\pm$ 0.28	2.77 $\pm$ 0.31	1.84 $\pm$ 0.45	2.22 $\pm$ 0.39	2.58 $\pm$ 0.32
	rPause	0.59 $\pm$ 0.13	0.59 $\pm$ 0.10	0.69 $\pm$ 0.11	0.58 $\pm$ 0.13	0.60 $\pm$ 0.12	0.68 $\pm$ 0.08
	rSpeech	0.58 $\pm$ 0.11	0.57 $\pm$ 0.10	0.68 $\pm$ 0.10	0.57 $\pm$ 0.11	0.58 $\pm$ 0.13	0.67 $\pm$ 0.09
Timing	nPVI − Con	69.5 $\pm$ 6.5	66.3 $\pm$ 9.8	65.5 $\pm$ 4.7	69.7 $\pm$ 8.4	66.7 $\pm$ 9.0	66.6 $\pm$ 6.4
	nPVI − Vow	69.3 $\pm$ 9.7	62.6 $\pm$ 8.9	63.4 $\pm$ 7.9	73.4 $\pm$ 8.8	64.2 $\pm$ 8.7	62.9 $\pm$ 7.3

nPVI − Con: Consonant timing. nPVI − Vow: Vowel timing.

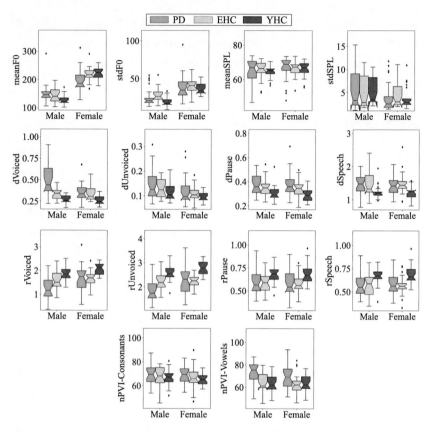

Figure 6.21: *Boxplots with the distribution of prosody-based features extracted from PD patients (light blue), elderly healthy speakers (light gray), and young healthy speakers (dark gray).*

than the young men and lower in female PD patients than the healthy elderly and young speakers. In the case of the duration of voiced sounds, male PD patients produced longer segments, followed by the healthy elderly controls and young speakers. However, there is not a clear difference between PD patients and elderly healthy speakers for the female speakers.

Tables 6.25 and 6.26 shows the results of the Mann–Whitney U-tests comparing female and male speakers, respectively. Significant differences were

Table 6.25: Mann–Whitney U-test to compare female PD patients, elderly healthy (EHC), and young healthy (YHC) speakers considering speech prosody features extracted from the reading text. The values highlighted in bold indicate significant differences.

Paramater	Feature	PD vs. EHC			EHC vs. YHC			PD vs. YHC		
		U-test	p-value	E. size	U-test	p-value	E. size	U-test	p-value	E. size
Pitch	meanF0	**153**	**<0.01**	**0.766**	277	0.497	0.127	**134**	**<0.01**	**0.888**
	stdF0	257	0.286	0.103	410	0.060	0.461	325	0.816	0.191
Loudness	meanSPL	386	0.157	0.119	317	0.938	0.028	383	0.174	0.101
	stdSPL	247	0.207	0.099	337	0.641	0.176	278	0.509	0.059
Duration	dVoiced	339	0.614	0.055	**501**	**<0.001**	**1.098**	**476**	**<0.01**	**1.012**
	dUnvoiced	306	0.907	0.250	385	0.162	0.419	371	0.260	0.537
	dPause	359	0.372	0.321	**464**	**<0.01**	**0.809**	**480**	**<0.01**	**0.961**
	dSpeech	300	0.823	0.112	**490**	**<0.01**	**0.982**	**454**	**<0.01**	**0.890**
Ratio	rVoiced	310	0.969	0.054	**109**	**<0.001**	**1.229**	**141**	**<0.01**	**0.955**
	rUnvoiced	331	0.727	0.060	**72**	**<0.001**	**1.728**	**123**	**<0.001**	**1.125**
	rPause	292	0.698	0.003	**155**	**<0.01**	**0.921**	**166**	**<0.01**	**0.813**
	rSpeech	311	0.985	0.060	**134**	**<0.01**	**1.096**	**142**	**<0.01**	**0.981**
Timing	nPVI – Con	382	0.181	0.367	330	0.742	0.110	**430**	**<0.05**	**0.684**
	nPVI – Vow	**438**	**<0.05**	**0.688**	278	0.509	0.084	**418**	**<0.05**	**0.643**

U-test: Mann-Whitney U statistic. E. size: Effect size. nPVI – Con: Consonant timing. nPVI – Vow: Vowel timing.

obtained for multiple parameters. However, the features that might differentiate between age and pathological-related speech disorders are limited. For instance, the variability in the duration of vowels (nPVI – Vow) was considerably higher in the PD group than in the EHC and YHC groups. However, such a difference was not found between the healthy elderly and young speakers (EHC vs. YHC), which indicates that this feature might exhibit abnormal values in the presence of the pathology but not due to age. In the case of the meanF0, female PD patients read the standard text with an average lower pitch than the healthy speakers (female: PD vs. EHC and PD vs. YHC), but there was no significant difference between the group of healthy speakers (female: EHC vs. YHC).

Another pattern observed in the male speakers is longer production of voiced segments in elderly speakers, which was even longer in the group of the PD patients. As discussed in Chapter 3, changes related to speech rates with aging have been well documented. One possible reason is the difficulty of controlling respiration during speech production (Linville, 1996). Evidence that supports such an argument in this thesis is the production of long pauses in

Table 6.26: Mann–Whitney U-test to compare male PD patients, elderly healthy (EHC), and young healthy (YHC) speakers considering speech prosody features extracted from the reading of the text. The values highlighted in bold indicate significant differences.

Parameter	Feature	PD vs. EHC			EHC vs. YHC			PD vs. YHC		
		U-test	p-value	E. size	U-test	p-value	E. size	U-test	p-value	E. size
Pitch	meanF0	299	0.801	0.056	**452**	**<0.01**	**0.906**	**465**	**<0.01**	**0.775**
	stdF0	**183**	**<0.01**	**0.291**	**528**	**<0.001**	**1.314**	414	0.050	0.672
Loudness	meanSPL	320	0.892	0.067	376	0.222	0.112	369	0.277	0.016
	stdSPL	314	0.985	0.037	265	0.362	0.006	278	0.509	0.035
Duration	dVoiced	**473**	**<0.01**	**1.050**	**481**	**<0.01**	**1.092**	**565**	**<0.001**	**1.540**
	dUnvoiced	341	0.587	0.336	373	0.244	0.325	386	0.157	0.554
	dPause	356	0.404	0.314	**453**	**<0.01**	**0.696**	**491**	**<0.01**	**0.991**
	dSpeech	340	0.600	0.002	**444**	**<0.05**	**0.734**	**455**	**<0.01**	**0.809**
Ratio	rVoiced	**182**	**<0.05**	**0.829**	**165**	**<0.01**	**0.827**	**84**	**<0.001**	**1.578**
	rUnvoiced	**163**	**<0.01**	**0.858**	**141**	**<0.01**	**0.988**	**58**	**<0.001**	**1.820**
	rPause	289	0.655	0.106	**174**	**<0.01**	**0.776**	**160**	**<0.01**	**0.846**
	rSpeech	287	0.628	0.109	**181**	**<0.05**	**0.763**	**142**	**<0.01**	**0.937**
Timing	nPVI − Con	351	0.461	0.339	332	0.712	0.012	371	0.260	0.408
	nPVI − Vow	**488**	**<0.01**	**1.008**	336	0.655	0.151	**507**	**<0.001**	**1.236**

U-test: Mann-Whitney U statistic. **E. size**: Effect size. **nPVI − Con**: Consonant timing. **nPVI − Vow**: Vowel timing.

elderly speakers (PD/EHC). However, this does not explain why PD patients have a higher duration variability in the production of vowels ($nPVI - Vow$) compared to the healthy speakers (EHC/YHC). It seems that this feature is more related to the patients' difficulties in controlling the movement of the vocal folds rather than problems controlling respiration.

Results: Phonemic analysis

Phoneme precision is evaluated by means of posterior probabilities. Table 6.27 shows the mean and standard deviation values obtained for PD patients, elderly, and young healthy speakers. Many phonemic features (e.g., palatal, postalveolar) for the DDK task are zero or close to zero. The reason is that only stop sounds and vowels are produced in this task. Figure 6.22 shows the radar plots with the average phoneme probabilities computed for each group. Tables 6.28 and 6.29 shows the results of the statistical analysis. In general, the phoneme precision of the elderly speakers (PD and EHC) was lower than young speakers. In the reading task, PD patients produced lower articulation precision than the

Table 6.27: Mean and standard deviation (Avg ± Std) values for phoneme precision features from PD patients, elderly healthy (EHC), and young healthy (YHC) speakers

Dimension	Features	Read text PD	Read text EHC	Read text YHC	DDK PD	DDK EHC	DDK YHC
Manner	Stop	0.73 ± 0.08	0.80 ± 0.05	0.83 ± 0.05	0.82 ± 0.09	0.91 ± 0.05	0.94 ± 0.04
	Nasal	0.71 ± 0.09	0.76 ± 0.08	0.85 ± 0.07	0.52 ± 0.21	0.42 ± 0.26	0.04 ± 0.15
	Trill	0.64 ± 0.13	0.70 ± 0.12	0.78 ± 0.09	0.37 ± 0.28	0.31 ± 0.26	0.20 ± 0.26
	Fricative	0.74 ± 0.13	0.82 ± 0.07	0.88 ± 0.06	0.35 ± 0.28	0.26 ± 0.31	0.27 ± 0.34
	Approximant	0.66 ± 0.21	0.71 ± 0.14	0.75 ± 0.11	0.03 ± 0.10	0.03 ± 0.12	0.00 ± 0.00
	Lateral	0.70 ± 0.10	0.77 ± 0.07	0.85 ± 0.08	0.25 ± 0.26	0.05 ± 0.15	0.02 ± 0.11
	Vowel	0.91 ± 0.05	0.95 ± 0.03	0.95 ± 0.02	0.93 ± 0.04	0.96 ± 0.03	0.99 ± 0.02
Place	Labial	0.71 ± 0.09	0.8 ± 0.07	0.83 ± 0.06	0.76 ± 0.15	0.87 ± 0.08	0.94 ± 0.05
	Alveolar	0.75 ± 0.07	0.82 ± 0.06	0.86 ± 0.04	0.71 ± 0.10	0.80 ± 0.10	0.92 ± 0.07
	Velar	0.59 ± 0.16	0.69 ± 0.11	0.76 ± 0.11	0.73 ± 0.19	0.89 ± 0.09	0.92 ± 0.08
	Palatal	0.74 ± 0.14	0.81 ± 0.12	0.85 ± 0.10	0.05 ± 0.16	0.03 ± 0.12	0.00 ± 0.00
	Postalveolar	0.45 ± 0.37	0.60 ± 0.37	0.88 ± 0.19	0.02 ± 0.11	0.00 ± 0.00	0.00 ± 0.00
	Central	0.80 ± 0.10	0.89 ± 0.07	0.89 ± 0.06	0.84 ± 0.11	0.91 ± 0.08	0.97 ± 0.02
	Front	0.81 ± 0.07	0.87 ± 0.05	0.88 ± 0.05	0.43 ± 0.25	0.27 ± 0.27	0.04 ± 0.14
	Back	0.76 ± 0.09	0.85 ± 0.06	0.83 ± 0.07	0.35 ± 0.28	0.22 ± 0.30	0.14 ± 0.28
Voicing	Voiceless	0.78 ± 0.07	0.84 ± 0.05	0.87 ± 0.04	0.85 ± 0.07	0.92 ± 0.04	0.96 ± 0.03
	Voiced	0.97 ± 0.02	0.99 ± 0.01	0.98 ± 0.02	0.99 ± 0.02	0.99 ± 0.01	0.99 ± 0.01

young speakers in all classes except for the approximants (/j/) and the EHC produced lower phoneme probabilities in stop (/p/, /t/), nasal (/m/, /n/), fricative (/f/), lateral (/l/), alveolar (/t/, /n/), velar (/k/, /g/), and postalveolar (/ʃ/) sounds. In the case of /pa-ta-ka/, elderly speakers produced lower phoneme precision than the young speakers in almost all classes except for voiced sounds. This result can be explained considering the radar plots in Figure 6.22 (Manner-

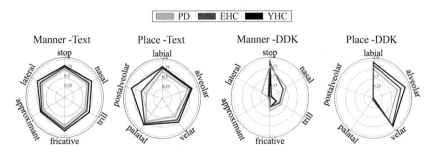

Figure 6.22: *Radar plots of the phoneme precision (*MaxPh*) in the reading task and the repetition of /pa-ta-ka/ (DDK) by PD patients, elderly (EHC) and young (YHC) healthy speakers*

DDK). In the figure, elderly speakers appear to have produced nasal, trill, and lateral sounds during the DDK task. The system misclassified some speech segments into phonemes that should not be in the signal (only stops and vowels are produced during this speech task). Thus, the model is confident that such speech segments are voiced sounds but is not able to identify if those sounds are vowels of voiced consonants. Furthermore, rather than an error of the system, this phenomenon appears to be related to articulation imprecision due to aging and PD. For instance, in the DDK task, elderly speakers have a high probability of nasal sounds. However, the young speakers have a probability close to zero for nasals, which indicates that the system is more confident in its prediction for the YHC group, probably due to higher precision in phoneme articulation. Low phoneme precision due to aging may be related to alterations in the temporal properties of the sounds (Benjamin, 1982). In the DDK task, acoustic properties of stop sounds may have been removed due to a prolongation of the preceding vowel, resulting in different phenomena such as voicing or consonant weakening (See Section 6.1.2). Figure 6.23 shows the bar diagrams of the average duration of consonants and vowels produced by the speakers of the three groups. In both cases, the elderly speakers produced longer vowels than the young speakers. In the case of the DDK, the difference in consonant duration is more evident, which may indicate that the elderly speakers remove the silence region during closure during this task.

Results: Regression analysis

The features previously analyzed are considered for the prediction of age. In the case of the phonemic features, the average duration durPH, the phoneme rate, and the phoneme log-likelihood (LLRPost) are also considered to train the SVR. Table 6.30 shows the results. Phonemic features seem to be suitable for capturing speech disorders caused by PD and changes related to aging. Once again, the DDK task proves to be suitable for detecting changes in speech, not only due to PD but also for changes caused by aging. The conclusions of this section should be taken carefully. One aspect not addressed in this thesis is

184

Table 6.28: Mann–Whitney U-test to compare male PD patients, elderly healthy (EHC), and young healthy (YHC) speakers considering phonetic features extracted from the reading of the text. The values highlighted in bold indicate significant differences.

Dimension	Features	Phonetic - Read text								
		PD vs. EHC			EHC vs. YHC			PD vs. YHC		
		U-test	p-value	E. size	U-test	p-value	E. size	U-test	p-value	E. size
Manner	Stop	669	<0.001	0.920	746	<0.01	0.667	389	<0.001	1.464
	Nasal	810	<0.01	0.587	549	<0.001	1.093	298	<0.001	1.656
	Trill	847	<0.01	0.485	792	<0.01	0.713	481	<0.001	1.225
	Fricative	715	<0.001	0.805	684	<0.001	0.851	397	<0.001	1.406
	Approximant	1060	0.191	0.322	1034	0.137	0.291	925	<0.05	0.564
	Lateral	711	<0.001	0.776	499	<0.001	1.184	278	<0.001	1.756
	Vowel	551	<0.001	1.004	1159	0.533	0.176	471	<0.001	1.157
Place	Labial	545	<0.001	1.069	988	0.071	0.437	352	<0.001	1.529
	Alveolar	559	<0.001	1.056	784	<0.01	0.669	269	<0.001	1.759
	Velar	696	<0.001	0.741	836	<0.01	0.602	412	<0.001	1.238
	Palatal	879	<0.05	0.499	976	0.059	0.412	676	<0.001	0.890
	Postalveolar	948	<0.05	0.403	655	<0.001	0.927	384	<0.001	1.438
	Central	540	<0.001	1.095	1327	0.598	0.043	528	<0.001	1.134
	Front	613	<0.001	0.943	1177	0.617	0.114	563	<0.001	1.039
	Back	482	<0.001	1.163	1473	0.125	0.262	632	<0.001	0.917
Voicing	Voiceless	636	<0.001	0.922	726	<0.001	0.831	264	<0.001	1.682
	Voiced	858	<0.01	0.637	1425	0.229	0.258	1005	0.092	0.428

U-test: Mann-Whitney U statistic. E. size: Effect size.

the possible influence of the training set in the phoneme recognition model. For instance, what would happen if the majority of the speakers used for training were elderly people? Would the speech of the young speakers then appear to be "disordered" to the model? Certainly, bias in this kind of model exists, which

Table 6.29: Mann–Whitney U-test to compare male PD patients, elderly healthy (EHC), and young healthy (YHC) speakers considering phonetic features extracted from the /pa-ta-ka/ task. The values highlighted in bold indicate significant differences.

Dimension	Features	Phonetic - /pa-ta-ka/								
		PD vs. EHC			EHC vs. YHC			PD vs. YHC		
		U-test	p-value	E. size	U-test	p-value	E. size	U-test	p-value	E. size
Manner	Stop	472	<0.001	1.234	708	<0.001	0.727	222	<0.001	1.760
	Vowel	688	<0.001	0.728	468	<0.001	0.940	166	<0.001	1.654
Place	Labial	599	<0.001	0.843	552	<0.001	1.017	172	<0.001	1.527
	Alveolar	633	<0.001	0.894	456	<0.001	1.283	148	<0.001	2.320
	Velar	479	<0.001	1.042	944	<0.05	0.372	297	<0.001	1.263
Voicing	Voiceless	508	<0.001	1.150	608	<0.001	0.953	192	<0.001	1.913
	Voiced	1217	0.823	0.320	1071	0.218	0.130	1049	0.167	0.214

U-test: Mann-Whitney U statistic. E. size: Effect size.

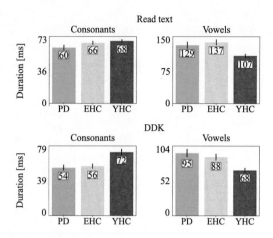

Figure 6.23: *Bar plots with the average duration of consonants and vowels measured in the read text (Top) and DDK (bottom) tasks. The numbers inside the bars indicate the average duration for each group.*

should be addressed to avoid wrong conclusions. Nevertheless, the results appear to be consistent with the hypothesis that changes in speech due to aging can be discriminated from changes due to a clinical condition such as PD.

Table 6.30: Estimation of the age of PD, EHC, and YHC. C and ϵ are the final parameters selected to test the performance of the SVR.

Task	Feat ID	Features	r	p-value	ρ	p-value	C	ϵ
Vowel	V1	Phonation	0.44	<0.001	0.42	<0.001	10	10
	V2	Articulation vowel	0.33	<0.001	0.30	<0.001	1	10
Read text	R1	Prosody	0.64	<0.001	0.61	<0.001	10	10
	R2	Phonemic Manner	0.76	<0.001	0.73	<0.001	1	10
	R3	Phonemic Place	0.74	<0.001	0.70	<0.001	1	1
	R4	Phonemic Voicing	0.77	<0.001	0.73	<0.001	10	10
	R5	R2+R3+R4	0.78	<0.001	0.71	<0.001	1	1
DDK	D1	Phonemic Manner	0.83	<0.001	0.76	<0.001	10	10
	D2	Phonemic Place	0.75	<0.001	0.69	<0.001	1	10
	D3	Phonemic Voicing	0.83	<0.001	0.75	<0.001	10	10
	D4	D1+D2+D3	0.83	<0.001	0.75	<0.001	1	10
Fusion	**F1**	**R5+D4**	**0.86**	**<0.001**	**0.76**	**<0.001**	**0.1**	**10**
	F2	V1+V2+R1+R5+D4	0.84	<0.001	0.76	<0.001	0.1	10

Fusion: Early fusion of features. r: Pearson's correlation coefficient. ρ: Spearman's correlation coefficient.

Conclusions

Aging influences phonation, articulation, and prosody aspects of speech. Although it is possible to capture differences between healthy elderly and young speakers, the exact cause of deviations in speech is unclear due to the lack of information about the physiological and anatomical changes produced by the normal aging process. Furthermore, it is not possible to demonstrate (with the data considered here) how these biological processes affect males and females. For instance, Linville (1996) reviewed different studies addressing the incidence of glottal gaps with aging as a result of changes in the laryngeal mechanism, which might account for differences in phonation intensity. In those studies, laryngoscopy and video stroboscopy data reported a higher incidence of glottal gaps in elderly male speakers compared to young men. In the case of the female speakers, both elderly and young speakers showed frequent glottal gaps. However, the configuration of the gaps seems to be different, e.g., anterior gaps for elderly females and posterior chinks for young females. Nevertheless, it was shown that for the speakers considered in this study, the elderly speakers exhibited deviations in some parameters such as F0, vowel space area, duration and ratio of voiced sounds and pauses, and phonemic articulation precision. Such deviations were even higher for PD patients. Furthermore, regression analysis showed the suitability of these features (and speech tasks) to obtain an estimate of the age of a person.

Another aspect not addressed in this thesis is the influence of such changes in automatic recognition systems. Nowadays, smartphones and some home devices contain virtual assistant technology that relies on automatic speech recognition to consult about the weather, get the news, and make internet searches. Here, it was shown that the phonemic precision was lower even for healthy elderly speakers. Thus, future work should consider analyzing the influence of phoneme imprecision in virtual assistant technology.

6.5   Smartphone-based applications for health care

One of the contributions of this thesis was the participation in the development of two Android applications for health care: Apkinson and CITA.

6.5.1   Apkinson

Apkinson (Orozco-Arroyave et al., 2020)[3] is an open-source application designed for motor evaluation and monitoring of PD patients. The application includes numerous daily exercises to capture gait, hand movement, dexterity, facial expression, and speech data. Apkinson was developed in a joint project between the University of Antioquia (Colombia) and the Friedrich-Alexander University of Erlangen-Nürnberg (Germany).

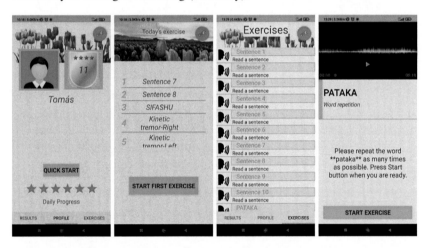

Figure 6.24: *Screenshots taken from Apkinson.*

Aim: To perform acoustic analysis on speech data captured with Apkinson.

---

[3]https://bit.ly/3iM03lu

188

Hypothesis

- It is possible to use smartphone applications to evaluate the speech production of PD patients.

- The smartphone used to capture data has an influence on the acoustic analysis.

Data

Speech recordings from 37 PD patients (17 females) and 37 healthy speakers (17 females) were considered for the experiments (Section 5.1.4). The recordings were captured in at the home of the speakers, the workplace, and in the Parkinson's foundation. Different smartphones were used to capture the data. In the case of the patients, 30 of the of the 7 patients were recorded with the same smartphone. For the healthy speakers, 10 different devices were used to capture the data. In order to analyze the influence of the microphone in the acoustic analysis, two standard speech tasks were considered: the repetition of /pa-ta-ka/ and the sustained phonation of the vowels /a/, /i/, and /u/.

Methods

Phonation and vowel articulation analyses were performed from the sustained phonation of the vowels /a/, /i/, and /u/. Articulation was also analyzed considering the onset/offset transitions extracted from the repetition of /pa-ta-ka/. Phonemic analysis was also performed in the DDK task by computing the average of the maximum phoneme posterior probability ($MaxPost$) of the relevant voicing, manner, and place of articulation phonemes i.e., stop, vowel, labial, alveolar, velar, voiced, and voiceless. Since the smartphone data was captured in different acoustic conditions, the noise reduction system presented by (Schröter et al., 2020), was used on all of the recordings to reduce the variability in the acoustic conditions. Automatic classification with a radial basis function SVM was considered for further analysis. The margin C and

189

kernel γ parameters are optimized through a grid search with $10^{-4} < C < 10^4$ and $10^{-4} < \gamma < 10^4$. The parameters are optimized as follows:

1. The Leave-One-Speaker-Out (LOSO) strategy was considered to train and test the model.

2. An internal 9-fold cross validation strategy is used to select the best set of parameters for testing.

3. After evaluating every fold, the medians of the resulting C and γ parameters are computed and LOSO was performed again with fixed parameters.

4. The performance of the bi-class SVM is evaluated using the accuracy, sensitivity, specificity, and AUC.

Results

The results of the automatic classification of PD patients vs. healthy speakers (with and without denoising) are reported in Table 6.31. The highest classifica-

Table 6.31: Results for automatic classification of PD patients and HC speakers using Apkinson's speech data. **Original:** Original speech recordings. **Denoising:** Denoised speech recordings.

Task	Feat ID	Features	Original				Denoising			
			Acc	Sen	Spe	AUC	Acc	Sen	Spe	AUC
Vowel	V1	Phonation	59	46	73	0.64	69	68	70	0.77
	V2	Articulation Vowel	59	30	89	0.60	64	62	65	0.65
	V3	V1+V2	62	43	81	0.64	70	78	62	0.71
DDK	D1	Articulation On	85	81	89	0.91	77	76	78	0.83
	D2	Articulation Off	81	81	81	0.83	61	62	59	0.71
	D3	Phonemic Manner	64	65	62	0.70	73	59	86	0.73
	D4	Phonemic Place	62	73	51	0.61	65	59	70	0.66
	D5	Phonemic Voicing	41	38	43	0.38	72	62	81	0.73
	D6	D3+D4+D5	66	76	57	0.66	73	81	65	0.72

Acc: Accuracy[%]. **Sen:** Sensitivity[%]. **Spe:** Specificity[%]. **AUC:** Area under the ROC curve.

tion performances were obtained using the original recordings and the features extracted from onset/offset transitions (filterbank analysis). However, using the same features, the performance decreases considerably when the denoised

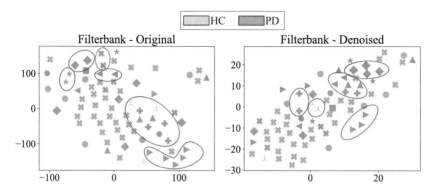

Figure 6.25: *Filterbank features (onset/offset transitions) distribution using t-SNE. Left: original speech recordings. Right: Denoised speech recordings. The shape of the markers represent the type of smartphone. The red circles indicate clusters formed by features extracted from the same device.*

signals are considered. On the contrary, the performance of the SVM improved when phonation, vowel articulation, and phonemic features were extracted from the denoised signals. The results indicate that acoustic analysis is affected by factors not related to the disease: noise and channel (microphone/smartphone). To analyze the influence of different devices in the recordings, the t-Distributed Stochastic Neighbor Embedding (t-SNE) algorithm was applied to the filterbank features extracted from the onset/offset transition (Van der Maaten and Hinton, 2008). Figure 6.25 shows the resulting t-SNE plots. The color of the markers represents the group of speakers (blue for PD and grey for HC), and the shape represents the type of smartphone. For instance, the smartphone represented by the cross symbol "**X**" (Figure 6.25) was used to capture the data of most patients and four of the healthy speakers. In the figure, it can be observed that there are small clusters formed even after noise reduction, which indicates that filterbank features are sensitive to channel conditions, i.e., the microphone of the device.

Figure 6.26 shows the triangular Vowel Space Areas (tVSA) and the radar plots obtained for patients and healthy controls using the original recordings and the denoised signals. In general, the healthy speakers have a higher tVSA and

191

phoneme posterior probabilities than the PD patients, which is consistent with the results obtained in previous sections of this thesis. Additionally, the vowel space area of the patients appears to have decreased after applying denoising, which indicates that the background noise influences formants; however, based on the results reported in Table 6.31, the type of device appears to have almost no influence on the tVSA.

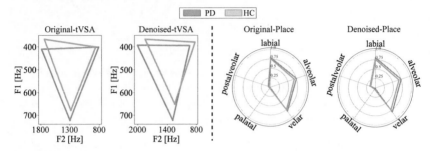

Figure 6.26: *Left: tVSA plots obtained from the sustained phonation tasks. Right: radar plots of the phoneme posterior probabilities of the place of articulation from the DDK task.*

6.5.2 Cochlear Implant Testing App - CITA

CITA (Popp, 2021)[4] is an open-source Android application developed to monitor speech perception and production of people with hearing loss. Hearing is evaluated using two different minimal pairs exercises: in the first one, the user has to repeat the word that he/she hears from the loudspeakers of the device. In the second one, four words are displayed in the screen of the phone. Then, one of them is reproduced trough the loudspeakers and the user should identify the correct one. Speech is evaluated using the reading of sentences, words, description of a picture, and the repetition of /pa-ta-ka/. Part of the source code of CITA is based on Apkinson.

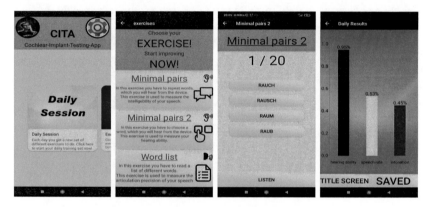

Figure 6.27: *Screenshots taken from CITA.*

Aim: To perform acoustic analysis on speech data captured with CITA.

Hypothesis

- It is possible to use smartphone applications to evaluate the speech production of CI users.

[4]https://bit.ly/3oX4SJm

193

Data

Due to the COVID-19 pandemic, only one CI user was recruited for data collection with CITA. The patient is a 50-year-old male which used CITA in four occasions in one month. The time between consecutive sessions were 1, 4, and 13 days. The baseline used for comparison is the 60 CI users (20 prelingual, 40 postlinguals) and 20 NH German native speakers described in Section 5.2.2. The speech task considered was the reading of a subset from the PLAKSS test (See Appendix A.2.3). Not all words were included due to the strategy used in CITA to capture speech: every day, a random set of 10 words are included in the daily evaluation for the user to read. Thus, only the following words were used to compare the CI users with the NH speakers. The subset used in the four sessions were:

- Day 1 (Session 1): Brief, Baum, Springt, Strumpf, Zange, Schlange, Frosch, Vogel, Haus, Fisch.

- Day 2 (Session 2): Anker, Eichhoernchen, Schiff, Unfall, Stuhl, Schuh, Schluessel, Spinne, Schornstein, Bank.

- Day 6 (Session 3): Kaputt, Fisch, Eichhoernchen, Vogel, Stuhl, Spritze, Schlange, Eimer, Schwein, Auto.

- Day 17 (Session 4): Erdbeere, Schiff, Hase, Heizung, Stuhl, Schlange, Schluessel, Spinne, Sonne, Gras.

Methods

Phoneme analysis was performed by computing the average of the maximum phoneme posterior probability (MaxPh) from the set of words. Due to the limited amount of data, no statistical tests nor automatic classification methods were considered in this section. Thus, only radar plots were used for analysis.

Results

Figure 6.28 shows the radar plots of the phoneme posterior probabilities from the manner and place of articulation. For the place of articulation, the CITA user has a higher posterior probability than the baseline CI users and lower than the NH speakers. However, the results obtained for the manner of articulation indicate that the CITA user produces a similar phoneme precision than the NH speakers, except for trills. By listening to the recordings, it was observed that the CITA user puts more emphasis on the /r/ sound than most of the speakers in the baseline (NH speakers and CI users). One possible explanation for this is the dialect. The baseline speakers were recruited in Munich (Southern Bavaria), whereas the CITA user was recruited from Nurnberg (Northern Bavaria), a region commonly known in Germany to "roll the /r/" more often. This thesis does not intend to address the implications of the different dialects in automatic speech recognition systems; however, based on the results, it seems that certain dialects may appear to sound "pathologic" when performing automatic analysis with speakers from different regions.

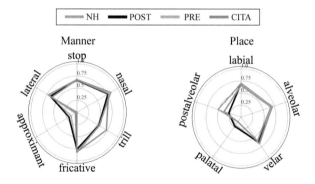

Figure 6.28: *Radar plots of the average maximum phoneme posterior probabilities computed from NH speakers, CI users (POST/PRE) and a CITA user.*

Conclusions (Apkinson and CITA)

Collecting data with a smartphone allows monitoring the progression of the speech symptoms. However, many of the acoustic features are affected by the acoustic conditions of the recordings. For instance, the filterbank features extracted from the onset/offset transitions are sensitive to the device used to capture the data and background noise. These results are not surprising, considering that MFCCs and GFCCs are features used to obtain a compressed spectrum representation. However, features such as the formant frequencies (used to construct the tVSA) and the phoneme posterior probabilities appeared to be more influenced by background noise. Thus, it is recommended to avoid features based on spectral representations when the acoustic conditions of the recordings are highly variable. Additionally, it is necessary to include a pre-processing stage to reduce the background noise and normalize the recordings' acoustic conditions. Future work should also focus on the multimodal analysis using the data captured with the smartphone to evaluate general motor impairments of the PD patients and the hearing status of the CI users. Additionally, it is necessary to evaluate the sensibility of different feature sets to the variable conditions of the data capture with different devices. One aspect not considered here is the influence of the strategy used for data collection in the acoustic analysis. This might be an issue when a patient does not receive clear instructions on how to perform every exercise or when the exercise becomes repetitive and thus influencing the outcome of the automatic evaluation.

Chapter 7

Summary

This thesis addressed the automatic acoustic analysis of speech characteristics resulting from Parkinson's disease (PD), hearing loss, and natural aging. Furthermore, this work gives an outlook to the suitability of data collected from smartphones for healthcare applications. The main motivation of this thesis is to show machine learning and speech processing techniques suitable for developing technology to support the clinical evaluation and the speech symptoms. The main finding of this work are summarized in the following subsections

7.1 Automatic methods for speech analysis

In this work, speech production was evaluated considering four aspects: phonation, articulation, prosody, and phonemic production. The speech tasks considered include a monologue, reading words, texts, and sentences, and the sequential repetition of /pa-ta-ka/. Phonation analysis was considered to capture voice production problems associated with abnormal vibration of the vocal folds during the sustained phonation of vowels. The set of phonation parameters used were pitch, loudness, and perturbation. Vowel articulation was used to measure the precision of movements graphically demonstrate on triangular vowel space areas. Articulation in the continuous speech was considered to detect problems to start or stop the movement of the vocal folds using the

197

onset and offset transitions. Prosody analysis is performed using pitch, loudness, duration, and timing parameters that were computed from continuous speech tasks. Finally, phonemic analysis was considered to evaluate precision, prolongation of speech sounds, phoneme rate, and Voice Onset Time (VOT).

For phonemic analysis, an RNN-based model was trained to automatically classify phonemes grouped according to three dimensions: voicing, manner, and place of articulation. Two automatic phoneme recognition systems were trained in German and Spanish. For the model trained with German speech recordings, the average classification performance was an F1-score of 0.85. For the model trained in Spanish, the average performance was F1-score=0.77. The performance of the German model was higher than the Spanish model because the phonetic transcriptions for German were manually corrected. In contrast, for the Spanish data, the phonetic transcriptions were obtained with forced alignment using an automatic speech recognition system. It was observed that using the German model as for weight initialization improved the accuracy of the Spanish model. It was also shown that the best way to use the pre-trained German model for parameter initialization is to train the Spanish model until the F1-score drops and not until the early stopping criterion is met. The output of the trained models is used analysis of speech production: the labels predicted were used to measure the average phoneme duration and rate and the probabilities of occurrence of the predicted phonemes were used to measure the phoneme articulation precision, i.e., the closer is the probability to 1, the better is the pronunciation.

A recurrent network was also considered for automatic detection of VOT in voiceless stop sounds produced during the rapid repetition of /pa-ta-ka/. Speech data from PD patients and healthy controls was considered to observe the influence of dysarthric speech on the model's performance. Automatic detection for VOT was possible with F1-scores of up to 0.78 for healthy speakers and 0.73 for PD patients. On average, the predictions deviated by 3.8 ms for healthy speakers and 5.6 ms for PD patients. The lower performance for PD patients was primarily caused by the consonant weakening phenomenon, which results from difficulties in controlling the vocal folds' movement when alternating from vowels to voiceless stop sounds. Although this phenomenon was also found in healthy speakers, the PD patients produced more weakened consonants. Future work should consider the detection of VOT in continuous speech tasks to analyze other acoustic phenomena. One of the limitations in this thesis is the relatively low number of recordings considered for training. Data augmentation techniques were considered to increase the sample size. However, the model's performance was better using noisy versions of the original signals. One reason might be that the noise component appears to remove part of the acoustic property that characterizes the stop consonants resulting in two different situations: On the one hand, the reduced phoneme precision of the patients combined with the Gaussian noise affects the model's performance to predict the correct sequence of consonants. On the other hand, the noise component improves the detection of vowels' onset, leading to higher F1-scores for the HC because they do not produce as many misarticulations as the patients, e.g., weakened consonants. Another limitation is that speech recordings of CI users were not included for automatic detection of VOT because the manual annotations were not available.

7.2 Parkinson's disease patients

Speech disorders resulting from PD were analyzed with three main tasks: (1) automatic classification of patients vs. healthy speakers, (2) regression analysis to predict the dysarthria level and neurological state, and (3) speaker embeddings to analyze the progression of the speech symptoms over time. The results showed that combining the information of different features sets and speech tasks improved the performance of automatic methods to detect disordered speech in PD patients. For the classification task, the highest performance (Accuracy: 84 %) was obtained with the combination of phonation, vowel articulation, offset transitions (monologue), and phonemic features (monologue and /pa-ta-ka/). For the regression analysis, two tasks were addressed: the prediction of the mFDA (dysarthria level) and the MDS-UPDRS-III (neurological state). The highest correlation between the predicted mFDA and the target scores was obtained with the combination of features from reading (phonemic), DDK (phonemic), and sustained phonation of vowels (Pearson's r = 0.80; Spearman's $\rho = 0.78$). In the case of the neurological state, the combination of articulation and phonemic features resulted in a better prediction of the MDS-UPDRS-III (Pearson's r = 0.40; Spearman's $\rho = 0.53$). The differences in the performances can be explained considering that the mFDA is a scale entirely focused on evaluating speech impairments. On the contrary, the MDS-UPDRS-III only includes speech in 1 item from 33. Thus, future work should consider the multimodal analysis of PD patients using other bio-signals such as writing, movement of the limbs, gait, among others. Nevertheless, automatic speech analysis shows a close relationship to the general clinical score.

The progression of speech symptoms of seven PD patients was evaluated considering recordings captured in the short-term (4 months) and long-term (5 years). The mFDA scores of the patients were predicted for every speech recording. For this, speaker embeddings, which are commonly used in speaker recognition and verification tasks, were combined with phonation, articulation, prosody, and phonemic features. Overall, it was possible to capture the progression of the speech symptoms over time. The highest results was obtained when the embeddings were combined with phonemic features extracted from /pa-ta-ka/ (Pearson's r = 0.75; Spearman's $\rho = 0.73$) indicating that it is possible to monitor the speech symptoms using automatic methods. However, this work did not consider other aspects such as medication intake, which may help to understand the short-term (during the day or week) and long-term (during the month or year) motor fluctuations. Another aspect that was not considered is the influence of the interviewer in the recording of the speech protocol. For instance, it might be the case that the attitude of one of the patients towards an interviewer resulted in a more familiar conversation during the monologue task or the interviewer with more experience will know when certain tasks were successful.

7.3 Cochlear implant users

Phonemic analysis was performed to evaluate the influence of the duration and onset of deafness in speech production. The duration of deafness refers to the duration of time between the onset of deafness and implantation: for a long duration, it was more than two years, and for a short duration, it was less than two years. The onset of deafness refers to whether the hearing loss occurred before (prelingual) or after (postlingual) the acquisition of spoken language. For automatic analysis, phoneme precision was quantified using the posterior probabilities computed from the RNN trained in German. The probabilities were computed from a list of 97 words containing every phoneme in different positions within the words (PLAKSS test). Compared to the Normal Hearing (NH) speakers, CI users produced velar (like /k/), palatal (/j/), and postalveolar (/ʃ/) sounds with lower precision (low posterior probability). Furthermore, there was a significant difference (p-value<0.05) in the production of postalveolar sounds; particularly, postlingually deafened CI users with long and short duration of deafness produce higher phoneme posterior probabilities than the prelingually deafened CI users. Deviations in the production of postalveolar sounds such as /ʃ/ have been linked to a limited spectral resolution of the implant in higher frequencies bands; thus, CI users shift the production of the sibilant sounds into the frequency range perceived by them. This frequency shift may also explain why the difference is more considerable between postlingually and prelingually deafened CI users, since the latter lost their hearing before speech acquisition and thus have always heard a "shifted" version of these sounds. On the contrary, postlingual CI users had heard the standard way to produce the sound before losing their hearing, but speech perception (and production) may have changed over time due to hearing loss and the device. This result reflects the role of auditory feedback in speech production. However, to validate this hypothesis, hearing status and data from the implant should be considered together with the speech analysis. The phonemic analysis appear to be suitability to identify which sounds are the most difficult for the CI users to produce. Thus, speech therapy can be more personalized by targeting these particular phonemes. Additionally, articulation, prosody, and phonemic analyses were performed to show that cochlear implant users present altered speech production even after hearing rehabilitation. For this, speech recordings of postlingually deafened adults were considered evaluated when reading a standard text. For speech prosody, CI users produced higher variability in the duration of vowels/consonants and read the text with a slower voiced rate than the NH speakers. On the one hand, male CI users produced longer voiced segments resulting in a slower voiced rate. On the other hand, a slow voiced rate in females was due to a prolongation of pauses and speech segments within the text. Future work should analyze if speech prosody deficits have a negative impact in the expression of emotions and the intended linguistic information provided, such as word focus and sentence stress to distinguish between questions and statements and phrase boundary marking. On the contrary, a slow speaking rate may positively impact overall intelligibility. However, this may not be the case for the CI users considered in this study. The phonemic analysis showed that CI users produced lower phoneme precision even for "visible" phonemes when reading a text. Furthermore, automatic classification of CI users vs. healthy speakers using onset/offset transitions showed that there are difficulties of the patients to start/stop movements like the vibration of the vocal folds. Some limitations include the lack of longitudinal data to monitor speech production over time. Additionally, specifics about the hearing state of the patients, ear side of implantation, insertion depth, active electrodes, manufacturer, filter settings of the input filters, and duration of CI usage should be taken into consideration, as well as possible influences on the acoustic parameters of speech production.

7.4 Aging and speech

The influence of aging in speech production was evaluated in the context of PD. For this, phonation, articulation, prosody, and phonemic analyses were performed in a group of PD patients, healthy elderly (EHC), and young speakers

(YHC). Phonation analysis appears to account more for the presence of PD rather than changes caused by aging (e.g., only the average SPL was significantly lower in females from the EHC group compared with young speakers: p-value<0.05). However, for acoustic features such as F0 and SPL, the voice of the elderly tends to be different from young speakers. Vowel articulation analysis revealed that the vowel space of the male elderly speakers (PD and EHC) has a smaller area than the young speakers, which indicates a reduction in the articulatory movements. While phonation features appear to be more suitable for discriminating between female PD patients and healthy speakers, the vowel space area highlights deficits in male PD patients. However, the exact cause of these results is unclear due to the lack of information about the physiological and anatomical changes produced by the normal aging process. The results of the prosody analysis showed that young speakers have a higher ratio of voiced, unvoiced, and pause segments than the elderly speakers (PD and EHC), which is associated with faster reading. Furthermore, PD patients produced longer pause segments than the healthy controls (EHC/YHC), and there was a tendency from the patients to produce higher vowel duration variability (nPVI − Vow). Also, male elderly speakers produced higher F0 values than the YHC group; however, PD patients exhibited higher F0 values than the age-matched healthy speakers. In the case of the duration of voiced sounds, male PD patients produced longer segments, followed by the healthy elderly controls and young speakers. However, for female speakers, there was no significant difference between PD patients and elderly healthy speakers. Phonemic analysis was performed in the reading and /pa-ta-ka/ tasks. In general, the phoneme precision of the elderly speakers (PD and EHC) was lower than young speakers. PD patients and healthy elderly speakers produced lower posterior probabilities than the young speakers in most phonemes. Low phoneme precision due to aging may be related to alterations in the temporal properties of the sounds, such as the consonant weakening phenomena observed in the automatic detection of VOT. Unfortunately, in this thesis, there was not sufficient data to analyze the aging process in the context of hearing loss. Future work should consider speech recordings of elderly CI users, age-matched healthy speakers, and young speakers to analyze phonation, articulation, prosody, and phonemic production.

7.5 Smartphone-based applications for health care

Smartphones are suitable to monitor the progression of speech symptoms. The acoustic analysis does not have to be done necessarily on the device. However, there is always the possibility of exporting audio files to a cloud service and performing a better pre-processing of the data. One of the main limitations is the variability in the acoustic conditions of the data captured with smartphones. It was shown that, for instance, the filterbank features extracted from the onset/offset transitions are sensitive to the device used to capture the data and to the background noise. The reason is that MFCCs and GFCCs are features used to obtain a compressed spectrum representation; thus, it is recommended to avoid features based on spectral representations when the acoustic conditions of the recordings are highly variable. Additionally, features such as the formant frequencies (used to construct the tVSA) and the phoneme posterior probabilities appeared to be affected by the background noise; however, using a denoising technique helped reduce its influence. Future work should also focus on the multimodal analysis using the data captured with the smartphone to evaluate general motor impairments of the PD patients and the hearing status of the CI users. Additionally, it is necessary to develop strategies for data collection that allow capturing data without influencing the patient's behavior. Some of them may learn the speech task over time, and measurements could be biased by the users' adaptability to the task, rather than detecting the progression or improvement of the speech disorder. Thus, data should be captured so that it is suitable for speech assessment, and at the same time, the user must not be aware of what kind of task is being evaluated.

Appendices

Appendix A

Speech tasks

A.1 Spanish speech protocol

A.1.1 Vowel phonation

The speakers were asked to produced the Spanish vowels in a sustained manner: /a/, /e/, /i/, /o/, /u/.

A.1.2 Sentences

The participants were asked to read the following sentences

- Rosita Niño, que pinta bien, donó sus cuadros ayer.

- Laura sube al tren que pasa.

- Mi casa tiene tres cuartos.

- Luisa Rey compra el colchón duro que tanto le gusta.

- Los libros nuevos no caben en la mesa de la oficina.

- Omar, que vive cerca, trajo miel.

- ¿Viste las noticias? Yo vi GANAR la medalla de plata en pesas. ¡Ese muchacho tiene mucha fuerza!

- Juan se ROMPIÓ una PIERNA cuando iba en la MOTO.

- Estoy muy triste, ayer vi MORIR a un amigo.

- Estoy muy preocupado, cada vez me es más difícil HABLAR!.

A.1.3 Read text

The participants were asked to read the following text:

Ayer fui al médico. ¿Qué le pasa? Me preguntó. Yo le dije: ¡Ay doctor! Donde pongo el dedo me duele. ¿Tiene la uña rota? Sí. Pues ya sabemos qué es. Deje su cheque a la salida.

A.1.4 Speech diadochokinesia

The participants were asked to produce the following syllable/words sequentially (during 3 to 5 seconds):

- /pa-ta-ka/

- /pe-ta-ka/

- /pa-ka-ta/

- /pa/

- /ta/

- /ka/

A.1.5 Monologue

The participants were asked to describe their daily routine.

A.2 German speech protocol

In this section are listed all the speech tasks considered to evaluate speech production from German speakers.

A.2.1 Read text

The participants were asked to read the following text.

Der Nordwind und die Sonne

Einst stritten sich Nordwind und Sonne, wer von ihnen beiden wohl der Stärkere wäre, als ein Wanderer, der in einen warmen Mantel gehüllt war, des Weges daherkam. Sie wurden einig, dass derjenige für den Stärkeren gelten sollte, der den Wanderer zwingen würde, seinen Mantel auszuziehen.

Der Nordwind blies mit aller Macht, aber je mehr er blies, desto fester hüllte sich der Wanderer in seinen Mantel ein. Endlich gab der Nordwind den Kampf auf. Nun wärmte die Sonne die Luft mit ihren freundlichen Strahlen, und schon nach wenigen Augenblicken zog der Wanderer seinen Mantel aus.

Da musste der Nordwind zugeben, dass die Sonne von ihnen beiden der Stärkere war.

A.2.2 Rhino sentences

The participants were asked to read the following sentences

- Nenne meine Mami Mimi.

- Peter spielt auf der Strasse.

- Das Pferd steht auf der Weide.

- Die Schokolade ist sehr lecke.

- Der Vater liest ein Buch.

A.2.3 PLAKSS words

The participants were asked to read the words in Table A.2.3 (not necessarily in that order).

Table A.1: List of words read by the German speakers

Anker	Feder	Kaputt	Quak	Stuhl
Apfel	Fenster	Katze	Rad	Tasche
Arzt	Fisch	Kiste	Roller	Tasse
Auto	Flasche	Kleid	Rutsche	Taucher
Ball	Frosch	Knöpfe	Sack	Telefon
Bank	Gabel	Korb	Schere	Teller
Baum	Gespenst	Krokodil	Schiff	Tiger
Berg	Gießkanne	Kuh	Schlange	Topf
Bett	Gitarre	Lampe	Schlüssel	Trecker
Bild	Glas	Löwe	Schmetterling	Unfall
Blume	Gras	Marienkäfer	Schnecke	Vogel
Brief	Grün	Milch	Schornstein	Wippe
Brille	Hase	Mond	Schrank	Wurst
Buch	Haus	Nagel	Schuh	Zange
Drachen	Heizung	Nest	Schwein	Zebra
Dusche	Hexe	Nuss	Sonne	Zitrone
Eichhörnchen	Hund	Pferd	Spinne	Zwerg
Eimer	Jacke	Pflaster	Spring	
Elefant	Jäger	Pilz	Spritze	
Erdbeere	Kanne	Punkt	Strumpf	

209

Appendix B

Publications

The following authored (and co-authored) publications were derived from this thesis:

B.1 Journal publications

- A. M. García, **T. Arias-Vergara**, J. C. Vásquez-Correa, E. Nöth, M. Schuster, A. E. Welch, Y. Bocanegra, A. Baena, and J. R. Orozco-Arroyave. *Cognitive Determinants of Dysarthria in Parkinson's Disease: An Automated Machine Learning Approach.* Movement Disorders, 2021.

- P. Klumpp, **T. Arias-Vergara**, J. C. Vásquez-Correa, P. A. Pérez-Toro, J. R. Orozco-Arroyave, A. Batliner, and E. Nöth. *The phonetic footprint of Parkinson's disease.* Computer Speech and Language. Vol 72. 2021.

- **T. Arias-Vergara**, P. Klumpp, J. C. Vásquez-Correa, J. R. Orozco-Arroyave, E. Nöth and M. Schuster. *Multi-channel spectrograms for speech processing applications using deep learning methods.* Pattern Analysis and Applications, 2020.

- **T. Arias-Vergara**, P. Arguello-Velez, J. C. Vásquez-Correa, E. Nöth, M. Schuster, M. C. González-Rátiva, and J. R. Orozco-Arroyave. *Automatic* *detection of Voice Onset Time in voiceless plosives using gated recurrent units.* Digital Signal Processing. Vol 104. 2020.

- P. A. Pérez-Toro, J. C. Vásquez-Correa, **T. Arias-Vergara**, E. Nöth, and J. R. Orozco-Arroyave. *Nonlinear dynamics and Poincaré sections to model gait impairments in different stages of Parkinson's disease.* Nonlinear Dynamics, Vol 100, pp 3253–3276, 2020.

- J. R. Orozco-Arroyave, J. C. Vasquez-Correa, P. Klumpp, P. A. Pérez-Toro, D. Escobar-Grisales, N. Roth, C. D. Rios-Urrego, M. Strauss, H. A. Carvajal-Castaño, S. Bayerl, L. R. Castrillón-Osorio, **T. Arias-Vergara**, A. Küderle, F. O. Lopéz-Pabón, L. F. Parra-Gallego, B. Eskofier, L. F. Gómez-Goméz, M. Schuster, and E. Nöth.. *Apkinson: the smartphone application for telemonitoring Parkinson's patients through speech, gait and hands movement.* Neurodegenerative Disease Management, 10(3), 137-157, 2020.

- J. C. Vasquez-Correa, **T. Arias-Vergara**, M. Schuster, J. R. Orozco-Arroyave, E. Nöth. *Parallel Representation Learning for the Classification of Pathological Speech: Studies on Parkinson's Disease and Cleft Lip and Palate*, Speech Communication, Vol 122, pp 56-67,2020

- F. O. López-Pabon, **T. Arias-Vergara**, J. R. Orozco-Arroyave. *Cepstral analysis and the Hilbert-Huang Transform for the automatic detection of Parkinson's disease.* TecnoLógicas, 23(47), 93-108, 2020.

- **T. Arias-Vergara**, J. C. Vásquez-Correa, J. R. Orozco-Arroyave, and E. Nöth. *Speaker models for monitoring Parkinson's disease progression considering different communication channels and acoustic conditions*, Speech Communication. Vol 101, pp 11-25, 2018.

- J. C. Vásquez-Correa, **T. Arias-Vergara**, J. R. Orozco-Arroyave, B. Eskofier, J. Klucken, and E. Nöth. *Multimodal assessment of Parkinson's*

211

disease: a deep learning approach. IEEE Journal of Biomedical and Health Informatics, 2018.

- **T. Arias-Vergara**, J. C. Vásquez-Correa, and J. R. Orozco-Arroyave. *Parkinson's Disease and Aging: Analysis of Their Effect in Phonation and Articulation of Speech.* Cognitive Computation, 9(6), p. 731-748., 2017.

B.2 Conference publications

- P. A. Pérez-Toro, J. C. Vásquez-Correa, **T. Arias-Vergara**, P. Klumpp, M. Sierra-Castrillón, M. E. Roldán-López, D. Aguillón, L. Hincapié-Henao, C. A. Tóbon-Quintero, T. Bocklet, M. Schuster, J. R. Orozco-Arroyave, and E. Nöth. *Acoustic and Linguistic Analyses to Assess Early-Onset and Genetic Alzheimer's Disease.* In ICASSP 2021-2021 IEEE International Conference on Acoustics, Speech and Signal Processing (ICASSP), pp. 8338-8342, 2021.

- J. C. Vásquez-Correa, **T. Arias-Vergara**, P. Klumpp, P. A. Perez-Toro, J. R. Orozco-Arroyave, and E. Nöth. *End-2-End Modeling of Speech and Gait from Patients with Parkinson's Disease: Comparison Between High Quality Vs. Smartphone Data.* In ICASSP 2021-2021 IEEE International Conference on Acoustics, Speech and Signal Processing (ICASSP), pp. 7298-7302, 2021.

- P. A. Pérez-Toro, J. C. Vásquez-Correa, **T. Arias-Vergara**, P. Klumpp, M. Schuster, E. Nöth, and J. R. Orozco-Arroyave. *Emotional State Modeling for the Assessment of Depression in Parkinson's Disease.* In International Conference on Text, Speech, and Dialogue, Springer, Champp. 457-468, 2021.

- L. F. Parra-Gallego, **T. Arias-Vergara**, and J. R. Orozco-Arroyave. *Robust Automatic Speech Recognition for Call Center Applications.* In

Workshop on Engineering Applications Springer, Cham, pp. 72-83, 2021.

- P. Arguello-Velez, **T. Arias-Vergara**, M. C. González-Rátiva, J. R. Orozco-Arroyave, E. Nöth., and M. Schuster. *Acoustic characteristics of vot in plosive consonants produced by parkinson's patients.* In Proceedings of Text, Speech, and Dialogue. Lecture Notes in Computer Science, Springer, Cham, , vol 12284, pp. 303-311, 2020.

- P. Klumpp, **T. Arias-Vergara**, J. C. Vásquez-Correa, P. A. Pérez-Toro, F. Hönig, E. Nöth, and J. R. Orozco-Arroyave. *Surgical mask detection with deep recurrent phonetic models.* In Proceeding of the 21th INTERSPEECH, pp 2057-2061. 2020.

- **T. Arias-Vergara**, J. R. Orozco-Arroyave, M. Cernak, S. Gollwitzer, M. Schuster, and E. Nöth. *Phone-attribute posteriors to evaluate the speech of cochlear implant users.* In Proceeding of the 20th INTERSPEECH, Graz, Austria, pp. 3108-3112, 2019.

- **T. Arias-Vergara**, S. Gollwitzer, J. R. Orozco-Arroyave, M. Schuster, and E. Nöth. *Consonant-to-Vowel/Vowel-to-Consonant Transitions to Analyze the Speech of Cochlear Implant Users.* In Proceedings of Text, Speech, and Dialogue. Lecture Notes in Computer Science, Springer, Cham , vol 11697, pp 299-306, 2019.

- **T. Arias-Vergara**, J. C. Vásquez-Correa, S. Gollwitzer, J. R. Orozco-Arroyave, M. Schuster, and E. Nöth. *Multi-channel Convolutional Neural Networks for Automatic Detection of Speech Deficits in Cochlear Implant Users.* Accepted to be presented at the 24th Iberoamerican Congress on Pattern Recognition, La Havana, Cuba. 2019.

- **T. Arias-Vergara**, S. Gollwitzer, J. R. Orozco-Arroyave, J.C. Vasquez-Correa, E. Nöth, C. Högerle, and M. Schuster. *Speech differences between CI users with pre- and postlingual onset of deafness detected by*

213

speech processing methods on voiceless to voice transitions. Laryngo-Rhino-Otologie; 98(S02), pp 305 – 305, 2019.

- J. C. Vásquez-Correa, **T. Arias-Vergara**, C. D. Rios-Urrego, M. Schuster, J. R. Orozco-Arroyave, and E. Nöth. *Convolutional Neural Networks and a Transfer Learning Strategy to Classify Parkinson's Disease from Speech in Three Different Languages.* Accepted to be presented at the 24th Iberoamerican Congress on Pattern Recognition, La Havana, Cuba. 2019.

- J. C. Vásquez-Correa, **T. Arias-Vergara**, P. Klumpp, M. Strauss, A. Küderle, N. Roth, S. Bayerl, N. García-Ospina, P. A. Perez-Toro, L. F. Parra-Gallego, C. D. Rios-Urrego, D. Escobar-Grisales, J. R. Orozco-Arroyave, B. Eskofier, and E. Nöth. *Apkinson: a Mobile Solution for Multimodal Assessment of Patients with Parkinson's Disease.* In Proceeding of the 20th INTERSPEECH, Graz, Austria, pp. 964-965, 2019.

- **T. Arias-Vergara**, P. Klummp, J. C. Vásquez-Correa, J. R. Orozco-Arroyave, and E. Nöth. *Unobtrusive Monitoring of Speech Impairments of Parkinson's Disease Patients Through Mobile Devices.* In 2018 IEEE International Conference on Acoustics, Speech and Signal Processing, Calgary, Canada, pp. 6004-6008, 2018.

- J.C. Vásquez-Correa, **T. Arias-Vergara**, J.R. Orozco-Arroyave, and E. Nöth. *A Multitask Learning Approach to Assess the Dysarthria Severity in Patients with Parkinson's Disease.* In Proceeding of the 19th INTER-SPEECH, Hyderabad, India, pp. 456-460, 2018.

- N. Garcia-Ospina, **T. Arias-Vergara**, J. C. Vásquez-Correa, M. Cernak, J. R. Orozco-Arroyave, and E. Nöth. *Phonological i-Vectors to Detect Parkinson's Disease.* In Text, Speech, and Dialogue: 21st International Conference, Brno, Czech Republic, 2018.

- P. A. Pérez-Toro, J. C. Vásquez-Correa, **T. Arias-Vergara**, N. Garcia-

Ospina, J. R. Orozco-Arroyave, and E. Nöth. *A Non-linear Dynamics Approach to Classify Gait Signals of Patients with Parkinson's Disease.* Communications in Computer and Information Science, Springer, 2018.

- L. F. Parra-Gallego, **T. Arias-Vergara**, J. C. Vásquez-Correa, N. Garcia-Ospina, J. R. Orozco-Arroyave and E. Nöth. *Automatic Intelligibility Assessment of Parkinson's Disease with Diadochokinetic Exercises.* Communications in Computer and Information Science, Springer, 2018

- **T. Arias-Vergara**, P. Klumpp, J. C. Vásquez-Correa, J. R. Orozco-Arroyave, and E. Nöth. *Parkinson's Disease Progression Assessment from Speech Using a Mobile Device-Based Application.* International Conference on Text, Speech, and Dialogue. Springer, Cham, pp. 371-379, 2017.

- J.C. Vásquez-Correa, R. Castrillón, **T. Arias-Vergara**, J.R. Orozco-Arroyave, and E. Nöth. *Speaker Model to Monitor the Neurological State and the Dysarthria Level of Patients with Parkinson's Disease.* International Conference on Text, Speech, and Dialogue. Springer, Cham, pp. 272-280, 2017.

- P. Klumpp, T. Janu, **T. Arias-Vergara**, J.C. Vásquez-Correa, J. R. Orozco-Arroyave, and E. Nöth, *Apkinson – A mobile monitoring solution for Parkinson's disease*, in Proceeding of the 18th INTERSPEECH, Stockholm, Sweden, pp. 1839-1843, 2017.

List of Figures

List of Tables

Acronyms

ANN Artificial Neural Network

APQ Amplitude Perturbation Quotient

ASR Automatic Speech Recognition

BCE Binary Cross-Entropy

BRNN Bidirectional Recurrent Neural Network

CARTs Classification And Regression Trees

CI Cochlear implant

CITA Cochlear Implant Testing App

CNN Convolutional Neural Network

DCT Discrete Cosine Transform

DDK Diadochokinese

DFT Discrete Fourier Transform

DIVA Directions Into Velocities of Articulators

DNN Deep Neural Network

EM Expectation Maximization

ERB Equivalent Rectangular Bandwidth

FCR Formant Centralization Ratio

FDA–2 Frenchay Dysarthria Assessment–2

FFT Fast Fourier Transform

GFCCs Gammatone-Frequency Cepstral Coefficients

GMM Gaussian Mixture Model

GPe Globus Pallidus external segment

GPi Globus Pallidus internal segment

GPI Global Proportions of Intervals

GRU Gated Recurrent Units

H&Y Hoehn & Yahr

HC Healthy Control

JFA Joint Factor Analysis

LASSO Least Absolute Shrinkage and Selection Operator

LSTM Long-Short Term Memory

MAE Mean Absolute Error

MAP Maximum A Posteriori

MDS-UPDRS Movement Disorder Society–Unified Parkinson Disease Rating Scale

MFCCs Mel-Frequency Cepstral Coefficients

mFDA modified Frenchay Dysarthria Assessment

MLP Multi-Layer Perceptron

NH Normal Hearing

NHR Noise to Harmonics Ratio

NN Neural Network

nPVI normalized Pairwise Variability Index

PD Parkinson's disease

PLP Perceptual Linear Prediction

PPQ Pitch Perturbation Quotient

RAP Relative Average Perturbation

RF Random Forest

RNN Recurrent Neural Network

rPVI raw Pairwise Variability Index

SGD Stochastic Gradient Descent

SNpc Substantia Nigra pars compacta

SNpr Substantia Nigra pars reticulata

SNR Signal-to-Noise Ratio

SPL Sound Pressure Level

STFT Short-Time Fourier Transform

STN Subthalamic nucleus

SVM Support Vector Machine

SVR Support Vector Regressor

tVSA triangular Vowel Space Area

UBM Universal Background Model

VAD Voice Activity Detection

VAI Vowel Articulation Index

VOT Voice Onset Time

WR Word Recognition Rate

Bibliography

Abu-Ghanem, S., Handzel, O., Ness, L., Ben-Artzi-Blima, M., Fait-Ghelbendorf, K., and Himmelfarb, M. (2016). Smartphone-based audiometric test for screening hearing loss in the elderly. *European archives of oto-rhino-laryngology*, 273(2):333–339.

Ackermann, H. and Ziegler, W. (1991). Articulatory deficits in Parkinsonian dysarthria: an acoustic analysis. *Journal of Neurology, Neurosurgery & Psychiatry*, 54(12):1093–1098.

Adams, D. (1991). Age changes in oral structures. *Dent Update*, 18(1):14–17.

Ahmed, N., Natarajan, T., and Rao, K. R. (1974). Discrete cosine transform. *IEEE transactions on Computers*, 100(1):90–93.

Albin, R. L., Young, A. B., and Penney, J. B. (1989). The functional anatomy of basal ganglia disorders. *Trends in neurosciences*, 12(10):366–375.

Almeida, J. S., Rebouças Filho, P. P., Carneiro, T., Wei, W., Damaševičius, R., Maskeliūnas, R., and de Albuquerque, V. H. C. (2019). Detecting Parkinson's disease with sustained phonation and speech signals using machine learning techniques. *Pattern Recognition Letters*, 125:55–62.

Argüello-Vélez, P., Arias-Vergara, T., González-Rátiva, M. C., Orozco-Arroyave, J. R., Nöth, E., and Schuster, M. E. (2020). Acoustic characteristics of VOT in plosive consonants produced by Parkinson's patients. In *International Conference on Text, Speech, and Dialogue*, pages 303–311. Springer.

Arvaniti, A. (2009). Rhythm, timing and the timing of rhythm. *Phonetica*, 66(1-2):46–63.

Asgari, M. and Shafran, I. (2010). Extracting cues from speech for predicting severity of Parkinson's disease. In *IEEE International Workshop on Machine Learning for Signal Processing (MLSP)*, pages 462–467. IEEE.

Baker, K. K., Ramig, L. O., Sapir, S., Luschei, E. S., and Smith, M. E. (2001). Control of vocal loudness in young and old adults. *Journal of Speech, Language, and Hearing research*.

Bayestehtashk, A., Asgari, M., Shafran, I., and McNames, J. (2015). Fully automated assessment of the severity of Parkinson's disease from speech. *Computer Speech and Language*, 29(1):172–185.

Benesty, J., Sondhi, M. M., and Huang, Y. (2007). *Springer handbook of speech processing*. Springer Science & Business Media.

Bengio, Y., Simard, P., and Frasconi, P. (1994). Learning long-term dependencies with gradient descent is difficult. *IEEE transactions on neural networks*, 5(2):157–166.

Benjamin, B. J. (1981). Frequency variability in the aged voice. *Journal of Gerontology*, 36(6):722–726.

Benjamin, B. J. (1982). Phonological performance in gerontological speech. *Journal of Psycholinguistic Research*, 1(11):159–167.

Bishop, C. M. (2006). *Pattern recognition and machine learning*. springer.

Blamey, P., Barry, J., Bow, C., Sarant, J., Paatsch, L., and Wales, R. (2001). The development of speech production following cochlear implantation. *Clinical Linguistics & Phonetics*, 15(5):363–382.

Boersma, P. et al. (1993). Accurate short-term analysis of the fundamental frequency and the harmonics-to-noise ratio of a sampled sound. In *Proceedings of the institute of phonetic sciences*, volume 17, pages 97–110. Citeseer.

Boersma, P. and Weenink, D. (2001). Praat, a system for doing phonetics by computer. *Glot International*, 5(9/10):341–345.

Bostan, A. C. and Strick, P. L. (2018). The basal ganglia and the cerebellum: nodes in an integrated network. *Nature Reviews Neuroscience*, 19(6):338–350.

Brant, J. A. and Eliades, S. J. (2020). Cochlear implant electrodes: design and characteristics. *Cochlear Implants and Other Implantable Hearing Devices*, page 23.

Brockmann, C. L. (2021). Anatomy of the Human Ear cs. https://en.wikipedia.org/wiki/File:Anatomy_of_the_Human_Ear_cs.svg.

Carlson, M. L. (2020). Cochlear implantation in adults. *New England Journal of Medicine*, 382(16):1531–1542.

Cernak, M., Orozco-Arroyave, J. R., Rudzicz, F., Christensen, H., Vásquez-Correa, J. C., and Nöth, E. (2017). Characterisation of voice quality of Parkinson's disease using differential phonological posterior features. *Computer Speech & Language*, 46:196–208.

Cernak, M., Potard, B., and Garner, P. N. (2015). Phonological vocoding using artificial neural networks. In *2015 IEEE International Conference on Acoustics, Speech and Signal Processing (ICASSP)*, pages 4844–4848.

Chiaramonte, R. and Bonfiglio, M. (2020). Acoustic analysis of voice in Parkinson's disease: a systematic review of voice disability and meta-analysis of studies. *Revista de neurologia*, 70(11):393–405.

Cho, K., Van Merriënboer, B., Gulcehre, C., Bahdanau, D., Bougares, F., Schwenk, H., and Bengio, Y. (2014). Learning phrase representations using RNN encoder-decoder for statistical machine translation. *arXiv preprint arXiv:1406.1078*.

Cohen, J. (1988). *Statistical power analysis for the behavioral sciences*. Academic press.

Colina, S. (2009). *Spanish phonology: A syllabic perspective*. Georgetown University Press.

Colton, R. H., Casper, J. K., and Leonard, R. (2011). *Understanding voice problems: A physiological perspective for diagnosis and treatment*. Lippincott Williams & Wilkins.

Cooley, J. W. and Tukey, J. W. (1965). An algorithm for the machine calculation of complex Fourier series. *Mathematics of computation*, 19(90):297–301.

Cortes, C. and Vapnik, V. (1995). Support-vector networks. *Machine learning*, 20(3):273–297.

Davis, S. and Mermelstein, P. (1980). Comparison of parametric representations for monosyllabic word recognition in continuously spoken sentences. *IEEE transactions on acoustics, speech, and signal processing*, 28(4):357–366.

De De Wet Swanepoel, K. C., Sousa, C. S., and David, R. M. (2019). Mobile applications to detect hearing impairment: opportunities and challenges. *Bulletin of the World Health Organization*, 97(10):717.

Dehak, N., Kenny, P. J., Dehak, R., Dumouchel, P., and Ouellet, P. (2011). Front-end factor analysis for speaker verification. *IEEE Transactions on Audio, Speech, and Language Processing*, 19(4):788–798.

Deliyski, D. and Gress, C. (1998). Intersystem reliability of MDVP for Windows 95/98 and DOS. In *Proceedings of the Annual Convention of the American Speech-Language-Hearing Association*, San Antonio, TX.

Denes, P. B. and Pinson, E. N. (1993). *The speech chain*. Macmillan.

Dieter, A., Keppeler, D., and Moser, T. (2020). Towards the optical cochlear implant: Optogenetic approaches for hearing restoration. *EMBO molecular medicine*, 12(4):e11618.

Diez, M., Varona, A., Penagarikano, M., Rodriguez-Fuentes, L. J., and Bordel, G. (2014). On the projection of PLLRs for unbounded feature distributions in spoken language recognition. *IEEE Signal Processing Letters*, 21(9):1073–1077.

Dubey, H. et al. (2015). EchoWear: Smartwatch technology for voice and speech treatments of patients with Parkinson's disease. In *Proceedings of the Conference on Wireless Health*, pages 15:1–15:8. ACM.

Duffy, J. R. (2000). Motor speech disorders: clues to neurologic diagnosis. In *Parkinson's Disease and Movement Disorders*, pages 35–53. Springer.

Dyagilev, K. and Saria, S. (2016). Learning (predictive) risk scores in the presence of censoring due to interventions. *Machine Learning*, 102(3):323–348.

D'haeseleer, E., Depypere, H., Claeys, S., Van Borsel, J., and Van Lierde, K. (2009). The menopause and the female larynx, clinical aspects and therapeutic options: a literature review. *Maturitas*, 64(1):27–32.

Elman, J. L. (1990). Finding structure in time. *Cognitive science*, 14(2):179–211.

Enderby, P. M. and Palmer, R. (2008). *FDA-2: Frenchay Dysarthria Assessment: Examiner's manual*. Pro-ed.

Eyben, F., Wöllmer, M., and Schuller, B. (2010). Opensmile: the munich versatile and fast open-source audio feature extractor. In *Proceedings of the 18th International Conference on Multimedia*, pages 1459–1462.

Fant, G. (1980). The relations between area functions and the acoustic signal. *Phonetica*, 37(1-2):55–86.

Fischer, E. and Goberman, A. M. (2010). Voice onset time in Parkinson's disease. *Journal of Communication Disorders*, 43(1):21–34.

Fletcher, H. (1940). Auditory patterns. *Reviews of modern physics*, 12(1):47.

Fox-Boyer, A. (2002). *PLAKSS: Psycholinguistische Analyse kindlicher Sprechstörungen*. Swets Test Services.

García, A. M., Arias-Vergara, T., C Vasquez-Correa, J., Nöth, E., Schuster, M., Welch, A. E., Bocanegra, Y., Baena, A., and Orozco-Arroyave, J. R. (2021). Cognitive determinants of dysarthria in Parkinson's disease: An automated machine learning approach. *Movement Disorders*.

García, A. M., Carrillo, F., Orozco-Arroyave, J. R., Trujillo, N., Bonilla, J. F. V., Fittipaldi, S., Adolfi, F., Nöth, E., Sigman, M., Slezak, D. F., et al. (2016). How language flows when movements don't: an automated analysis of spontaneous discourse in Parkinson's disease. *Brain and language*, 162:19–28.

García, N., Orozco-Arroyave, J., D'Haro, L., Dehak, N., and Nöth, E. (2017). Evaluation of the neurological state of people with Parkinson's disease using i-vectors. In *Proceeding of the 18th Annual Conference of the International Speech Communication Association (INTERSPEECH)*, pages 299–303.

Gautam, A., Naples, J. G., and Eliades, S. J. (2019). Control of speech and voice in cochlear implant patients. *The Laryngoscope*, 129(9):2158–2163.

Glasberg, B. R. and Moore, B. C. (1990). Derivation of auditory filter shapes from notched-noise data. *Hearing research*, 47(1-2):103–138.

Goetz, C. G. et al. (2008). Movement disorder society-sponsored revision of the unified Parkinson's disease rating scale (MDS-UPDRS): scale presentation and clinimetric testing results. *Movement disorders: official journal of the Movement Disorder Society*, 23(15):2129–2170.

Gold, T. (1980). Speech production in hearing-impaired children. *Journal of Communication Disorders*, 13(6):397–418.

Gollan, T. H. and Goldrick, M. (2019). Aging deficits in naturalistic speech production and monitoring revealed through reading aloud. *Psychology and aging*, 34(1):25.

Gómez-Vilda, P., Palacios-Alonso, D., Rodellar-Biarge, V., Álvarez-Marquina, A., Nieto-Lluis, V., and Martínez-Olalla, R. (2017). Parkinson's disease monitoring by biomechanical instability of phonation. *Neurocomputing*, 255:3–16.

Gould, J., Lane, H., Vick, J., Perkell, J. S., Matthies, M. L., and Zandipour, M. (2001). Changes in speech intelligibility of postlingually deaf adults after cochlear implantation. *Ear and hearing*, 22(6):453–460.

Goy, H., Fernandes, D. N., Pichora-Fuller, M. K., and Van Lieshout, P. (2013). Normative voice data for younger and older adults. *Journal of Voice*, 27(5):545–555.

Grabe, E. and Low, E. L. (2002). Durational variability in speech and the rhythm class hypothesis. *Papers in laboratory phonology*, 7(515-546).

Graves, A. (2012). Supervised sequence labelling. In *Supervised sequence labelling with recurrent neural networks*, pages 5–13. Springer.

Graves, A., Fernández, S., Gomez, F., and Schmidhuber, J. (2006). Connectionist temporal classification: labelling unsegmented sequence data with recurrent neural networks. In *Proceedings of the 23rd international conference on Machine learning*, pages 369–376.

Grósz, T., Busa-Fekete, R., Gosztolya, G., and Tóth, L. (2015). Assessing the degree of nativeness and Parkinson's condition using Gaussian processes and deep rectifier neural networks. In *Proceeding of the 16th Annual Conference of the International Speech Communication Association (INTERSPEECH)*, pages 919–923.

Guenther, F. H. (1994). A neural network model of speech acquisition and motor equivalent speech production. *Biological cybernetics*, 72(1):43–53.

Guenther, F. H. and Hickok, G. (2016). Neural models of motor speech control. In *Neurobiology of language*, pages 725–740. Elsevier.

Guenther, F. H., Perkell, J. S., Maassen, B., Kent, R., Peters, H., van Lieshout, P., and Hulstijn, W. (2004). A neural model of speech production and its application to studies of the role of auditory feedback in speech. *Speech motor control in normal and disordered speech*, pages 29–49.

Gupta, R., Chaspari, T., Kim, J., Kumar, N., Bone, D., and Narayanan, S. (2016). Pathological speech processing: State-of-the-art, current challenges, and future directions. In *2016 IEEE International Conference on Acoustics, Speech and Signal Processing (ICASSP)*, pages 6470–6474. IEEE.

Häggström, M. (2021). Basal ganglia circuits. `https://commons.wikimedia.org/wiki/File:Basal_ganglia_circuits.svg`.

Hanson, D. G., Gerratt, B. R., and Ward, P. H. (1984). Cinegraphic observations of laryngeal function in Parkinson's disease. *The Laryngoscope*, 94(3):348–353.

Hardcastle, W. J., Laver, J., and Gibbon, F. E. (2012). *The handbook of phonetic sciences*, volume 119. John Wiley & Sons.

Hassan, S. M., Malki, K. H., Mesallam, T. A., Farahat, M., Bukhari, M., and Murry, T. (2012). The effect of cochlear implantation on nasalance of speech in postlingually Hearing-Impaired Adults. *Journal of Voice*, 26(5):669.e17 – 669.e22.

Havelock, D., Kuwano, S., and Vorländer, M. (2008). *Handbook of signal processing in acoustics*. Springer Science & Business Media.

Hemmerling, D. and Wojcik-Pedziwiatr, M. (2020). Prediction and estimation of Parkinson's disease severity based on voice signal. *Journal of Voice*.

Ho, A. K., Iansek, R., Marigliani, C., Bradshaw, J. L., and Gates, S. (1999). Speech impairment in a large sample of patients with Parkinson's disease. *Behavioural neurology*, 11(3):131–137.

Hochreiter, S. and Schmidhuber, J. (1997). Long short-term memory. *Neural computation*, 9(8):1735–1780.

Hoehn, M. M., Yahr, M. D., et al. (1998). Parkinsonism: onset, progression, and mortality. *Neurology*, 50(2):318–318.

Holdsworth, I., McKeown, D., Zhang, C., and Allerhand, M. (1992). Complex sounds and auditory images. In *Auditory Physiology and Perception: Proceedings of the 9th International Symposium on Hearing Held in Carcens, France on 9-14 June 1991*, volume 83, page 429.

Hornykiewicz, O. (1998). Biochemical aspects of Parkinson's disease. *Neurology*, 51(2 Suppl 2):S2–S9.

Hudgins, C. V. and Numbers, F. C. (1942). An investigation of the intelligibility of the speech of the deaf. *Genetic psychology monographs*.

Israel, H. (1973). Age factor and the pattern of change in craniofacial structures. *American Journal of Anthropology*, 39(1):111–128.

Jones, H. N. (2009). Prosody in Parkinson's disease. *Perspectives on Neurophysiology and Neurogenic Speech and Language Disorders*, 19(3):77–82.

Kahane, J. (1981). Anatomic and physiologic changes in the aging peripheral speech mechanism. In Beasley, D. and Davis, G., editors, *Aging Communication Process and Disorders*. Grune & Stratton, New York.

Karan, B., Sahu, S. S., Orozco-Arroyave, J. R., and Mahto, K. (2020). Hilbert spectrum analysis for automatic detection and evaluation of Parkinson's speech. *Biomedical Signal Processing and Control*, 61:102050.

Kato, Y. and Yoshino, T. (1988). Segmental aspects in the speech of the hearing impaired. *Bulletin of defectology*, 13(1):65–71.

Kelly, F., Alexander, A., Forth, O., and Vloed, D. (2019). From i-vectors to x-vectors: A generational change in speaker recognition illustrated on the NFI-FRIDA database. In *Proc. 25th Int. Assoc. Forensic Phonetics Acoust.(IAFPA)*, pages 1–28.

Kenny, P., Ouellet, P., Dehak, N., Gupta, V., and Dumouchel, P. (2008). A study of interspeaker variability in speaker verification. *IEEE Transactions on Audio, Speech, and Language Processing*, 16(5):980–988.

Kingma, D. P. and Ba, J. (2014). Adam: A method for stochastic optimization. *arXiv preprint arXiv:1412.6980*.

Lane, H., Wozniak, J., Matthies, M., Svirsky, M., and Perkell, J. (1995). Phonemic resetting versus postural adjustments in the speech of cochlear implant users: An exploration of voice-onset time. *The Journal of the Acoustical Society of America*, 98(6):3096–3106.

Langereis, M., Dejonckere, P., Van Olphen, A., and Smoorenburg, G. (1997). Effect of cochlear implantation on nasality in post-lingually deafened adults. *Folia phoniatrica et logopaedica*, 49(6):308–314.

LeCun, Y., Haffner, P., Bottou, L., and Bengio, Y. (1999). Object recognition with gradient-based learning. In *Shape, contour and grouping in computer vision*, pages 319–345. Springer.

Leder, S. B. and Spitzer, J. B. (1990). A perceptual evaluation of the speech of adventitiously deaf adult males. *Ear and hearing*, 11(3):169–175.

Leder, S. B., Spitzer, J. B., and Kirchner, J. C. (1987). Speaking fundamental frequency of postlingually profoundly deaf adult men. *Annals of Otology, Rhinology & Laryngology*, 96(3):322–324.

Lenarz, T. (2017). Cochlear implant–state of the art. *GMS current topics in otorhinolaryngology, head and neck surgery*, 16:1–29.

Linares-Del Rey, M., Vela-Desojo, L., and Cano-de la Cuerda, R. (2019). Mobile phone applications in Parkinson's disease: A systematic review. *Neurología (English Edition)*, 34(1):38–54.

Linville, S. E. (1996). The sound of senescence. *Journal of voice*, 10(2):190–200.

Loizou, P. C. (1999). Introduction to cochlear implants. *IEEE Engineering in Medicine and Biology Magazine*, 18(1):32–42.

Lombard, E. (1911). Le signe de l'elevation de la voix. *Ann. Mal. de L'Oreille et du Larynx*, pages 101–119.

Louzada, T., Beraldinelle, R., Berretin-Felix, G., and Brasolotto, A. G. (2011). Oral and vocal fold diadochokinesis in dysphonic women. *Journal of Applied Oral Science*, 19(6):567–572.

Madhero (2021). Midbrain section. `https://commons.wikimedia.org/wiki/File:Midbrainsection.svg`.

McCulloch, W. S. and Pitts, W. (1943). A logical calculus of the ideas immanent in nervous activity. *The bulletin of mathematical biophysics*, 5(4):115–133.

Mermelstein, P. (1976). Distance measures for speech recognition, psychological and instrumental. *Pattern recognition and artificial intelligence*, 116:374–388.

Milardi, D., Quartarone, A., Bramanti, A., Anastasi, G., Bertino, S., Basile, G. A., Buonasera, P., Pilone, G., Celeste, G., Rizzo, G., Bruschetta, D., and Cacciola, A. (2019). The cortico-basal ganglia-cerebellar network: past, present and future perspectives. *Frontiers in systems neuroscience*, 13:61.

Miller, N. (2017). Communication changes in Parkinson's disease. *Practical Neurology*, 17(4):266–274.

Montaña, D., Campos-Roca, Y., and Pérez, C. J. (2018). A diadochokinesis-based expert system considering articulatory features of plosive consonants for early detection of Parkinson's disease. *Computer methods and programs in biomedicine*, 154:89–97.

Neumeyer, V., Harrington, J., and Draxler, C. (2010). An acoustic analysis of the vowel space in young and old cochlear-implant speakers. *Clinical linguistics & phonetics*, 24(9):734–741.

Neumeyer, V., Schiel, F., and Hoole, P. (2015). Speech of cochlear implant patients: An acoustic analysis of sibilant production. In *ICPhS*.

Novotný, M., Pospíšil, J., Čmejla, R., and Rusz, J. (2015). Automatic detection of voice onset time in dysarthric speech. In *2015 IEEE International Conference on Acoustics, Speech and Signal Processing (ICASSP)*, pages 4340–4344. IEEE.

Obeso, J. A., Rodriguez-Oroz, M. C., Rodriguez, M., Lanciego, J. L., Artieda, J., Gonzalo, N., and Olanow, C. W. (2000). Pathophysiology of the basal ganglia in Parkinson's disease. *Trends in neurosciences*, 23:S8–S19.

Olah, C. (2021). Understanding LSTMs. http://colah.github.io/posts/2015-08-Understanding-LSTMs/.

Olusanya, B. O., Davis, A. C., and Hoffman, H. J. (2019). Hearing loss grades and the International classification of functioning, disability and health. *Bulletin of the World Health Organization*, 97(10):725.

Orozco-Arroyave, J. R. (2016). *Analysis of speech of people with Parkinson's disease*. Logos Verlag Berlin, Germany.

Orozco-Arroyave, J. R., Arias-Londoño, J. D., Vargas-Bonilla, J. F., Gonzalez-Rátiva, M. C., and Nöth, E. (2014). New Spanish speech corpus database for the analysis of people suffering from Parkinson's disease. In *Proceedings of the 9th International Conference on Language Resources and Evaluation*, pages 342–347.

Orozco-Arroyave, J. R., Vásquez-Correa, J. C., Hönig, F., Arias-Londoño, J. D., Vargas-Bonilla, J. F., Skodda, S., Rusz, J., and Nöth, E. (2016). Towards an automatic monitoring of the neurological state of Parkinson's patients from speech. In *Proceedings of the IEEE International Conference on Acoustics, Speech and Signal Processing (ICASSP)*, pages 6490–6494.

Orozco-Arroyave, J. R., Vásquez-Correa, J. C., Klumpp, P., Pérez-Toro, P. A., Escobar-Grisales, D., Roth, N., Ríos-Urrego, C. D., Strauss, M., Carvajal-Castaño, H. A., Bayerl, S., et al. (2020). Apkinson: the smartphone application for telemonitoring Parkinson's patients through speech, gait and hands movement. *Neurodegenerative Disease Management*, 10(3):137–157.

Orozco-Arroyave, J. R., Vásquez-Correa, J. C., Vargas-Bonilla, J. F., Arora, R., Dehak, N., Nidadavolu, P. S., Christensen, H., Rudzicz, F., Yancheva, M., Chinaei, H., et al. (2018). NeuroSpeech: An open-source software for Parkinson's speech analysis. *Digital Signal Processing*, 77:207–221.

Osberger, M. J. and McGarr, N. S. (1982). Speech production characteristics of the hearing impaired. *Speech and language*, 8:221–283.

Oster, A. (1990). The effects of prosodic and segmental deviations on intelligibility of deaf speech. *Speech Transmission Laboratory-Quarterly Progress and Status Reports*, 31(1):65–86.

Pérez-Toro, P. A., Bayerl, S. P., Arias-Vergara, T., Vásquez-Correa, J. C., Klumpp, P., Schuster, M., Nöth, E., Orozco-Arroyave, J. R., and Riedhammer, K. (2021). Influence of the interviewer on the automatic assessment of Alzheimer's disease in the context of the ADReSSo challenge. In *Proceeding of the 22th Annual Conference of the International Speech Communication Association (INTERSPEECH)*, pages 478–482.

Perkell, J., Lane, H., Svirsky, M., and Webster, J. (1992). Speech of cochlear implant patients: A longitudinal study of vowel production. *The Journal of the Acoustical Society of America*, 91(5):2961–2978.

Perkell, J. S., Denny, M., Lane, H., Guenther, F., Matthies, M. L., Tiede, M., Vick, J., Zandipour, M., and Burton, E. (2007). Effects of masking noise on vowel and sibilant contrasts in normal-hearing speakers and postlingually deafened cochlear implant users. *The Journal of the Acoustical Society of America*, 121(1):505–518.

Perkell, J. S., Guenther, F. H., Lane, H., Matthies, M. L., Perrier, P., Vick, J., Wilhelms-Tricarico, R., and Zandipour, M. (2000). A theory of speech motor control and supporting data from speakers with normal hearing and with profound hearing loss. *Journal of Phonetics*, 28(3):233–272.

Pernambuco, L., Espelt, A., and de Lima, K. C. (2017). Screening for voice disorders in older adults (RAVI) - Part III: Cutoff score and clinical consistency. *Journal of Voice*, 31(1):117.e17–117.e22.

Pisoni, D. B., Kronenberger, W. G., Harris, M. S., and Moberly, A. C. (2017). Three challenges for future research on cochlear implants. *World journal of otorhinolaryngology-head and neck surgery*, 3(4):240–254.

Plant, G. and Oster, A. (1986). The effects of cochlear implantation on speech production. a case study. *Speech Transmission Laboratory-Quarterly Progress and Status Reports*, 27(1):65–86.

Poewe, W. (2008). Non-motor symptoms in Parkinson's disease. *European journal of neurology*, 15:14–20.

Pomaville, F. M. and Kladopoulos, C. N. (2013). The effects of behavioral speech therapy on speech sound production with adults who have cochlear implants. *Journal of Speech, Language, and Hearing Research*, 56(2):531–541.

Popp, C. (2021). CITA: An android-based application to evaluate the speech of cochlear implant users. Bachelor's thesis - Friedrich-Alexander University of Erlangen-Nürnberg, Germany.

Potgieter, J.-M., Swanepoel, D. W., Myburgh, H. C., Hopper, T. C., and Smits, C. (2016). Development and validation of a smartphone-based digits-in-noise hearing test in South African English. *International Journal of Audiology*, 55(7):405–411.

Purcell, D. W. and Munhall, K. G. (2006). Adaptive control of vowel formant frequency: Evidence from real-time formant manipulation. *The Journal of the Acoustical Society of America*, 120(2):966–977.

Ramig, L. O., Sapir, S., Countryman, S., Pawlas, A. A., O'Brien, C., Hoehn, M., and Thompson, L. L. (2001). Intensive voice treatment (lsvt®) for patients with parkinson's disease: A 2 year follow up. *Journal of Neurology, Neurosurgery & Psychiatry*, 71(4):493–498.

Ramus, F., Nespor, M., and Mehler, J. (1999). Correlates of linguistic rhythm in the speech signal. *Cognition*, 73(3):265–292.

Redgrave, P., Rodriguez, M., Smith, Y., Rodriguez-Oroz, M. C., Lehericy, S., Bergman, H., Agid, Y., DeLong, M. R., and Obeso, J. A. (2010). Goal-directed and habitual control in the basal ganglia: implications for Parkinson's disease. *Nature Reviews Neuroscience*, 11(11):760–772.

Reubold, U., Harrington, J., and Kleber, F. (2010). Vocal aging effects on F0 and the first formant: A longitudinal analysis in adult speakers. *Speech Communication*, 52(7-8):638–651.

Reynolds, D. A., Quatieri, T. F., and Dunn, R. B. (2000). Speaker verification using adapted Gaussian mixture models. *Digital signal processing*, 10(1):19–41.

Rosenblatt, F. (1958). The perceptron: a probabilistic model for information storage and organization in the brain. *Psychological review*, 65(6):386.

Ruff, S., Bocklet, T., Nöth, E., Müller, J., Hoster, E., and Schuster, M. (2017). Speech production quality of cochlear implant users with respect to duration and onset of hearing loss. *ORL*, 79(5):282–294.

Sapir, S., Ramig, L. O., Spielman, J. L., and Fox, C. (2010). Formant centralization ratio: A proposal for a new acoustic measure of dysarthric speech. *Journal of Speech, Language, and Hearing research.*

Schröter, H., Rosenkranz, T., Escalante-B., A. N., and Maier, A. (2020). CLC: Complex linear coding for the DNS 2020 challenge.

Schuller, B., Steidl, S., Batliner, A., Hantke, S., Hönig, F., Orozco-Arroyave, J. R., Nöth, E., Zhang, Y., and Weninger, F. (2015). The INTERSPEECH 2015 computational paralinguistics challenge: Nativeness, Parkinson's & eating condition. *Proceeding of the 16th Annual Conference of the International Speech Communication Association (INTERSPEECH)*, pages 478–482.

Schultz, G. and Grant, M. (2000). Effects of speech therapy and pharmacologic and surgical treatments on voice and speech in Parkinson's disease: a review of the literature. *Journal of Communication Disorders*, 33(1):59–88.

Schuster, M. and Paliwal, K. K. (1997). Bidirectional recurrent neural networks. *IEEE transactions on Signal Processing*, 45(11):2673–2681.

Skodda, S., Grönheit, W., Mancinelli, N., and Schlegel, U. (2013). Progression of voice and speech impairment in the course of Parkinson's disease: a longitudinal study. *Parkinson's Disease*, 2013. Art. ID 389195.

Skodda, S., Visser, W., and Schlegel, U. (2010). Short- and long-term dopaminergic effects on dysarthria in early Parkinson's disease. *Journal of Neural Transmission*, 117(2):197–205.

Skodda, S., Visser, W., and Schlegel, U. (2011). Vowel articulation in Parkinson's disease. *Journal of voice*, 25(4):467–472.

Slaney, M. et al. (1993). An efficient implementation of the Patterson-Holdsworth auditory filter bank. *Apple Computer, Perception Group, Tech. Rep*, 35(8).

Smith, C. R. (1975). Residual hearing and speech production in deaf children. *Journal of Speech, Language, and Hearing Research*, 18(4):795–811.

Smola, A. J. and Schölkopf, B. (2004). A tutorial on support vector regression. *Statistics and computing*, 14(3):199–222.

Snyder, D., Garcia-Romero, D., Sell, G., Povey, D., and Khudanpur, S. (2018). x-vectors: Robust DNN embeddings for speaker recognition. In *2018 IEEE International Conference on Acoustics, Speech and Signal Processing (ICASSP)*, pages 5329–5333. IEEE.

Stevens, K., Nickerson, R., Boothroyd, A., and Rollins, A. (1976). Assessment of nasalization in the speech of deaf children. *Journal of Speech and Hearing Research*, 19(2):393–416.

Stuart, A., Kalinowski, J., Rastatter, M. P., and Lynch, K. (2002). Effect of delayed auditory feedback on normal speakers at two speech rates. *The Journal of the Acoustical Society of America*, 111(5):2237–2241.

Švec, J. G. and Granqvist, S. (2018). Tutorial and guidelines on measurement of sound pressure level in voice and speech. *Journal of Speech, Language, and Hearing Research*, 61(3):441–461.

Sztahó, D., Tulics, M. G., Vicsi, K., and Valálik, I. (2017). Automatic estimation of severity of Parkinson's disease based on speech rhythm related features. In *2017 8th IEEE International Conference on Cognitive Infocommunications (CogInfoCom)*, pages 000011–000016. IEEE.

Tao, F., Daudet, L., Poellabauer, C., Schneider, S., and Busso, C. (2016). A portable automatic PA-TA-KA syllable detection system to derive biomarkers for neurological disorders. In *Proceedings of the Seventeenth Annual*

Conference of the International Speech Communication Association, pages 362–366.

Taylor, S., Dromey, C., Nissen, S. L., Tanner, K., Eggett, D., and Corbin-Lewis, K. (2020). Age-related changes in speech and voice: Spectral and cepstral measures. *Journal of Speech, Language, and Hearing Research*, 63(3):647–660.

Teixeira, J. P. and Gonçalves, A. (2016). Algorithm for jitter and shimmer measurement in pathologic voices. *Procedia Computer Science*, 100:271–279.

Titze, I., Riede, T., and Mau, T. (2016). Predicting achievable fundamental frequency ranges in vocalization across species. *PLoS computational biology*, 12(6):e1004907.

Todd, A. E., Edwards, J. R., and Litovsky, R. Y. (2011). Production of contrast between sibilant fricatives by children with cochlear implants. *The Journal of the Acoustical Society of America*, 130(6):3969–3979.

Torre, P. and Barlow, J. A. (2009). Age-related changes in acoustic characteristics of adult speech. *Journal of Communication Disorders*, 42(5):324–333.

Tourville, J. A., Reilly, K. J., and Guenther, F. H. (2008). Neural mechanisms underlying auditory feedback control of speech. *Neuroimage*, 39(3):1429–1443.

Trail, M., Fox, C., Ramig, L. O., Sapir, S., Howard, J., and Lai, E. C. (2005). Speech treatment for Parkinson's disease. *NeuroRehabilitation*, 20(3):205–221.

Tremblay, P., Deschamps, I., Bédard, P., Tessier, M.-H., Carrier, M., and Thibeault, M. (2018). Aging of speech production, from articulatory accuracy to motor timing. *Psychology and aging*, 33(7):1022.

Tsanas, A., Little, M., McSharry, P. E., and Ramig, L. (2010). Accurate telemonitoring of Parkinson's disease progression by noninvasive speech tests. *IEEE Transactions on Biomedical Engineering*, 57(4):884–893.

Tykalova, T., Rusz, J., Klempir, J., Cmejla, R., and Ruzicka, E. (2017). Distinct patterns of imprecise consonant articulation among Parkinson's disease, progressive supranuclear palsy and multiple system atrophy. *Brain and language*, 165:1–9.

Ubrig, M. T., Goffi-Gomez, M. V. S., Weber, R., Menezes, M. H. M., Nemr, N. K., Tsuji, D. H., and Tsuji, R. K. (2011). Voice analysis of postlingually deaf adults pre-and postcochlear implantation. *Journal of Voice*, 25(6):692–699.

Van den Berg, J. (1958). Myoelastic-aerodynamic theory of voice production. *Journal of speech and hearing research*, 1(3):227–244.

Van der Maaten, L. and Hinton, G. (2008). Visualizing data using t-SNE. *Journal of machine learning research*, 9(11).

Vapnik, V. (1995). *The nature of statistical learning theory*. Springer-Verlag, New York.

Vásquez-Correa, J. C., Klumpp, P., Orozco-Arroyave, J. R., and Nöth, E. (2019). Phonet: A tool based on gated recurrent neural networks to extract phonological posteriors from speech. In *Proceedings of the 20th Annual Conference of the International Speech Communication Association*, pages 549–553.

Vásquez-Correa, J. C., Orozco-Arroyave, J. R., Bocklet, T., and Nöth, E. (2018). Towards an automatic evaluation of the dysarthria level of patients with Parkinson's disease. *Journal of communication disorders*, 76:21–36.

Vipperla, R., Renals, S., and Frankel, J. (2010). Ageing voices: The effect of changes in voice parameters on ASR performance. *EURASIP Journal on Audio, Speech, and Music Processing*, 2010:1–10.

Volkmann, J., Stevens, S., and Newman, E. (1937). A scale for the measurement of the psychological magnitude pitch. *The Journal of the Acoustical Society of America*, 8(3):208–208.

Wahlster, W. (2013). *Verbmobil: foundations of speech-to-speech translation.* Springer Science & Business Media.

Waldstein, R. S. (1990). Effects of postlingual deafness on speech production: implications for the role of auditory feedback. *The Journal of the Acoustical Society of America*, 88(5):2099–2114.

Weber, P. C. and Klein, A. J. (1999). Hearing loss. *Medical Clinics of North America*, 83(1):125–137.

White, L. and Malisz, Z. (2020). Speech rhythm and timing. In *The Oxford Handbook of Language Prosody*. Oxford Handbooks Online.

Xue, S. A. and Deliyski, D. (2001). Effects of aging on selected acoustic voice parameters: Preliminary normative data and educational implications. *Educational Gerontology*, 27(2):159–168.

Yang, W., Hamilton, J. L., Kopil, C., Beck, J. C., Tanner, C. M., Albin, R. L., Dorsey, E. R., Dahodwala, N., Cintina, I., Hogan, P., et al. (2020). Current and projected future economic burden of Parkinson's disease in the US. *npj Parkinson's Disease*, 6(1):1–9.

Zaino, C. and Benventano, T. (1977). Functional involutional and degenerative disorders. In Zaino, C. and Benvetano, T., editors, *Radiographic Examination of the Oropharynx and Esophagus*. Springer-Verlag, New York.

Zhan, A., Little, M. A., Harris, D. A., Abiola, S. O., Dorsey, E., Saria, S., and Terzis, A. (2016). High frequency remote monitoring of Parkinson's disease via smartphone: Platform overview and medication response detection. *arXiv preprint arXiv:1601.00960*.

Zhan, A., Mohan, S., Tarolli, C., Schneider, R. B., Adams, J. L., Sharma, S., Elson, M. J., Spear, K. L., Glidden, A. M., Little, M. A., et al. (2018). Using smartphones and machine learning to quantify Parkinson's disease severity: The mobile Parkinson's disease score. *JAMA neurology*, 75(7):876–880.

Zhang, A., Zachary, C., Lipton, M. L., and Smola, A. J. (2021). Dive into deep learning. `https://d2l.ai/index.html`.

Zwicker, E. (1961). Subdivision of the audible frequency range into critical bands (frequenzgruppen). *The Journal of the Acoustical Society of America*, 33(2):248–248.

In der Reihe *Studien zur Mustererkennung,*
herausgegeben von
Prof. Dr.-Ing Heinricht Niemann und Herrn Prof. Dr.-Ing. Elmar Nöth
sind bisher erschienen:

| 19 | Georg Stemmer | Modeling Variability in Speech Recognition |
| | | ISBN 978-3-8325-0945-3, 2005, 270 S. 40.50 € |

20 Frank Deinzer   Optimale Ansichtenauswahl in der aktiven
Objekterkennung

ISBN 978-3-8325-1054-1, 2005, 370 S. 40.50 €

21 Radim Chrastek   Automated Retinal Image Analysis for Glaucoma
Screening and Vessel Evaluation

ISBN 978-3-8325-1191-3, 2006, 233 S. 40.50 €

22 Jochen Schmidt   3-D Reconstruction and Stereo Self-Calibration for
Augmented Reality

ISBN 978-3-8325-1422-8, 2006, 283 S. 40.50 €

23 Marcin Grzegorzek   Appearance-Based Statistical Object Recognition
Including Color and Context Modeling

ISBN 978-3-8325-1588-1, 2007, 230 S. 40.50 €

24 Lothar Mischke   Teilautomatisierte Verschlagwortung von in alt-
deutschen Schriftfonts gesetzten Texten mit Hilfe
lernender Verfahren

ISBN 978-3-8325-1631-4, 2007, 302 S. 40.50 €

25 Tino Haderlein   Automatic Evaluation of Tracheoesophageal
Substitute Voices

ISBN 978-3-8325-1769-4, 2007, 238 S. 40.50 €

26 Ingo Scholz   Reconstruction and Modeling of Static and
Dynamic Light Fields

ISBN 978-3-8325-1963-6, 2008, 254 S. 38.50 €

27 Richard Ottermanns   Mustererkennung, Dimensionsreduktion und
statistische Modellierung in der Ökologie –
dargestellt am Beispiel der Lebensgemeinschaften
grasiger Feldraine in deutschen Agrarlandschaften

ISBN 978-3-8325-2032-8, 2008, 499 S. 47.00 €

28 Stefan Steidl   Automatic Classification of Emotion-Related User
States in Spontaneous Children's Speech

ISBN 978-3-8325-2145-5, 2009, 260 S. 43.50 €

Alle erschienenen Bücher können unter der angegebenen ISBN im Buchhandel oder direkt beim Logos Verlag Berlin (www.logos-verlag.de, Fax: 030 - 42 85 10 92) bestellt werden.